Da
Pla

**The Restoration of Arnold Middleton,
In Celebration, The March on Russia**

'David Storey is our best, most original and satisfying playwright. My
best times in the theatre have always been when I have had the good
luck to direct his plays – which combine intelligence and feeling in a
unique way.'
Lindsay Anderson

The Restoration of Arnold Middleton: 'The best first play produced by
the English Stage Company since *Look Back in Anger*.'
Harold Hobson, *Sunday Times*

In Celebration: 'Profoundly moving play . . . puts him unquestionably
in the front rank of today's playwrights.' *Financial Times*

'A play of nobility and compassion . . . the great themes of guilt and
atonement are handled with skill, insight and a weight not often
displayed on the English stage.' *Daily Express*

'*The March on Russia* is an elegy for the lost hopes of both our postwar liberal-left generation and the harder left one that preceded it, and
for its two central characters Storey has provided some of the most
true and moving moments of marital ambivalence to be seen on any
stage today.'
Ian Herbert, *London Theatre Record*

David Storey
Unique in his generation of writers, David Storey's achievements are
divided equally between his work as a novelist and as a playwright.
Born in 1933, the third son of a mineworker, he was educated at the
Queen Elizabeth Grammar School at Wakefield and Slade School of
Fine Art in London. He had various jobs in his youth, ranging from
farm labouring and showground tent-erecting to professional rugby
league football and schoolteaching. Among his novels are *This Sporting
Life*, which won the Macmillan Fiction Award in 1960 and was filmed,
Flight Into Camden, which won the John Llewelyn Rhys Memorial
Prize, and *Radcliffe*, which won the Somerset Maugham Award in
1963. Later novels include *Pasmore*, a Booker Finalist and winner of
the Faber Memorial Prize, and *Saville*, winner of the Booker Prize in
1976. His plays include *The Contractor*, *Home* and *The Changing
Room* – each of which won the New York Critics Best Play of the Year
Award – *In Celebration*, which was filmed, *Life Class* and *The Farm*:
all of these plays were premièred at the Royal Court Theatre; his two
later plays, *Early Days* and *The March on Russia*, were presented at
the National Theatre in the 1980s. *Stages* was premièred at the Royal
National Theatre in 1992. David Storey lives in London. He was
married in 1956 and has four children.

DAVID STOREY

Plays: Two

The Restoration of Arnold Middleton
In Celebration
The March on Russia

with an introduction by the author

Methuen Drama

METHUEN WORLD CLASSICS

This collection first published in Great Britain in 1994
by Methuen Drama
an imprint of Reed Consumer Books Ltd
Michelin House, 81 Fulham Road, London SW3 6RB
and Auckland, Melbourne, Singapore and Toronto
and distributed in the United States of America
by Heinemann, a division of Reed Elsevier Inc.
361 Hanover Street, Portsmouth, New Hampshire NH 03801 3959

The Restoration of Arnold Middleton first published by Penguin Books
1970 copyright © David Storey 1970
In Celebration first published by Jonathan Cape 1969
copyright © David Storey 1969
The March on Russia first published by Samuel French Ltd 1989
copyright © David Storey 1989
Introduction copyright © David Storey 1994
This collection copyright © David Storey 1994
The author has asserted his moral rights.

ISBN 0–413–68610–8

A CIP catalogue record for this book is available from the British Library

The front cover shows artwork by David Storey for the curtain for
The March on Russia at the National Theatre, London 1989

Phototypeset in 9½/11 pt Sabon by Wilmaset Ltd, Birkenhead, Wirral
Printed and bound in Great Britain
by Cox & Wyman Ltd, Reading, Berkshire

CAUTION
All rights whatsoever in these plays are strictly reserved and application for
professional performance should be made before rehearsals begin to Peters,
Fraser and Dunlop, Fifth Floor, The Chambers, Chelsea Harbour, Lots
Road, London SW10 0XF. For amateur performance contact Samuel
French Ltd, 52 Fitzroy Street, London W1P 6JR. No performance may be
given until a licence has been obtained.

Contents

A Chronology

of plays, novels and poetry

This Sporting Life (Novel), pub. Longman (Penguin, 1962). U.S. Macmillan Fiction Award. (Filmed 1963). **1960**

Flight into Camden (Novel), pub. Longman (Penguin, 1964). John Llewelyn Rhys Memorial Prize.

Radcliffe (Novel), pub. Longman (Penguin, 1965). Somerset Maugham Award. **1963**

The Restoration of Arnold Middleton (Play), pub. Jonathan Cape (Penguin 1970). First presented at The Traverse Theatre, Edinburgh, 22 September 1966. Royal Court Theatre, London, 4 July 1967. *Evening Standard* Drama Award. **1967**

In Celebration (Play), pub. Jonathan Cape (Penguin 1971). First presented at the Royal Court Theatre, 22 April 1969. (Filmed 1974). **1969**

The Contractor (Play), pub. Jonathan Cape (Penguin 1971). First presented at the Royal Court Theatre, 20 October 1969. Variety Club of Great Britain Best Play of the Year Award. New York Critics Best Play of the Year Award. **1970**

Home (Play), pub. Jonathan Cape (Penguin 1972). First presented at the Royal Court Theatre, 17 June 1970. *Evening Standard* Drama Award. New York Critics Best Play of the Year Award.

Pasmore (Novel), pub. Longman (Penguin, 1976). Faber Memorial Prize. Booker Prize finalist. **1972**

The Changing Room (Play), pub. Jonathan Cape (Penguin, 1973). First presented at the Royal Court Theatre, 9 November 1971. New York Critics Best Play of the Year Award.

A Temporary Life (Novel), pub. Allen Lane (Penguin, 1978). 1973

Cromwell (Play), pub. Jonathan Cape. First presented at the Royal Court Theatre, 15 August 1973.

The Farm (Play), pub. Jonathan Cape (Penguin 1982). First presented at the Royal Court Theatre, 26 September 1973.

Edward (Humour), pub. Allen Lane.

Life Class (Play), pub. Jonathan Cape (Penguin 1975
1980). First presented at the Royal Court Theatre, 9 April 1974.

Saville (Novel), pub. Jonathan Cape (Penguin 1978). 1976
Booker Prize.

Mother's Day (Play), pub. Penguin, 1978. First presented at the Royal Court Theatre, 22 September 1976.

Sisters (Play), pub. Penguin, 1980. First produced 1978
at the Royal Exchange Theatre, Manchester, 12 September 1978.

Early Days (Play), pub. Penguin, 1980. First 1980
produced at the National Theatre, 22 April 1980.

A Prodigal Child (Novel), pub. Jonathan Cape 1982
(Penguin, 1984).

Present Times (Novel), pub. Jonathan Cape (Penguin, 1984
1985).

The March on Russia (Play), pub. Samuel French, 1989
1989. First presented at the National Theatre, 6 April 1989.

Storey's Lives (Poems: 1951–1991), pub. Jonathan 1992
Cape, 1992.

Stages (Play), pub. Methuen Drama, 1992. First presented at the Royal National Theatre, November 1992.

Caring (Play), pub. Methuen Drama, 1992.

Note: Dates refer to first publication.

Introduction

A period of twenty-seven years spans the writing of these three plays. As the Introduction to Volume One describes, *The Restoration of Arnold Middleton* was written in 1958 when, at the age of twenty-four, I was teaching in a school at the back of Kings Cross Station in London.

My 'assault' upon London, which had begun on my arrival at the Slade School of Fine Art five years before, had come to a halt. Seven novels, not to mention several short stories and essays, had, over the previous half decade, been rejected by everyone to whom they had been sent. Somewhat in despair I resorted, over a school half-term weekend, to putting my frustrations into a play: it wouldn't – and didn't – take long to write and, where extrapolations of character and prose descriptions had clearly failed, dialogue on its own might, if only by its economy, succeed.

The combination of circumstances which resulted in the play finally being produced eight years later, first at the Traverse Theatre, Edinburgh, directed by Gordon McDougall, with David Collings in the leading role, and, one year later, at the Royal Court Theatre, London, in a production by Robert Kidd, with Jack Shepherd and Eileen Atkins in the principal roles, is described in the Introduction to Volume One.

The play itself, at the time of its composition, had been triggered off by a remark made to me in a Wakefield side-street some years before. 'There,' said my companion, 'is old so-and-so, a teacher at our school,' pointing out a fair-haired man in his early twenties approaching us with a young woman on one arm and an older woman on the other. 'He sleeps with both of them,' my companion added. 'One is his wife, the other her mother.'

This extraordinary arrangement – convened within the conventions associated (at least at that time) with the teaching profession – caught my imagination: on the one hand, a sense of civic responsibility (the enlightenment of the young), on the other, the violation of a moral code which this teacher's public life was there to endorse. 'What,' I mentally enquired, 'went on indoors? What inversion – or conversion – of social (and sexual) practices, not to mention music-hall ribaldry, occurred within the patterning of an otherwise normal marriage? How did they relate to one another – the women to the man, the man to the women, the women to one another?'

Coming home from another racking day in front of a Kings Cross 'C' stream class to find yet another rejection slip waiting for me for yet another novel, I sat down to write what I could only then conceive of as a schoolteacher's saga: the constant interplay of childish demands, interests and misbehaviour, with the equally constant request for probity (not to mention maturity) and common sense. The anarchic response to this seemingly irreconcilable conflict suggested by the provincial schoolteacher walking arm-in-arm with his lovers down a Wakefield side-street some years before came to mind with an unexpected vigour.

It was after seeing *The Restoration of Arnold Middleton* on the Royal Court stage – and convincing myself that I had finally found an artistic home – that I was prompted to write five other plays. The first of these was *The Contractor*, published in Volume One, the second was *In Celebration* (followed immediately by *Home*).

My career as a novelist, at this time (three volumes to my name), was in the doldrums. I had spent the previous five years writing what I had, if surreptitiously, conceived of as the definitive postwar British novel. To my despair it had come to nothing. The distraction of *Arnold Middleton*, the excitement of seeing it on the Royal Court stage, unblocked a dramaturgical dam.

In Celebration was written in three days. Its subject was one which had preoccupied me long before the occasion when, at the age of seventeen, I had announced to my parents my intention of becoming an 'artist'. Art, to their minds, was not only a waste of time but an explicit rejection of all their sacrifices and efforts. How, for instance, was I to equate the enlightenment afforded by my education with the exigencies and deprivations of working-class life? The conflict between the injustices of the latter and the privileges associated with the former had never been more apparent. Having initially endeavoured to encapsulate my native dilemma in a series of novels, I now attempted to do so in a play.

Converging on their old, back-street home to celebrate their parents' fortieth wedding anniversary, the three educated sons of the Shaw family (their father a miner) discover that what unites them as surely as anticipation is pain: grief underscores pleasure, loss counters gain: the ambiguities of familial love become increasingly, and despairingly, apparent.

This second 'family' play, written ten years after the first, expressed, at least for me, a similar immediacy of feeling. Directed by Lindsay Anderson, at the invitation of the artistic director of the Royal Court, Bill Gaskill, it began a theatrical collaboration which was to extend itself over the next three decades. Cast in the original production with Bill Owen, Constance Chapman, Brian Cox, James Bolam, Gabrielle Daye, Fulton Mackay and Alan Bates, it not only established a method of working – empirical, lyrical, naturalistic – but brought together a group of actors several of whom were to be used in subsequent memorable productions. In the final play in this volume, for instance, Bill Owen and Constance Chapman also play the parents – the siblings, on this occasion, Frank Grimes and Rosemary Martin, who had both appeared in several previous plays, and – a newcomer to me but not to Lindsay's productions – Patsy Rowlands.

In the seventeen years which had elapsed between the writing of *In Celebration* and *The March on Russia*, my definitive postwar British novel had been stripped of its excesses and published in two separate fragments: *Pasmore* in 1972, *A Temporary Life* in 1973.

As a sequel to the conflict between morality and art – between a man who sells his health by working down a mine and a man who spends his time writing novels and plays, and painting pictures – I picked on the family described in the novel *Pasmore*, moving their situation on by two decades.

The protagonist of the novel is a college lecturer who, from an early age, having submitted to the educational (and other) aspirations of his working-class parents, finds himself in adult life alienated not only from them, his wife and his children, but, more potently, as he sees it, from himself. Abandoning his family and, temporarily, his job, he searches for some form of reclamation.

In the play, in the manner of the sons in *In Celebration*, he, together with his two sisters, returns, twenty years on, to his parents' retirement bungalow to celebrate their sixtieth wedding anniversary. The battle between social justice and individual choice is re-engaged, seen, in this context, more specifically through the eyes of the parents. The father's rhapsodic recollection of his youthful march on Russia (to free the Tsar) is paralleled with his commentary on the 'march' that has gone on ever since – of 'progress', of emancipation – of affluence. An epilogue – a codicil – an elegy, it brings the lifelong issues of the previous play up against what might be described as a final dying of the light.

Written over a period of almost thirty years, these three 'family' plays contain much of what, I suspect, has been my own experience over a rather longer period of time: the conflict between filial and parental truths, between rebellion and loyalty, between the destruction of the past and the reconstruction of the present; between chance and resolution; between destiny and choice – between what binds us together and, just as surely, by the same measure, drives us apart.

David Storey, 1994

THE RESTORATION OF
ARNOLD MIDDLETON

The Restoration of Arnold Middleton was first presented at the Traverse Theatre, Edinburgh, on 22 November 1966. The cast was as follows:

MRS EDIE ELLIS	June Watson
JOAN MIDDLETON	Marian Diamond
ARNOLD MIDDLETON	David Collings
JEFFREY HANSON	Paul Williamson
SHEILA O'CONNOR	Ann Holloway
MAUREEN WILKINSON	Rosemary McHale

Directed by Gordon McDougall

Subsequently presented at the Royal Court Theatre, London, on 4 July 1967. The cast was as follows:

MRS EDIE ELLIS	Noel Dyson
JOAN MIDDLETON	Eileen Atkins
ARNOLD MIDDLETON	John Shepherd
JEFFREY HANSON	Tenniel Evans
SHEILA O'CONNOR	Gillian Hills
MAUREEN WILKINSON	Andree Evans

Directed by Robert Kidd

ACT ONE

Scene One

*A cosy, well-furnished, scrupulously clean living-room,
equipped with dining table and chairs as well as a three-
piece suite and sideboard.*

*Arranged round the room, on the walls and furniture, are
various objects, mounted and in excellent state of
preservation: a stuffed eagle, a sword, a ship, a model
aeroplane, a model engine, etc., which may suggest the
rudiments of a museum, but bereft of any specific human
connotation. Over the mantlepiece hangs a Lee-Enfield rifle.*

*The centre of the room is dominated by a full-size suit of
armour, standing in a pile of brown paper and string from
which it has just emerged. A two-handed sword runs down
from its hands.*

*Regarding this object with a mixture of amazement and
distaste are two women: JOAN, an attractive, good-
humoured if tenacious-looking woman in her early thirties,
and MRS ELLIS, her mother, a rather unconsciously sensual
woman in her late fifties. Like her daughter, she is neatly
and prettily dressed. They are also both wearing pinafores:
JOAN's full, MRS ELLIS's petite and frilly and fastened
around her waist.*

JOAN has a label in her hand.

MRS ELLIS. Well . . . They must have sent it here by
mistake.

JOAN (*glancing at the label*). It's the right address.

MRS ELLIS. But it should have gone to the school, surely?
That's where he has all the others.

JOAN. The man said that he'd asked for it to be delivered
here.

MRS ELLIS. Here? But why here? We've nowhere to keep it
here. Whoever would want a thing like that in their
house?

JOAN. Perhaps it's his idea of a joke. (*She looks round the
room.*) At this rate we shan't be here at all soon.

MRS ELLIS. He must *mean* it to go to the school, Joan.

Eventually. That's where all the others are. And he's had it sent here so we can see it.

JOAN. Well, it's strange if he has, because it's the only one I've seen. Queen Elizabeth, George V and all the rest. I'm the only person who hasn't been allowed in. 'Some other time. Some other time.' While any schoolchild can go in and out as he pleases.

MRS ELLIS. I'm sure that's where this will end up. The history museum. Just you see.

JOAN. Clean the paper up, Mother, will you? I'll put his tea on. (*Goes through into the kitchen; she treats her mother strictly, as she would a servant.*)

MRS ELLIS (*clearing up*). Well, it's a surprise, and no mistake.

JOAN (*calling through*). Have you got all the string? I don't want bits left lying about.

MRS ELLIS (*looking up at the armour as she stoops*). Of course . . . it's as you say. His idea of a joke. (*She laughs uneasily.*)

JOAN (*reappearing with the tea-tray to set the table*). Or an insult.

MRS ELLIS. Insult? It needs time to sink in. I can see now . . .

JOAN. Could you put it all in the kitchen. There's a piece of string.

MRS ELLIS, *her arms full of brown paper, stoops down, retrieves the last morsel of string and carries her load into the kitchen.*

JOAN *is setting the table: as she goes to the sideboard during this conversation to get the tablecloth she passes the armour one way, then changes her mind and goes the other, as though it were a person to be avoided.*

MRS ELLIS (*calling through*). Of course, if you were really stuck for somewhere to put it, you could keep it in the bedroom.

JOAN. In the bedroom!

MRS ELLIS (*calling through*). No one would see it, would they?

JOAN. No one?

MRS ELLIS. Not in the bedroom.

JOAN. What about me?

MRS ELLIS (*reappearing*). Well. I'm sure I don't want to quarrel about it.

JOAN (*lightly*). Well, then, at least I'm glad of that.

MRS ELLIS. I do live here as well, Joan.

JOAN (*disregarding*). Could you do the bread? (*Checks her watch with the clock.*) He'll have forgotten altogether that we're going out tonight.

MRS ELLIS. You're so inconsiderate, Joan.

JOAN. It would be different, wouldn't it, if he ever showed any interest in them. But he spreads them all over the place then never looks at them again. Accidentally move one and he comes down on you as though it were the house you'd shifted.

MRS ELLIS. Why can't you let it rest? He doesn't give you anything else to grumble about. You can't complain about him. Not really.

JOAN. He's never out of the damned house. (*She picks up one or two of the pieces.*) He puts on his coat, goes out to school, and leaves them like this. They're like spies. He never lets you rest. Everywhere you look there's some part of him watching and waiting. Even in the bathroom . . .

MRS ELLIS. It's just you, Joan, that.

JOAN. Two slices. That's enough. Well, it's not staying there.

MRS ELLIS. Where are you going to put it?

JOAN. Don't just stand there.

She's taken hold of it, leaning it back, and with MRS ELLIS she drags it over to a built-in cupboard near the kitchen door.

In the cupboard.

MRS ELLIS. In the cupboard! Do you think we should?

JOAN. It's obscene. Something like this in the house. It makes you feel terrible just to touch it . . . These houses weren't built for things like this. Mother: will you open the door?

They put it in the cupboard and JOAN *hands out a few brushes, mops and an umbrella which she gives to* MRS ELLIS *before shutting the cupboard doors on the armour.*

Put those in the kitchen, will you?

MRS ELLIS. Are you going to hide it from him?

JOAN. It'll do for now. Why did he have to have it here? Aren't there enough people here already?

MRS ELLIS *has gone to the kitchen.* JOAN *goes to the door to talk in at her, instructionally.*

No, in the cupboard, Mother. There's his mother and father coming in two days' time. Can you imagine what *they* are going to think?

MRS ELLIS (*re-emerging*). They'll hardly complain, Joan.

JOAN. Coming to somebody's house only to find out as you step through the door it's a museum. It's not a home, it's an institution.

MRS ELLIS. They've never seen *either* of you all these years. They're hardly in a position to judge anybody.

JOAN. But that's just what they will do. They're just about total strangers, aren't they? Come to that, it's just as well they are.

MRS ELLIS. I don't know . . .

JOAN *turns restlessly about the room,* MRS ELLIS *watching her concernedly.*

If only you had something.

JOAN (*beginning to rearrange the tea-table already scrupulously prepared by both of them*). Had something what?

MRS ELLIS. An interest.

JOAN. Interest! I have an interest.

MRS ELLIS. You could go out to work, get a job. You're qualified to do any number of things.

JOAN. This is my house.

MRS ELLIS. I know it's your house, Joan.

JOAN. And it takes some looking after.

MRS ELLIS *doesn't answer.*

I run this as I want it.

MRS ELLIS. All I'm saying is I could run the house while you do something else.

JOAN sits down: MRS ELLIS begins to rearrange the table now.

And there would be so much more coming in.

JOAN. And your widow's pension.

MRS ELLIS. I don't just mean money. But all those opportunities for other interests as well.

JOAN. You think, then, we'd all be better off if we each had an interest?

MRS ELLIS. What's life for if you can't have an interest?

JOAN (*examines her mother shrewdly*). You know, Mother, you're too much like me.

MRS ELLIS. People can laugh at interests, but it's like religion. He who laughs . . .

JOAN (*shouting*). We've got an interest here already! *His!* It's scattered in every cranny of this building. You can't sit down without finding a stone 'with an interesting mark' on it, or a bit of wood that fell off Noah's ark, or a rotten old nail that dropped out of somebody's rotten old chariot. And just look at that thing. Standing behind that cupboard door listening to every word I say. It's not fair. It's not fair.

MRS ELLIS. Joan, I do my work here.

They are silent a moment. Then, contemplative:

JOAN. Do you remember once when you bought him a little statue – a man's head and shoulders? God only knows where his body had got to. And he accidentally knocked it off the sideboard and broke it?

MRS ELLIS. He was more concerned with my feelings than with the thing.

JOAN. He wanted to get rid of it.

MRS ELLIS. He did not.

JOAN. He wanted to get rid of it. It was the only thing that resembled a human being in the entire house.

MRS ELLIS. You've never understood him, Joan. You never have.

JOAN. And now he brings this thing. There's something

strange about it. It's the first lifelike thing he's ever had here. He usually keeps them all at school. (*She gets up.*)

MRS ELLIS. Joan. You don't understand my position here.

JOAN *begins preparations to go out.*

Where are you going?

JOAN. Out. (*She goes to the door leading to the hall.*)

MRS ELLIS (*alone*). If you're hoping to go to the cinema you'll have to leave almost as soon as he comes in . . . He'll be back any time now.

JOAN (*calling through*). I won't be long. (*She enters with a coat she puts on over her pinafore.*) He's not going to find me waiting here, that's all.

MRS ELLIS. Waiting here?

JOAN. Stuck here amongst his trophies.

MRS ELLIS *watches* JOAN *make up her face in the mirror.*

I'll go down to the corner, or something.

MRS ELLIS. It's ridiculous.

JOAN (*turning to her*). I'll go out the back way, then there's no chance of meeting.

MRS ELLIS. Joan. This is silly. (*Suddenly, looking at the cupboard.*) You won't be long, will you, Joan?

JOAN. Don't mention *that* until I come in. (*She indicates the cupboard.*) Do you understand?

MRS ELLIS. Yes. But . . .

JOAN. And for God's sake don't say I've just gone out. Say I've been gone an hour. All right? (*She leaves by the kitchen door.*)

MRS ELLIS. You won't be long, love, will you?

MRS ELLIS *glances at the cupboard again, then goes to the table, fingers and rearranges the various tea-things, then moves uncertainly about the room, avoiding the cupboard area completely. Finally she comes face to face with the mirror, glances at it, then becomes increasingly interested in her reflection. She begins to examine her face, its various expressions of hope and dismay, glee and uncertainty, unconsciously producing animal noises, purring and cooing. She becomes lost in herself; her body heaves for a sigh, then suddenly relaxes in a huge, vaguely grotesque smile.*

ARNIE, *a well-built man in his thirties, has appeared in the hall doorway. He watches a while, expressionless, then comes quietly into the room until he is almost behind MRS ELLIS. Then he suddenly barks like a dog.*

MRS ELLIS *gives a scream of fright. Then:*

MRS ELLIS. Oh, Arnie! Arnie!

ARNIE. Loved one!

MRS ELLIS (*recovering*). It's just what you'd expect from a schoolmaster.

ARNIE (*takes off his old raincoat*). Master, Edie. Master. Watch this, Edie. (*Using his coat as a whip he begins to beat the floor.*)

MRS ELLIS *watches this with interest and pleasure, yet as though she's seen it all before. She sits down at the table to watch.*

Take that. And that. And that – you sniffling snot-gobbling little crat. And *that*. I'll teach you to take my stick of chalk. (*He growls and roars as he drives the imaginary child into the floor. He steps on the spot and spreads the remnants thoroughly over the carpet.*) Got it! Got it! Now. How do you like that, Edie? I know how to take care of these little crats.

MRS ELLIS. I don't know. It's a wonder any of them stay alive.

ARNIE. Know? Edie! You know. You know everything.

MRS ELLIS (*pleased*). What! Me!

ARNIE. You.

MRS ELLIS. More than a schoolteacher?

ARNIE. Yes.

MRS ELLIS. Well . . . I don't know . . . (*She holds her cheek with pleasure.*)

ARNIE *watches her, suddenly intent. Then:*

ARNIE. Look . . . (*His mood relaxes again.*) Did you see his face? The way he looked when I hit him the first time. He thought I didn't mean it. He thought I'd *let him off* for taking my stick of chalk. Mind you – he'd every reason to think I wouldn't beat his lousy head in. These *dwarfs* think you're frightened of being reprimanded, of being handed over to the . . .

MRS ELLIS. And will you get the sack?

ARNIE. No such fortune for me. (*He sits down and begins to tug off his shoes. His mood changes again. Reflective.*) If I rape two, or perhaps it may have to be three, I might be asked if I'd mind being moved to another school. But chances of promotion like that are increasingly rare. (*He gets his last shoe off with a struggle.*) Rape apart, it's all a question of dead men's shoes, Edie.

MRS ELLIS (*concernedly*). I wish you wouldn't use language like that, Arnie.

ARNIE (*holding up his shoes*). Ill-will; that's the cargo these shoes carry. Along, that is, with my own personal misfortunes. (*He searches round, sees MRS ELLIS's feet and, on hands and knees, crawls across to them as though they were shoes he was hunting.*) Why . . . Why, these are full of hopes.

MRS ELLIS. Oh, now . . .

ARNIE. Can't you feel them: growing beneath your feet? Why, Edie, your shoes are full of hope. It's sprouting through your toes . . .

MRS ELLIS. All I feel is how glad I am I didn't know what teachers were like when our Joan went to school.

ARNIE. Where is SHE, by the way? Not gone off on my bike, her dress tucked into her bloomers.

MRS ELLIS. Really, Arnie . . . She's just gone out. I mean, *merely* gone out.

ARNIE. Merely gone out?

MRS ELLIS. She's only gone out. That's what I mean.

ARNIE. Only gone out. Not merely gone out.

MRS ELLIS. She's . . . out.

ARNIE. I see.

MRS ELLIS. Your tea's on the table.

ARNIE. We're supposed to be going to the cinema. Let me see. (*Consults his wrist-watch.*) Half an hour ago.

MRS ELLIS. She'll only be a few minutes . . . (*Hurries into the kitchen.*)

ARNIE (*knowingly and quickly searching the room*). It all seems carefully timed. What's going on?

MRS ELLIS (*calling through*). She's so restless. She can't sit down two minutes these days without getting up again because there's something not satisfactory. I don't know . . . it's just everything.

ARNIE *turns at this and goes to the table. He sits down and begins to put some jam on the bread.*

MRS ELLIS (*calling through*). How's your play going at school?

ARNIE *plays with the bread abstractedly.* MRS ELLIS *reappears in the kitchen door with a teapot.*

You. Can't you hear me when I talk to you?

ARNIE. What's that, chump-chops?

MRS ELLIS. None of your cheek. Haven't you been rehearsing this afternoon?

ARNIE *breaks his mood to give a dramatic recitation.*

ARNIE.
    Said Robin Hood to Friar Tuck,
    'How are you my fat fellow?'
    'I'm very well,' said the cheerful monk,
    'But I'm sorry you're looking yellow.'

    'Is that a jest or would you dare
    To challenge your captain staunch?'
    'Nay,' said the Friar, 'don't threaten me,
    Or I'll kill you with my paunch.'

MRS ELLIS (*giggles*). Is that it?

ARNIE. A generous portion of it, Edie. On the whole, I think it will appear neither conspicuous nor insignificant on the contemporary theatrical scene.

MRS ELLIS (*pouring his tea*). Is it going very well?

ARNIE. A minor alarm this morning when the Lionheart tripped over his scabbard. He'll appear on stage with a bandage round his leg – a wound sustained, while fighting the Turks outside Damascus.

MRS ELLIS. They're only boys. What are you calling the play?

ARNIE. I don't know. (*Thoughtfully.*) 'Hands up, Sheriff, your Money or your Wife.'

MRS ELLIS. Oh, now.

ARNIE. 'The Good King Richard and the Bad King John!' Probably, 'Robin Hood and His Merry Men', Edie.

MRS ELLIS. Oh, that's nice. (MRS ELLIS *sits down opposite* ARNIE *and watches him eat his tea.*) And is it adpated from William Shakespeare, then?

ARNIE. No. Jeffrey Hanson. He's the head of the English Department. He's coming round tomorrow evening to discuss the less serious aspects of the play. So that'll be tea for two, Edie.

MRS ELLIS. Oh, I'll be out late tomorrow, getting things in. (*Silence.*) Are you looking forward to them coming? Are you listening?

ARNIE. Yes.

MRS ELLIS. What are they like?

ARNIE. Who?

MRS ELLIS. You know. Silly.

ARNIE. Oh. (*Dismisses it.*)

MRS ELLIS. Of course, I only met them that once at the wedding. Ten years. (*She broods.*) It's not often you meet decent people nowadays. (*Suddenly.*) You complain that they never come to see you. Yet you've never been to see them.

ARNIE. No.

MRS ELLIS. Did you have a happy childhood, Arnie?

ARNIE. Did you?

MRS ELLIS (*laughs*). No: I'm asking you. I bet you were a model child.

ARNIE (*pleasantly*). I was. Facsimiles of me could be seen all over the place at one time, Edie.

MRS ELLIS *becomes preoccupied with her thoughts, getting up and wandering round the room distractedly.*

MRS ELLIS. You know, Arnie . . .

ARNIE *is getting out a pipe and looking round.*

Joan. She's been in such a funny mood today.

ARNIE. Yes.

MRS ELLIS. You've stopped listening, haven't you?

ARNIE. I have not.

MRS ELLIS. She's been suggesting, you know . . . that I wasn't much use to anyone.

ARNIE. You know, Edie, I've told you before. I'm not stepping in between your women's fights.

MRS ELLIS (*coming to the table*). Do you want another cup?

ARNIE. Thanks.

MRS ELLIS *pours a cup*. ARNIE *fusses with his pipe*.

It would be nice to have a proper job and a decent home, wouldn't it?

MRS ELLIS. Arnie! You have a decent home. And it could be even better if you'd let me.

ARNIE. Better?

MRS ELLIS. Cleaner and neater.

ARNIE. Cleaner than this?

He stirs up his tea with milk and sugar. MRS ELLIS watches him acutely, the teapot still in her hand.

MRS ELLIS. In a way.

ARNIE. In a way! Why can't we ever hold a decent conversation in this house? I teach in a madhouse all day, then come home to another at night.

MRS ELLIS (*outraged*). Arnie!

ARNIE. It's not right. You and Joan . . . If you would only say what you meant. Just once.

MRS ELLIS. You don't begrudge me staying here, do you?

ARNIE. No.

MRS ELLIS. I could go away. I'm not so old . . .

ARNIE. Edie. What are you talking about? (*He gets up from the table and moves about the room, apparently looking for matches.*)

MRS ELLIS. Fancy . . . Do you remember that little statue I bought you once as a present? That was accidentally broken?

ARNIE. What? (*Taps out his pipe abstracted.*)

MRS ELLIS. Joan said – this afternoon – that you broke it deliberately. Because you didn't like it. And you hadn't the heart to tell me.

ARNIE. Now, look. I don't have to stand here and listen to

all this, Edie. You're a woman in your own right: you must stick up for yourself.

MRS ELLIS. I don't want to cause any bother. I don't. But Joan's always making me feel I haven't got anything at all . . . nothing.

She's clearly upset. ARNIE watches her. Then crosses to her, and takes her shoulders.

ARNIE. I didn't break it on purpose, Edie. And it wasn't a statue. It was a piece of pottery made to look like stone. I appreciated you giving it to me. All right?

She looks into his eyes, then nods.

So there's no need to start an argument, is there?

MRS ELLIS. No.

The front door bangs, and ARNIE releases her.

ARNIE. Quick. Hide under the table and tickle her knees.

MRS ELLIS. Get on with you, you devil!

She's laughing as JOAN comes in: then goes to clear the table.

ARNIE has taken a comic from his pocket and propped it on the mantelpiece to read aloud.

JOAN looks at them both, then goes to the mirror and takes off her coat.

ARNIE (*reading like a child*). G . . . g . . . g . . . gooood . . . ness g . . . g . . . g . . . gra . . . gra . . . gracious! Ssss . . . ssss . . . ssssaid th . . . th . . . th . . . the F . . . Ffff . . . Ffff . . . Fairy Qu . . . Qu . . . Qu . . . Queen . . .

JOAN. That girl's followed you home from school again. I suppose you realise.

ARNIE goes casually to the window.

ARNIE. What?

JOAN. O'Connor. Isn't that her name?

ARNIE (*looking out*). I don't know what I'd do without her. Always that faithful twenty-five yards behind . . . Like a progressive following the revolution.

MRS ELLIS joins him to look out too.

JOAN. She moved smartly across the road when I came in. And no wonder.

MRS ELLIS. What does she hope to get out of it?

ARNIE. Some people do things, Edie, not for what they can get but for what they can give . . .

JOAN. Oh, very nice. For two damn pins I'd go out there and give *her* something she *wouldn't* be grateful for!

As ARNIE turns from the window.

And I thought we were going out tonight?

ARNIE. I'm ready when you are. I'll just finish this instalment then I'll be right with you.

JOAN. Is that a child's magazine?

ARNIE. It's all right. I didn't buy it. I stole it from a desk. (*He takes the comic and goes to the stairs: the sound of his feet ascending, then a door closing.*)

JOAN goes to the window.

JOAN. Has he seen that?

MRS ELLIS. No.

JOAN. Are you sure?

MRS ELLIS. I'm positive.

JOAN. What have you been crying about?

MRS ELLIS. I haven't been crying. (*She finishes clearing the table.*)

JOAN. It doesn't look like that.

MRS ELLIS. We were talking about his parents, if you must know.

JOAN. What about his parents?

MRS ELLIS. Nothing you would understand.

JOAN watches her intently. Then:

JOAN. I don't like this. I don't.

MRS ELLIS. What?

JOAN. This! *This!* (*She grabs and tugs at her mother's pinafore.*)

MRS ELLIS. What?

JOAN doesn't answer.

What's the matter with . . .

JOAN. It's all wrong! (*She swings on the room. Neither can speak.*)

MRS ELLIS. I'll take mine off, then.

JOAN. Take *yours* off?

MRS ELLIS *takes her apron off slowly: she lays the petite-looking thing absent-mindedly on* ARNIE's *raincoat on the chair.*

Not there! Not there! (*She snatches it up and throws it on the floor.*)

MRS ELLIS. Joannie . . .

JOAN. I don't like this. I don't.

MRS ELLIS. What is it, pet?

JOAN. Don't *pet* me.

MRS ELLIS. Joan . . .

JOAN. You weren't talking about his parents. You were talking about *me*.

MRS ELLIS. Do you think we've nothing better . . .

JOAN. Don't say *we*! You were talking about me. You were talking to him about me. Did you tell him . . . did you say anything about that? (*She gestures at the cupboard.*)

MRS ELLIS. No.

ARNIE's *feet are stamping down the stairs:* JOAN *goes to stand by the cupboard doors.*

ARNIE *comes in smoking a pipe. He begins to put on his shoes.*

ARNIE. Well, ready?

JOAN. I have a surprise for you first.

ARNIE (*genially*). Yes.

JOAN. Are you ready?

ARNIE. Yes . . . Just a minute. Right.

JOAN. All right?

ARNIE. Yes.

JOAN *swings open the cupboard doors.*

JOAN. There.

ARNIE (*smokes on*). Oh, that's where it is.

JOAN. How do you mean, that's where it is?

ARNIE. I couldn't imagine where you'd hidden it. It wasn't upstairs; I've just looked.

JOAN (*crying out at* MRS ELLIS). You told him! You liar!

ARNIE. As a matter of fact, I asked the man to ring up the school and let me know when he delivered it.

JOAN. You *sneak*!

ARNIE. I'm not sneaking. I've been waiting for it to come.

JOAN. You rotten, bloody sneak. I've been walking around out there . . .

ARNIE. Walking round?

JOAN. What's it doing here?

ARNIE. Walking round?

JOAN. What's it doing *here*?

ARNIE. Walking *round*?

JOAN. *What's it doing here*?

ARNIE. It looks to me as though it's standing in a cupboard. (*To armour.*) Aren't you coming in, old man?

JOAN. I mean *here*! Here! At this house. You usually have all this junk thrown into your mausoleum at school.

ARNIE. But I didn't buy this with school funds.

JOAN. What?

ARNIE *is smoking still.*

ARNIE. It's mine. I bought it myself.

JOAN. Yours? (*Pause.*) What sort of tale is this, Arnold?

ARNIE. I've always wanted one. (*He puts his pipe in his mouth, and eases the armour out of the cupboard: he sets it upright in the room.*)

JOAN. When did you buy it?

ARNIE. What?

JOAN. When did you buy it?

ARNIE. A few days ago.

JOAN. Why? What for? Don't you think we've enough with this already?

ARNIE. You're very aggressive, Joan. Has it assaulted you or something behind my back?

JOAN. It's going back where it came from.

ARNIE. It even smokes a pipe. I told you it was respectable. I don't know. It might easily entertain political ambitions.

JOAN. I've tolerated everything else, Arnie. But not this.

ARNIE *takes no notice: he's detaching the sword.*

Can't you see? The place isn't built for a thing like this.

ARNIE *leaps with a shout and swings the sword at* MRS ELLIS, *who escapes with a scream.*

MRS ELLIS. Arnie!

ARNIE *snorts at her.*

JOAN. Where do you think you're going to keep it for one thing? In the garden?

MRS ELLIS (*standing behind a chair*). Oh. We can't keep it there. (*Jumps.*) Joan! Everybody would see it.

JOAN. And I'm not having it in the kitchen, peering over my shoulder. And not in the bathroom, the bedroom, the living-room or the hall.

ARNIE *stalks* MRS ELLIS: 'No, Arnie! No!'

ARNIE (*holding the blade to her*). D'you think it's blood?

JOAN. It's not staying here, Arnie. It's ugly. That's enough!

ARNIE. Well. Are we ready? (*He fits the sword back into place.*)

JOAN. Ready?

ARNIE. To go out.

JOAN. Are we going out now? And leave this?

ARNIE. What do you want me to do? Hug it and give it a kiss? It won't run away. Well, Edie . . . how about you then?

MRS ELLIS. Going out? I don't mind going out. Why, it's ages . . .

JOAN. It's all right. (*She goes to her coat.*) Tomorrow, first thing: that's going.

ARNIE. Aren't you going to take your apron off?

JOAN. What?

ARNIE. Your how d'you do.

JOAN *sees she's still got on her pinafore.*

Don't you want to come, Edie?

MRS ELLIS. Well . . .

JOAN *has almost wrenched off her pinafore and, watching her mother, pulls on her coat.*

JOAN. She'll be quite all right at home.

MRS ELLIS. I wouldn't have minded going out. I don't really fancy being left alone with this, Arnie.

ARNIE. Get your coat, Granny, and away we go!
MRS ELLIS. Ay, now . . .

ARNIE *puts his arm round* JOAN *as* MRS ELLIS *gets her coat.*

ARNIE. It's not half as bad as it seems.
JOAN. It's too much, Arnie, that's all. (*But she is appeased by his coaxing gestures.*) Stop playing around . . .
ARNIE.
O sing us a song, you hearty woman,
Of all your dark crimes and your fears;
And we'll swallow your pride and lie down by your side,
And digest all your grief in our tears.
JOAN. Do you hear . . .

MRS ELLIS *has returned with her coat.*

ARNIE. Ah, now, a gorgeous old lady of twenty-one . . .
MRS ELLIS. Inches round the neck. I know.
ARNIE. Oh, now Edie. You enlarge yourself . . . (*He goes to help her with her coat.*)
MRS ELLIS. Oh, I know. Don't worry. I wasn't born yesterday.
ARNIE. If you insist.
MRS ELLIS. There you are, you see . . . And I ought to have done my face.
ARNIE. Only a disservice, my dear.
MRS ELLIS. Goodness. What's got into him?

ARNIE *takes her hand.*

ARNIE.
Pray take advantage of my goodwill:
Let us share it between the two;
Take all you can and in return
I'll do the same for you.
JOAN. Come on, we better be going out before he breaks into song.
ARNIE. A moment. (*He sidles with exaggerated caution to the window, carefully lifts the curtain, and looks out.*) The coast's clear. (*To* JOAN.) Your glance spoke as eloquently as your thoughts, my dear. Her loyalty knew no bounds — and now you've presented it with several.

JOAN. At least we can go out now, without being molested.

ARNIE. You always could. It's me who is the loser. (*He puts his arm about the two women. As they go out:*)
Gay Robin Hood to town did ride
With maidens fair on either side:
The evil Sheriff and the bad King John
Ne'er recognized the gentlemon.

JOAN *waits patiently.*

(*Hesitates.*) . . . Yes. (*He sweeps them out of the room. A moment later, however, he dashes back in, knocks his pipe out on the armour, boxes it briefly, pats it, then hurries out.*)

ARNIE's *voice is heard crying with pleasure, then a door crashes to, and it's silent.*

The room slowly darkens.

Scene Two

The door bursts open, there's giggling and laughter: then MRS ELLIS *and* ARNIE *enter, followed a moment later by* JOAN.

ARNIE. We should . . . we should . . . we should . . .

MRS ELLIS. But we didn't. (*She breaks into outrageous laughter.*)

ARNIE. But we should have!

JOAN. We'd have been home a damn sight sooner if we had. Weee! (*She throws her shoes into the air and runs across the furniture.*)

ARNIE (*instructionally*). If we had we wouldn't have had to stand all the way back. (*He belches.*)

JOAN. I'll be sick if I drink any more.

MRS ELLIS. It was your idea.

ARNIE. She doesn't have ideas, Mother. Only prejudices.

JOAN *barks angrily like a dog at* ARNIE, *snarling then growling.*

MRS ELLIS. Whatever anybody says, I enjoyed myself. I enjoyed myself. (*Telling herself.*) How about you, Joan?

JOAN. All the time . . . All the time . . . asking each other if

we've had a good time? All the way back (*Mimicking.*)
'Have you had a good time, *Arnie*?' 'Have you had a good
time, Edie?'

ARNIE. Well, have you had a good time, Edie?

JOAN. What did you call me?

*ARNIE has turned from her and taken MRS ELLIS by the
shoulders, looking into her face.*

You called me Edie!

*ARNIE turns from MRS ELLIS, one hand still holding her
shoulder, and he begins to recite with a boy's mechanical,
tutored gestures to an imaginary audience.*

ARNIE.

I have lived a long time, mother,
And seen strange sights beyond the seas,
But never a one have I seen, mother,
To match the dimples in your knees.

MRS ELLIS has burst out laughing.

JOAN (*calling out*). You called me Edie, you swab.

ARNIE.

There are women who shout and women who moan,
And women who titter down the phone,
But the only women that I ever see
Are the ones that need hanging from the nearest tree.

JOAN (*calling*). You're disgusting!

ARNIE.

My wife Joan has a heart of stone,
And eyes as black as charcoal,
She wouldn't have looked bad
If she hadn't have had
A mouth the shape of her arsehole.

JOAN. I'll kill you!

*MRS ELLIS attempts to drag her back: ARNIE has leapt
with great alacrity behind the Knight who, until now, has
gone unnoticed.*

ARNIE. If you touch me I'll set him on to you.

JOAN. And tomorrow that thing's going first thing.

ARNIE. He'll tear you to pieces!

For a moment they stand poised, silent. Then:

MRS ELLIS. I think you both better get to bed.

ARNIE. Did you hear . . . (*He steps cautiously from behind the Knight, reassures himself from* JOAN's *look that he's safe.*) Did you hear, as we passed them in the street, what those . . . *children* called me? Children – I might add – whom I teach and instruct in my own classroom.

MRS ELLIS. It's nothing I'd care to repeat.

ARNIE. And it's nothing, I can assure you, Mother, that I've taught them. Those words are not in the curriculum. I even thought once that they liked me.

JOAN. You shouldn't go round getting plastered where they can see you.

ARNIE *takes* MRS ELLIS's *hand suddenly.*

ARNIE. Here . . . here darling.

He leads her to the arm of a chair, sitting beside her to recite:

There are things in your life
Not even your wife
Would think could pass through your brain.
But give me a light
And I'll show you a sight
That would turn even Satan insane.

MRS ELLIS *laughs, shocked, and breaks away.*

MRS ELLIS. I think I'll be getting to bed . . .

JOAN. Oh, no, Mother.

MRS ELLIS. What?

JOAN. You're not going to bed till you've helped me shift this.

ARNIE. Where to?

JOAN. I'm not going to bed, I'm not. I'd never rest. Not with this wandering loose in the house.

ARNIE. What's it going to get up and do?

JOAN. It's going back in its kennel. And tomorrow . . .

ARNIE. . . . . morning it's going out first thing. (*They finish the phrase together.*)

JOAN has begun to struggle with it back to the cupboard, MRS ELLIS *going to help her.* ARNIE *watches them ironically, arms folded, though he's still bleary with drink.*

Rub-adub-dub, three nuts in a tub,
Who do you think they can be?

JOAN (*struggling*). I've told you. Tomorrow morning . . .

ARNIE (*together*). . . . it's going out first thing. (*He has switched on the wireless.*)

JOAN. You don't seem to believe me. But it is. The minute you've gone to school.

Dance music has started as the women haul the armour slowly to the cupboard. ARNIE has begun to dance, taking a bottle to drink.

And I don't want to see it again. Do you hear? (*She hiccups.*)

ARNIE dances on, oblivious to them. As JOAN fastens the cupboard doors, MRS ELLIS turns to watch ARNIE dance, amused.

MRS ELLIS. That's a sight for sore eyes. He can hardly put two feet together. (*Laughs. Then claps.*)

ARNIE looks up at her with sultry affection, eyes half-closed.

ARNIE. Oh, I don't know . . . all that there and so forth. Hup-dee. Hup-dee.

JOAN (*hiccups*). Do you hear?

ARNIE takes MRS ELLIS's hand and they dance loosely together, MRS ELLIS laughing still.

ARNIE (*swaying his hips*). That's it, Edie. That's it. Swill it all around . . . Give it a good shake.

JOAN has picked up a bottle: she seems about to use it both on the wireless and ARNIE, then some instinctive coquettishness overcomes her and, bottle dangling, she puts her arm round ARNIE, who's spouting his own bottle to his lips.

JOAN. Move over, babe. (*She bumps her mother.*) Let's have a dance, honey.

The three of them, holding together, dance slowly and lugubriously.

ARNIE. Sing us a song, Joannie.

JOAN. I can't sing . . . (*Hiccups.*) I can't sing. (*She makes several near-noises approximating to the music.*)

ARNIE. Oh, lovely, beautiful. (*He belches.*)

MRS ELLIS *dances away on her own; a slow waltz, not ungraceful. She holds her skirt and dances with a slow nostalgia.*

Oh, lovely, Edie. Lovely.

MRS ELLIS *dances on.* JOAN *and* ARNIE *stop to watch her, intrigued.*

JOAN. Go on, Mother. Let 'em have it. (*Hiccup.*)

MRS ELLIS (*dancing*). Do you like it?

ARNIE. Go on, Edie. Don't stop. She's good. She's good. Oh, she's good. Just look at her little old legs going!

MRS ELLIS. What's the matter with my legs?

JOAN. You should see yourself, darling.

ARNIE. Take no notice of her, Edie. They're all right. You can take my word for it.

MRS ELLIS (*stopping, looking down at her legs*). I've got good legs . . . I always have had, since I was a young woman.

JOAN. Mother!

MRS ELLIS. What's the matter? (*She lowers her skirt.*)

JOAN (*with sudden bravado*). Those (*Hiccup.*) are legs, if you want them! (*Lifts her skirt discreetly and poses her legs.*) There's no comparison . . . Lift your skirt up. Lift. Come on. (*She pulls at her mother's skirt.*) You just look. Arnie. What do you say? (*Hiccup.*)

ARNIE *has already turned away.*

Hold it up, Mother. (*She turns round, for the first time aware of* ARNIE'*s lack of attention.*) Go on. What do you think? (*Pause.*) Arnie, for God's sake!

ARNIE *blearily turns round.*

ARNIE. What . . .

JOAN. What do you say?

MRS ELLIS *turns to him, holding her skirt like a child paddling, her mood a vague stupor between elation and tiredness.*

ARNIE. What . . .
JOAN. Look, damn you!

ARNIE *is overcome with weariness.*

Tell her, for God's sake. (*She has still one hand guardedly holding her mother's skirt, the other her own.*)
ARNIE. Tell her . . . ?
JOAN. What you think.
ARNIE. You want me to, Edie?
MRS ELLIS. I don't mind, love. (*Giggles.*) It's getting draughty here.
JOAN. Look, look. We're walking. How's it look?

ARNIE *sits down, drunkenly and tired. He watches, frowning, and belches.*

ARNIE. Like a camel. (*He finishes off the bottle, toasting the cupboard doors.*)
JOAN. Just look at her, then. Mother, you walk up and down. And keep your skirts up. (*Suddenly aware of ARNIE's diversion.*) You're not watching! (*Hiccup.*) For God's sake. We're walking! Here! Give me that! (*She snatches the bottle from him.*) All gone. Pig. (*She throws the bottle down, and suddenly snatches his hair.*) NOW – choose!

ARNIE *sinks down in the chair, calling out.*

Who's got the best legs! (*Hiccup.*)
ARNIE. Help! Let go! You're hurting . . . Yarooo!
JOAN. I'm going to hurt you. Open your great mouth and tell her.
ARNIE. Edie! Tell her to let go. She's drunk. She doesn't know. OW!
MRS ELLIS. Why don't you do as she says, Arnie?
ARNIE. OW!

The chair slips: JOAN's grip tightens: ARNIE falls to his knees, calling out, more helpless than he'd realised, his humour, however, still apparent.

For God's sake let go, Joan. I'm an historian.

JOAN. Choose. (*Hiccup.*)

ARNIE. If you don't let go I'll maim you.

JOAN. You try, then.

MRS ELLIS *has picked up some sewing scissors from the sideboard. She's laughing, holding her skirt still with one hand as though she were paddling.*

MRS ELLIS. If you hold him still I can cut his hair!

JOAN. Go on, then, Mam . . .

MRS ELLIS. I'll cut it all off, Arnie!

ARNIE. Get off!

JOAN. Go on, Mam. Give him a cut. (*Hiccup.*)

She pulls at his hair and ARNIE *gives a real cry of pain, and can only bend more ineffectually to the floor.* JOAN *holds up the hair while, one-handed – her other holding up her skirt –* MRS ELLIS *cuts it off.*

MRS ELLIS. There! . . . There! He looks younger already!

JOAN. And another. Go on, Mam!

ARNIE. Let go. Or I'll kill you. Both of you.

JOAN. Go on, then. You stupid devil.

MRS ELLIS. Choose, Arnie. Then she'll let you go.

JOAN. Choose!

ARNIE. Edie! She's got the best legs. All the way.

JOAN. What? (*Hiccup.*)

ARNIE. Edie's! Edie's, all the way.

JOAN *has released him.*

JOAN. You prefer *her* to me!

ARNIE. Completely. (*He's still kneeling, clutching his head, still humoured, considering how best to take his revenge.*)

JOAN (*hiccup*). You don't love *me*!

ARNIE. No!

JOAN. You've never loved me.

ARNIE. Never!

JOAN. You just wanted *that* (*Hiccup.*) and then it was all over.

ARNIE. Absolutely.

JOAN. You don't love me.

MRS ELLIS (*chastened*). Let's get to bed. For goodness sake. We're not in our senses. Come on. Let's get up.

JOAN. Yes. Yes! I know . . . I know . . . (*Implying.*)

MRS ELLIS. Joan . . .

JOAN *hiccups.*

ARNIE. Make way! Make way! Move back!

JOAN. You've never loved me.

ARNIE. Oh! Oh! Oh!

JOAN. I know what's going on. Don't worry.

ARNIE. Why. Why. Why. All the time. Nothing but this, baby!

MRS ELLIS. Take no notice. None of you. It doesn't mean anything. It's nothing.

JOAN (*to* MRS ELLIS). Well, what are you doing here, then? (*Hiccup.*) Come on. Come on. You be honest just this once.

MRS ELLIS. Joannie! Joannie!

JOAN. History or no bloody history. Don't think I haven't noticed. (*Hiccup.*) And that *thing*! All the time. Stuck in there listening to every word. (*She gestures at the cupboard.*)

ARNIE. I'm going up . . .

JOAN. Arnie. Tell her. Tell her to go.

ARNIE *pauses on his way to the stairs.*

Tell her to go. (*Hiccup.*)

ARNIE (*pauses, then*). If your Bob doesn't pay our Bob that bob that your Bob owes our Bob our Bob will give your Bob a bob on the nose.

JOAN. Arnie! Tell her! Tell her!

ARNIE.

Tiger, tiger, burning bright,
In the forests of the night,
If you see a five-pound note
Then take my tip and cut your throat.

JOAN. Tell her to go!

MRS ELLIS. No, Arnie!

ARNIE.

The man in the moon has a chocolate spoon,
And eyeballs made of custard;

His big fat head is a loaf of bread,
And his whiskers are peppered with mustard.
JOAN. Arnie!

ARNIE *pauses again, bows to them with a flourish. Then:*

ARNIE. Ladies. Ladies. Ladies. (*He goes.*)
JOAN. Arnie!
MRS ELLIS. Arnie!

Lights fade.

ACT TWO

Scene One
Late afternoon.

JEFF HANSON *slumps in an easy chair. He's dressed in sports coat and flannels, a very long college scarf with tassels, bowler hat and yellow gloves: the eternal student. The gloves he eventually peels off, but the bowler hat remains on his head. He also retains a stout walking-stick which he uses to amplify and reinforce his conversation. He is about forty, a middle-aged man with certain, perhaps obsessive desires to retain his youth.*

Standing behind him is the suit of armour.

ARNIE *himself sits at the table smoking a pipe.*

JOAN *is out of sight, cleaning the stairs with a hand-brush and pan.*

HANSON (*raised voice*). My dear Joan, I wouldn't believe a word of it.
JOAN (*heard*). It was absolutely nothing at all.
HANSON. Absolutely.
JOAN. We were drunk.
HANSON. Of course.
JOAN (*heard*). We'd all had too much.
HANSON. Naturally.

   JOAN *appears in the door.*

JOAN. So whatever he's told you . . .
HANSON. My dear china, he's told me nothing. All we've heard are hints from you.
JOAN. You never know . . . (*Watching* ARNIE *suspiciously.*)
HANSON. And if he had it would be of no account. Our long friendship (*Indicating* ARNIE.) is based on the simple precaution that I never believe a single word he says. I hate to indulge in scepticism of any sort but events have always justified my foresight.
ARNIE. He's lying as dextrously himself . . .
HANSON. Arnold, I'm the last person to step between a

man and his mother-in-law, as well you know. Despite all
your accounts of domestic felicities I have always
refrained from intruding. The only reason I don't agitate
my hands about my ears is the faint hope that I may hear
an explanation . . . (*He is looking steadfastly at* ARNIE.)

JOAN. Of what?

HANSON. A remarkable occurrence that took place at
school this morning, my dear. (*Suddenly looking up at*
JOAN.) I'm astonished you're not already acquainted with
it.

JOAN (*watching* ARNIE). Well, I'm not.

ARNIE. It was nothing.

HANSON. Nothing!

ARNIE. A slight miscalculation.

HANSON. My dear Joan – hardly were we assembled in the
hall – eight hundred *youthful* spirits about to make the
most *hearty* obeisances to the one and only – when what
should we glimpse through the door backing on to the
stage but the most incredible apparition you can imagine!
Beyond the Headmaster's stout and noble figure – its eyes
raised, somewhat prematurely it now appears, towards the
Heavens – could be discerned a man accompanied by a
suit of armour, stealthily creeping by under the obvious
delusion that our devotions concealed him from our view.
At first our benevolent autocrat mistook the huge and
hideous roar that greeted this astonishing sight for one of
religious fervour, his eyes travelling quickly downwards in
a mixture of horror and surprise. (*Pause.*) Standing there
in all his furtive glory was Arnold, smiling shyly in the
arms of his new-found friend, and making unmistakable
gestures with his one free hand that we should ignore his
presence as best we may. God in Heaven, I said to myself,
is this a manifestation – the not-unforeseen consequence
of our rigorous vocation – or has Arnold, my dearest and
closest friend, taken complete and utter leave of his
senses?

ARNIE. She wanted to get rid of it. I had to protect it the
only way I could. If I hadn't taken it to school, she'd have
thrown it away.

JOAN. They must have laughed themselves sick!

HANSON. Except for the Head, my dear. Assuming it to be

a comment upon his own austere régime – perhaps even on the strenuous nature of his religious practices – he ordered its immediate seizure and removal from the premises. It spent the remainder of its day, I believe, in the coal cellar, until its owner could take it home. (*He looks expectantly at* ARNIE.) Well?

ARNIE *puffs contentedly at his pipe.*

Aren't you going to tell us? (*Pause.*) Is it some cheap means, Arnold, of publicising your subject at the expense of others on the curriculum? (*Pause.*) Perhaps an indication to us of the kind of company you actually prefer.

ARNIE. I've told you why I took it to school.

JOAN. You won't get anything out of him.

HANSON. What is this, Arnold? Are we no longer sufficient for you? Your dear wife, your friends, your devoted pupils . . . Or is it that you feel a sword is necessary to prompt us to a proper admiration of your extraordinary talents? Ungrateful may be the world, but, Arnold, surely not those who know you.

ARNIE. It won't be here much longer. You better take advantage of it while you can.

JOAN. Not here? (*Pause.*) Where's it going?

HANSON. Not – back to school?

ARNIE. No.

JOAN. Where, then?

ARNIE. As a matter of fact it's a present.

JOAN. A present!

HANSON. A present. Not for . . . (*Gestures at himself.*)

ARNIE. No.

HANSON. Nor . . . (*He gestures at* JOAN.)

ARNIE *moves away.*

ARNIE. For my parents.

JOAN. Your parents!

ARNIE. That's the last I want to hear of it.

HANSON. But . . . of course, I'm not acquainted with the couple . . . and far be it from me to judge from preconceptions. But are they . . . I mean, is it something

they've always wanted? Do they have a fondness for
metallic men?

JOAN. You've never said it was a present. You never said it
was.

ARNIE. I take it I'm entitled to a little privacy of intention.

JOAN. Privacy of *what*?

HANSON. You mean they collect suits of armour?

JOAN. You let me shout down the house. (*Catching hold of
him.*) Look . . . have you just invented this?

ARNIE. That's all I want to hear of it. I've told you. Now
you know. It's a present.

JOAN. He's always inventing things when he thinks it suits
him. Why . . .

ARNIE. It's over.

JOAN. My God!

HANSON. All these alarums, then, were merely to conceal
the natural benevolence of your heart. What stratagems
men will go to to disguise their proper virtues!

JOAN, *however, is watching* ARNIE *with a mixture of
disbelief and condemnation.*

JOAN. Do you expect me to believe that? What's the point
of buying them that? Of all things.

ARNIE *doesn't answer.*

Aren't you going to *talk*? (*Pause.*) All right. Just do as you
damn well please. (*To* ARNIE.) And tell him to take his
hat off in the house. (*She goes to the kitchen: sound of
cups.*)

HANSON. Have at you, man! (*He thrusts at him with his
stick.*)

ARNIE. Have at you!

They fight with much groaning and exertion, ARNIE *with
his invisible sword,* HANSON *with his stick.*

Back! Back! Th . . . th . . . th . . . i . . . i . . . i . . . ssss . . .
sssss THIS! i . . . i . . . i . . . ssss . . . IS! g . . . g . . . g . . .
gay! r . . . r . . . r . . . r . . . ROBIN h . . . h . . . h . . . h
. . . HOOD!

HANSON *gives a great and ugly scream and dies
writhingly in a chair.*

HANSON. Actually, could you lend me five pounds?

ARNIE. I haven't a cent. It all went on this.

HANSON has got up. He eyes the armour suspiciously.

HANSON. Oh. (*Pause.*) Actually. Why did you buy it?

ARNIE. As a present.

HANSON. For your parents?

ARNIE nods.

Mmmmm! (*Watches him a moment. Then:*) The purpose of the loan was to entertain a lady. Temporarily, I'm without the wherewithal without.

ARNIE. A lady?

HANSON. A Miss Wilkinson, to be precise.

ARNIE. Not our Miss Wilkinson? From school?

HANSON. 'Fraid so. (*He talks a little in* JOAN's *direction.*) Naturally the school premises – where normally I make assignations of this nature – are the most propitious place for the dalliances I have in mind. But of late Old Thompson, despite rheumatism, a protopsic condition of the right eye, and an audibly leaking bucket, has acquired in stealth what he has so patently forfeited in spontaneity. The Park, though ample in resources, and open to all classes and creeds of men, is constant victim to the inclemency of the weather; the lady herself lives with elderly parents in a charming country cottage several miles from town; and my landlord resents frivolities of every nature.

ARNIE (*watching him cautiously*). She's a damn fit woman, I'm told, Jeffrey.

HANSON. You were correctly informed. While we clamber daily through the portals of our plight, she is nimbly leaping over bucks, vaulting-horses and horizontal bars as lightly as . . . a frog, say.

ARNIE. I had always assumed her to be the soul of integrity, Jeffrey.

HANSON. I have a curriculum to straighten out with her.

ARNIE. That would be nice.

HANSON. And her permission to examine the subject on an evening suitable to both.

ARNIE. I see.

HANSON *finally turns from the armour just as* JOAN *re-enters carrying a tea-try.*

HANSON. So what's to do?

ARNIE (*perceiving* JOAN). Entertain her here.

HANSON. In public?

ARNIE. A party. Or whatever festivities you feel she might approve.

HANSON. Tonight?

JOAN (*setting down the tray*). Is someone coming here tonight?

ARNIE. It is a debt of honour I am endeavoring to pay with a frenzied bout of hospitality. Nothing more.

JOAN. What do you think all this is for?

ARNIE. All what?

JOAN. This! All this tidying up!

ARNIE. Any evidence of the pleasures we may have sustained will have been long removed by then.

JOAN *stares at him in silence. Then:*

JOAN. What *is* all this about, Arnie?

ARNIE (*to* HANSON). You might bring a few bottles with you, Jeffrey. No reason why your pleasures should not entertain our own particular miseries.

HANSON. Oh, but of course.

JOAN. There's your tea. If you want anything else help yourselves. (*She returns to the kitchen.*)

ARNIE (*loudly*). Talking of religious fervours, Miss O'Connor followed me home again today. The distance of twenty-five yards has increased slightly to thirty, perhaps even thirty-five. Idolatry, I fear, has given way to something verging on detachment.

HANSON. Sheila O'Connor . . .

ARNIE. The one.

HANSON (*leaning on kitchen door*). Is a girl . . .

JOAN (*heard*). I've seen enough of that.

HANSON. . . . . Upon whom a mischievous deity has bestowed two attributes, the largeness of which – in all humble deference – must be an embarrassment even to Himself. (*He salaams to the ceiling.*)

JOAN (*reappearing with cleaning utensils*). Is that how you talk about the children?

HANSON. A child in the eyes of the State, my dear, but a woman in the eyes of God.

ARNIE. She actually approached me at four o'clock, just as I was entering the staff-room prior to retrieving my armour, and asked me to take her out. Tonight. (*Pause.*) Those are the first words that have passed between us.

HANSON. Oh, she's never asked me that. She never has.

JOAN. What arrangements did you come to?

ARNIE. I suggested we rendezvous at the picture palace at nine o'clock. 'Nine o'clock sharp, mind!' I said sternly, if not officiously – reminding her as casually as I could that I had a position to maintain. As it so happened, she would have followed me into the staff-room there and then if it hadn't been for the fact that old Manners was marking her arithmetic book along with several thousand others. 'Oh, Sheila,' he said, looking up obliquely from his tattered ledgers, 'I've just got to yours, my dear. Would you like to stand by me while I glance through your problems?' Wherein she vanished in the twinkle of an eye.

HANSON. There are incentives to the profession the Minister never dreamed of.

JOAN. Yes.

She goes to the stairs but ARNIE takes her shoulders.

ARNIE. You're very contained, my little sparrow.

JOAN. I've to fly up there and finish the stairs if you don't mind, then fly back down and tidy here.

HANSON. A woman's work is never done!

JOAN. *What*!

HANSON. I . . . Merely a tribute, my dear, to your . . . profession.

JOAN releases herself from ARNIE.

JOAN. God, I love you, honey. (*She blows a kiss and goes.*)

ARNIE goes to the table, gets his pot, and sits down. He doesn't drink. HANSON watches him. Then:

HANSON. Say, old man. Isn't your hair somewhat oddly arranged for an historian? Or, indeed, for a man?

ARNIE. What?

HANSON. You're not short of food, I take it? It appears someone has consumed two mouthfuls of your tonsure.
ARNIE. It was a slight accident on the way to the kitchen.

HANSON holds up his walking-stick guardedly.

HANSON. Ah.
ARNIE. Mind your own business, loppy-lugs.
HANSON. Snot-nose.
ARNIE. Carpet-breath.
HANSON. That's revolting.

ARNIE turns away to his tea.

By such inadvertent gestures cancer is induced. Secrets go bad and affect the very flesh.
ARNIE. Cabbage knuckles.
HANSON (*with his stick*). Have at you, Gay Robin!
ARNIE (*without gesture*). Have at you, Big John.

Pause. HANSON taps the armour reflectively. Then he glances at ARNIE.

HANSON. You think, then, it's conceivable I'm mistaken about Miss Wilkinson. One grave disadvantage is that she's physically so very *fit*. It would be imprudent continually to have recourse to this stout staff while she merely relies upon the dexterity of her limbs. But my daily exercises are entirely cerebral, whereas hers, day in, day out, are designed exclusively to extend the already phenomenal resilience of her physique.
ARNIE. It could be an advantage, no doubt, in one way. And then again, in another . . .
HANSON. But you do not think it strange . . . (*He glances round.*) . . . that women are gradually acquiring a physcial superiority to men? Do you think . . . (*Goes to the stairs, listens, then returns to say slowly, putting his arm round the armour:*) Do you think there's some sort of organisation behind it?
ARNIE. A conspiracy . . .
HANSON. Which we are very foolish to ignore. (*He glances quickly behind him.*) I mean, one hears so much of judo and professional equality these days.
ARNIE. Does the King know?

HANSON. The King? My dear Arnold, the very sources are corrupt. (*Moves away thoughtfully flexing his stick.*) I mean, it can't have failed to have reached your attention that we – that is men *and* women alike – emerge at some point of our lives from the body of a woman. But has it also occurred to you that whereas we are always under this obligation to them, they are never under a reciprocal obligation to us? They, as it were, *divulge* us: whereas we – we are simply *exposed*. This is an extraordinary advantage bestowed on one sex at the expense of the other.

As he talks he reapproaches ARNIE *who takes* HANSON's *stick and, as he listens, flexes it over his shoulders.* HANSON *leans over him with the confidence of a spy.*

Have you noticed that women live longer than men? (*Pause.*) They do not fight wars, only occasionally do they murder their fellows, and they seldom, unfortunately, commit rape. Relate this to our original observation that it is *they* who breed *us*, then things like politics and finance, even philosophy and art, become like playthings bestowed on us by women merely to amuse and divert our unbreeding functions!

ARNIE. What time are you meeting her?

HANSON. What? (*Glances at his watch.*) Yes, I shall have to go.

JOAN *has re-entered from the stairs.*

HANSON. It is one thing to sit there and smile at present danger. It's quite another to rest there until you are *gobbled up*.

ARNIE (*quickly*). You have caught Jeffrey in the very act of leaving.

HANSON. Ah, I did not hear you dismount, madam. (*He takes his stick from* ARNIE, *and pulls on his gloves.*) I must be about my business before it is about me. (*He suddenly turns round on* ARNIE *with his stick.*) On guard!

ARNIE. To be sure.

HANSON salutes with his stick. ARNIE has stood up and now he stands by JOAN, putting an arm about her shoulders. HANSON glances at them a moment.

HANSON. I shall take my leave quickly. Imagine I am killed in the street the moment I have stepped beyond the door, and allow that poignancy to inform your farewells. (*He takes JOAN's hand and kisses it, salaams to ARNIE, then crosses to the armour. He taps it lightly with his stick.*) That, Arnold. That I'm not altogether sure of. Well . . . (*He regards it thoughtfully for a moment. Then, turning briskly.*) Remember, no fisticuffs when I introduce Miss Wilkinson to this abode. And may all our cavortings be as discreet and as anonymous as alcohol allows. (*He ceremoniously bows and exits backwards, closing the door. A moment later there's the sound of the outer door shutting.*)

ARNIE releases JOAN. She watches him a moment. Then:

JOAN (*lenient*). You needn't be afraid.
ARNIE. Afraid?
JOAN. Of showing in private the affection you display in public. (*Pause.*) I could have told him.
ARNIE. You could?
JOAN. I heard your 'discussion' from the stairs. I could have told him how you came to lose your hair.
ARNIE. An embarrassment to both of us I would have thought.
JOAN. Doesn't *he* ever grow sick of it?
ARNIE. Of what?
JOAN (*pause*). You despise him really.
ARNIE. I do not.

She watches him a moment, then goes to the kitchen.

ARNIE sits down at the table. A moment later JOAN reappears.

JOAN. Has something sunk through all those layers at last?
ARNIE (*pause*). Has what sunk through which layers?
JOAN. Disgust.
ARNIE. You're being boring.
JOAN. Isn't it that underneath . . .

ARNIE (*calling out*). You're being boring! I've never known anyone make such commonplace observations in so revelationary a tone!

They're both silent.

JOAN (*quietly*). Do you have any feeling left for me at all?

ARNIE. Are you trying to be frivolous?

JOAN (*pause*). You make me feel I don't exist. You hide away. You don't look. You show nothing but a parody of yourself. You deride even your own weakness. Isn't that self-contempt?

ARNIE. You're sickening.

JOAN. Am I . . .

ARNIE. You're sickening. Your allegories are sickening, woman.

JOAN (*crying out and gesturing at the room*). And what's this, then, but sickening! What's this!

ARNIE *makes no response.* JOAN *watches him. Then, more quietly:*

If you'd just break up this – pretence!

ARNIE. What? What? What? What?

JOAN. Anything so long as you don't have to step up here. (*Gestures at herself.*)

ARNIE. You think that's an eminence worthy of ascent?

JOAN. You did once. (*Silence.*) Why do you stay with me, Arnie?

ARNIE *watches her intently.*

Go on.

ARNIE. Go knot your nose.

JOAN. Tell me. Why do you stay here?

ARNIE. Run up a flag.

JOAN. Try and answer me.

ARNIE. Leave me alone.

JOAN (*slowly*). Why do you stay with me, Arnie?

ARNIE *glances round at the doors.*

Well, off you go then.

ARNIE. I can detect a piece of dust. Wait a minute, yes. It's under the near left-hand leg of the dressing-table in your

mother's bedroom: a quick outflanking manoeuvre and it
will be within your grasp.

Silence. Then:

JOAN. You must make yourself so *sick*.
ARNIE.
Ladybird, Ladybird, fly away home:
Your house is on fire and your children have gone.

Silence. JOAN waits patiently.

*ARNIE suddenly shouts with burlesque affectation,
slamming the table.*

Will somebody get me out of here!
Help! Help! . . . HELP!

JOAN watches a while. Then:

JOAN. It's not a game is it?
ARNIE. Leave me alone.
JOAN. No. You run away instead.
ARNIE. All right. (*He doesn't move. After a while:*) Assume
I've run away.
JOAN. You insulting little *snot*!

ARNIE closes his eyes.

Come on. Get down on your knees and cry. Do something
to attract some *pity*! Come on. Get down! Cry! Come on.
Cry, *baby*, cry!

ARNIE turns his head away.

Nobody's going to love you unless you show us
something.
ARNIE. Go away.
JOAN. Let's have some rage. Isn't there anything in this
world, Arnold, that you'd like to put right?
ARNIE. Go away.
JOAN. Come on, baby. Isn't there anything that offends
you? Isn't there some tiny little wrong that can rouse your
indignation?
ARNIE. Get out.

JOAN. Come on. Make me sickening.
ARNIE. Hop it!

She comes and studies his face more closely.

JOAN. Just look. For God's sake, Arnie.

They're silent. Then:

What are you frightened of?

He makes no response. Then quietly:

All right. All right. (*She watches him, waiting for a
response. Quietly, she goes.*)

ARNIE *sits remotely at the table.*

After a while JOAN *re-enters. She watches him a moment,
sitting exactly as she left him.*

As a start, Arnie . . . I suggest we get rid of all these.
(*Indicating the objects.*)
ARNIE. Yes.
JOAN. You agree, then?

Pause. ARNIE *looks up.*

ARNIE. Certainly.
JOAN. We get rid of all this.
ARNIE. Yes.

She seems about to start.

Not yet.
JOAN. Isn't this the best time?
ARNIE (*pause*). No.
JOAN. All right. When?
ARNIE. Tomorrow.
JOAN. After *they've* been?
ARNIE. Er . . . Yes.
JOAN. You promise that?
ARNIE. Yes.
JOAN. And this? (*Indicating armour.*)

ARNIE *regards it in silence. Then:*

ARNIE. That's going in any case.
JOAN. As a present.

ARNIE *makes no response.*

And if they won't have it?
ARNIE. What?
JOAN. I can't imagine they will. (*Pause.*) If that's what you
really intend to do with it.

Pause.

ARNIE. They'll have it because I'm giving it to them.
JOAN. Oh.
ARNIE. I like it.
JOAN. Yes.
ARNIE. And I'd like them to have it.
JOAN. Suppose they don't.

Pause.

ARNIE. This is not a battle.
JOAN. No.
ARNIE. They'll be pleased with it because I am. And the
other way round.

She watches him.

Some people are actually like that.
JOAN. Yes.
ARNIE. All right?
JOAN. I'll believe it when I see it.
ARNIE. I doubt it.
JOAN. Well, then, while we're clearing everything away,
there's one other thing. It's time my mother left and went
and lived on her own.
ARNIE. What?
JOAN. In this case you'll just have to accept *my* word if you
don't believe it.
ARNIE. She's harmless.
JOAN. It's time she went for all our sakes. You'll be better
off for it. I will. And so will she.
ARNIE. I don't want her to go. It'd break her bloody heart.
JOAN. I'm sorry. But she'll have to.

The outside door bangs.

That's her now.

ARNIE. Well, don't say anything to her. Not yet.

JOAN. It's my decision.

ARNIE. I've told you. Don't. (*He waits, almost threatening.*) You understand?

JOAN *makes no response. There are sounds outside the door, and ARNIE's mood changes abruptly as MRS ELLIS appears. She's smartly dressed, a fur round her shoulders, and she carries a full shopping basket which she puts on the table. ARNIE greets her with a dashing gesture.*

Here comes a spy to parry at our scheme:
I shall retire, and make it – all a dream.

MRS ELLIS (*pleased*). Oh . . .

ARNIE *goes with a flourish.*

What's got into him?

JOAN *doesn't answer.*

It's a lovely evening out. A beautiful sunset.

Pause. The two women confront each other; MRS ELLIS with some perplexity.

What's the matter?

JOAN (*goes to her*). Let me help you off with your coat, Mother.

MRS ELLIS. What?

JOAN. Your coat.

Surprised, she submits.

The light fades.

Scene Two
The same evening.

ARNIE, *in shirtsleeves, tieless, lies on a couch. The suit of armour has gone.*

JOAN (*heard*). Aren't you going to get changed?

*There are sounds of her working in the kitchen. ARNIE
makes no response: his eyes are closed, apparently in
sleep.*

(*Entering.*) Aren't you going to get shaved?

ARNIE (*eyes still closed*). I thought you wanted no one here.
The place kept tidy and clean.

*JOAN has dressed herself attractively, and her hair is tied
in a ribbon.*

JOAN (*briefly and briskly tidying the room*). I've changed
my mind . . . Aren't you going to get ready at all?

ARNIE. Oh? (*He opens his eyes, watches her a moment.*)
They might never get here.

JOAN. My mother's gone out for nothing, then.

ARNIE. She didn't have to go out.

JOAN. She didn't feel like meeting people this evening.
That's all.

Pause.

ARNIE. The sacrifice of one old woman . . .

JOAN. She can look after herself.

ARNIE rouses himself, sitting up.

ARNIE. You can't turn people out like that, that's all. Not
when they rely on you. You either do it at the beginning
or not at all.

JOAN. I'm not arguing about it.

ARNIE. That's settled then. (*Sitting on the couch, slaps his
thighs and looks around contentedly. Then he puts his
hands together and blows between them, hooting like an
owl.*)

After a while:

JOAN. You know . . .

ARNIE hoots.

(*Pause.*) With my mother it's my decision whether she
goes or not. She's *my* mother.

ARNIE. I've told you.

JOAN. But it's my decision, Arnie. I make it!

The door is crashed back on its hinges and HANSON *puts his head round.*

HANSON.
  Pray! Hold thy hand good Robin Hood,
  And your merry men each one,
  For you'll swear this is the finest maid
  That e'er your eyes fell on.
JOAN. Don't you usually knock when you come in?
HANSON (*taking her hand*).
  If thou wilt forsake, housewife, thy craft,
  And wend to the greenwood with me (*Kisses her hand.*)
  Thou shalt have loving all the year long,
  And forty gold crowns for thy fee.
ARNIE. All right. All right.
HANSON (*to* ARNIE).
  And Robin leapt up full thirty good foot,
  'Twas thirty good foot and one,
  And he cleft the rude fellow with a blow of his fist —
  And his light went out like the sun.

  HANSON *disappears immediately through the door. His voice is heard.*

  Go on, dear. Straight ahead.

  SHEILA O'CONNOR, *a precociously developed girl, though by no means loutish, enters. She's dressed in slacks and a bright sweater. Her shyness tends to disappear first when she sees* ARNIE, *then the interior.*

SHEILA. Hello, sir.

  ARNIE *is up quickly from the couch where he's been lounging.*

ARNIE. Oh, hello, Sheila. Didn't expect to see you here.
HANSON. Odd thing. Passing the gate just as we came in.
  Thought: what a coincidence! Then: why one be damned
  when rest sanctified by celebration!
ARNIE. Yes. (*To* JOAN.) This is Sheila O'Connor, Joan.
  This is my wife, Sheila.

SHEILA. Hello, Miss.
JOAN. Hello, Sheila.

> MAUREEN WILKINSON *and* HANSON *have followed*
> SHEILA *in. The schoolmistress is dressed tastefully: a*
> *respectable and fairly attractive woman in her late*
> *twenties.*

ARNIE. Evening, Maureen. I don't think you know my wife.
Joan – this is Maureen.
MAUREEN. It's very nice meeting you, Joan.

They shake hands.

JOAN. Let me take your coat.
ARNIE (*to* HANSON). Well, let's sit down, and so forth.
HANSON. Look here, Arnold, would you mind awfully if
Sheila and I betook ourselves to the hostelry to purchase
an armful of drinks? Things came up. Distracted the
intention . . .
ARNIE (*to* SHEILA). So soon arrived, so soon departed.
HANSON. You don't mind, do you, Sheila? I swear I heard
you had been appointed milk monitor this term for the
Lower Fifth.
SHEILA. It's not far, is it?
HANSON. Good girl! We shan't be long. Adios, caballeros.
ARNIE. Shall I . . .
HANSON. Oh, we'll manage, old man.

They go. ARNIE *has got up to go with them but, rejected,*
returns.

JOAN. Does that irritate you?
MAUREEN. Oh, you get used to it.
JOAN. What is it, do you think?
MAUREEN. The school play this year is 'Robin Hood and
His Merry Men'.
JOAN. No, I meant . . .
ARNIE. You're being unnecessarily adventurous, aren't you,
coming out with Jeffrey?
MAUREEN. He's asked me out so often it's less tedious to
agree.
ARNIE. Is that all?
MAUREEN. I'm sorry.

JOAN *watches* ARNIE's *almost vindictive manner with* MAUREEN, *curious and intrigued.*

There was nothing I could do about him bringing Shelia in. It's very foolish.

ARNIE. It'll give her a break from her usual sentry-go. I never know whether she's keeping me in, or keeping the others out.

JOAN. It's inviting trouble: walking through the streets with her like that, and going into pubs.

MAUREEN (*pleasantly*). Oh, he'll take a pleasure in it.

JOAN. After all, we're partly responsible for it.

ARNIE. Of those two, the only one who can be violated is Jeffrey.

MAUREEN. You're not responsible. That's absurd.

JOAN (*indicating* ARNIE). Oh, he has ways of encouraging her. Don't worry.

ARNIE. She asked *me* out.

JOAN (*to* MAUREEN). Some days they say it's because they teach in a school; then on other days they say it's the world.

MAUREEN. I never knew you had a philosophy, Arnold. As well as a suit of armour. (*Stretching round.*) Where is it, by the way?

ARNIE. Yes. (*He gets up and wanders uneasily about the room.*)

JOAN (*to* MAUREEN). Are all your men staff alike?

MAUREEN. Oh, very nearly!

JOAN. Doesn't it wear you down?

MAUREEN (*laughing*). I shouldn't worry about it, Joan!

ARNIE. Watch this. (*Does a handstand against the wall, balancing precariously.*)

The women pause to watch.

JOAN. Would you like some tea, Maureen?

MAUREEN. Love some.

JOAN. I'll just put the kettle on. I was hoping to make some sandwiches as well. Won't be a minute. (*Goes into the kitchen.*)

MAUREEN *looks round at the objects in the room for the first time.*

MAUREEN. Are all these yours?

ARNIE. Yes.

MAUREEN. Don't you want me here?

ARNIE. You?

MAUREEN. Us?

ARNIE. It was *my* party. Joan has appropriated it.

MAUREEN (*laughs*). Yes.

ARNIE *lowers himself from his handstand.*

ARNIE. Do you know what happened to the Early Christian martyrs the moment they stopped throwing them to the lions, and loved them instead?

MAUREEN. They went off into the desert to live in caves, haunted by demons.

ARNIE. What?

MAUREEN *waits.*

I've told you before. (*Pause.*) Are you sure?

MAUREEN. Yes.

ARNIE. I see. (*Pause.*) Don't you think it's extraordinary?

MAUREEN. In what way?

ARNIE. In what way? (*Pause.*) I don't know really. It seemed extraordinary at the time . . .

Pause.

MAUREEN. Where is . . .

JOAN (*returning*). I'm making some sandwiches then perhaps one or two people won't get so drunk. Where are you going?

ARNIE *has gone to the door, picking up his jacket.*

ARNIE. Out. See if Hanson needs any help.

JOAN. I should think he'd be able to manage well enough on his own.

ARNIE *still goes.*

You won't be long?

ARNIE. No.

JOAN. Give us a kiss, Arnie.

ARNIE (*to* MAUREEN). You'll notice. Always the
diminutive.

*JOAN waits. ARNIE, after a moment, comes back, takes
her shoulder and kisses her on the cheek.*

JOAN. You won't be long, Arnold?
ARNIE. No.

He goes. A pause. JOAN tentatively re-tidies the room.

JOAN. His parents are coming tomorrow. We haven't seen
them for years.
MAUREEN. The best thing is to ride with it, isn't it? I still
live with my parents: I know what a trouble they can be.
JOAN. When *we* got married and his mother came up to
kiss me as we were leaving the church, she said, 'Well,
you'll look after my only son, won't you, Joan?' And he
said, quick as a flash, 'Your only sin, Mother.' And she
smiled as sweetly as anything; he laughed out loud; and
God did I feel a fool! You can see just what a state I'm in.
Would you like to see round the house?
MAUREEN. Yes, I'd love to.

They move to the stairs.

JOAN. I'll show you upstairs. You've seen nearly all there is
to see down here. Considering how small they look from
the outside it's surprising how large they are.

*They go. Heard is MAUREEN: 'Do you intend staying on
here, then?' Then JOAN: 'Oh, I suppose so. We've lived
here since we got married. There's no point in moving
into something smaller . . . This is the main bedroom . . .'*

*Their voices grow fainter, then disappear. After a short
interval there's the sound of the back door opening in the
kitchen and, a moment later, the kitchen door is
cautiously opened. MRS ELLIS enters. She's drunk. She
puts a bottle on the table and stands aimlessly looking
round, stifling her sobs with a handkerchief. Then she*

moves to the mirror and stares distractedly at herself, moaning.

From above come the voices of the women as they move about: 'the bathroom there, and this is the spare room . . . ' 'Well, that's convenient . . . Goodness. Is that all Arnold's too?' 'And this my mother's room . . '

MRS ELLIS *swings round, hurries to the kitchen door, then across to the door leading to the hall. Then, as the women begin to descend the stairs, she remembers the bottle, hurriedly retrieves it and goes out by the hall door, leaving it open.*

MAUREEN (*re-entering*). His classroom's extraordinary. More like the court of King Arthur than a schoolroom. Have you seen his museum?

JOAN (*re-entering*). No.

MAUREEN. The children love it. What it has to do with history I've no idea. They seem to spend all their time building model castles, singing ballads and doing great big pictures of William the Conqueror . . . It's strange we've never met at school, isn't it? You've never been to any of the plays Arnold's produced, have you? They're very good.

JOAN. He prefers me to stay away.

MAUREEN. Whatever for?

JOAN (*shrugs*). He prefers it, that's all. He's full of prejudices, you know, Maureen.

MAUREEN. Prejudices?

JOAN. We better do the sandwiches, by the way, before they get back. The kettle should be boiling. You promise . . .

They go into the kitchen.

After a moment MRS ELLIS reappears and stands hesitantly in the room, uncertain whether to go into the kitchen herself. She stifles a sob, staring at the door. Then, at the sound of a door opening and whispers from the hall, she glances wildly round and, with her bottle, departs unsteadily to the stairs.

The sound of the women's laughter comes from the kitchen, and MAUREEN's shout of 'Joan!' HANSON appears in the hall door, looks left and right, then signals behind him. Giggling, SHEILA follows him in, a carrier bag with bottles in her arms. HANSON puts his finger to his lips and gestures at the kitchen.

HANSON (*whispers*). Excellent. Very good, O'Connor. Next week, as a very special reward, you can be in charge of the ink *and* the chalk – and if you're extra good I'll let you clean the blackboard.

SHEILA. Oh, thank you, sir! (*Taking off her coat.*)

HANSON (*aware*). I think for that you deserve a red star. Or is it a green one? (*He pins an imaginary medal on her chest, then kisses her on either cheek.*)

SHEILA takes him round the neck and kisses him more directly.

ARNIE has entered quietly. HANSON looks up in mid-kiss to see him.

There you are, dear fellow.

ARNIE. Saw you down the street. Thought: bound to resent my intrusion. Kept my distance. Circumspect. All that.

HANSON. Absolutely, old boy.

ARNIE. Not at all.

JOAN (*heard*). Arnie?

She enters from kitchen, followed by MAUREEN, carrying a tray of tea and sandwiches.

There you are.

MAUREEN. Arrived back all together.

HANSON. Are we supposed to drink out of our hands?

JOAN. You can help yourself in the kitchen.

SHEILA. Can I find the glasses?

HANSON. You find them, love. Anything that will hold liquid. You know what liquid is, don't you?

SHEILA. Course I do, silly.

HANSON and SHEILA giggle.

JOAN (*to ARNIE*). What are you doing?

ARNIE *stands at the back of the room rubbing his hands energetically, nodding his head at everybody, his face set in a pleased grin.*

ARNIE. Just getting it all organised. Shipshape. Everyone on the best of terms. Pleasantries, cordialities, sparks within a fire.

JOAN. What's got *into* you?

MAUREEN (*to* HANSON). I hope you know what you're doing with that girl.

HANSON. Oh, definitely.

JOAN. Better leave him alone, Maureen.

MAUREEN. He needs reminding.

HANSON. On whose authority, Miss Wilkinson?

MAUREEN. Those people who hire you to educate the . . .

HANSON. That's their fault for serving up dishes like her. We're not sticks of chalk.

MAUREEN. I never said you were.

HANSON. So put that over your shoulder and start marching.

There's a cry from the kitchen and the sound of breaking glass. JOAN *rushes out.*

Relax, Maureen. Relax.

ARNIE (*cheerfully*). *Relax.*

MAUREEN. I am relaxed. There's a question of behaviour, isn't there?

HANSON. My behaviour's strictly human . . .

ARNIE. It's strictly human.

HANSON. Or are you against that too?

ARNIE. Are you against that too?

HANSON (*to* ARNIE). What's the matter with you?

JOAN (*re-entering*). One broken glass, that's all.

SHEILA (*following with tray of glasses*). I broke a glass!

HANSON. Right, then . . . (*He starts pouring out the drinks.*)

ARNIE (*to* MAUREEN). What's got *into* you?

MAUREEN. What?

HANSON. Joan? Maureen? A little for you, Sheila?

JOAN. I'll have a glassful . . .

HANSON. But certainly.

MAUREEN. I'll make do with tea.

HANSON. Naturally. (*To* JOAN.) We have a little whisky here for the menfolk. If you like . . .

JOAN. Oh, beer will do.

HANSON. And Arnold?

JOAN. Don't give him whisky. One glass knocks him off his feet.

HANSON. Aha!

He hands a glass of whisky to ARNIE *who downs it in one swallow.*

JOAN. I've warned you.

HANSON *tots it up again, and* ARNIE *drinks it off.*

ARNIE *screws his face, holds his stomach, then his head, gesticulates with violent, staccato motions, lurches erratically one way then another, goes boss-eyed, knock-kneed . . .*

All right. All right.

. . . ARNIE *stands motionless in the centre of the room.*

HANSON (*expressionless*). Oh dear. Oh dear, I haven't laughed so much for ages . . . Are you sure you're old enough, Sheila?

SHEILA. Course I am.

HANSON. I meant for alcohol, my dear. (*He slaps his thigh.*) Oh, my!

ARNIE. My *friends*!

HANSON. *What*?

ARNIE. I would like to address you, if I may.

HANSON. Oh.

ARNIE (*swallows his next whisky. Hesitates. Then*). This . . . *celebration* . . . is not an ordinary celebration. Oh, you may say, it *looks* an ordinary celebration. And I admit. It has all the signs, the characteristics, all the *moeurs*, as they say in German. Of a celebration. But the fact is . . . What? . . . What? (*He looks round questioningly.*)

JOAN. Is that the end?

ARNIE. I have always in my life attempted to deal . . .
  fairly, with my fellow men.

HANSON. And women.

ARNIE. Ah. (*Holds up an admonitory finger.*) And it would,
  indeed, be mealy-mouthed . . .

HANSON. It would.

ARNIE. Of me. Ungracious. Prevaricating. To let you
  assume that this is merely a celebration. This is in fact . . .
  What is this? (*He holds up his glass.*)

HANSON *holds up the whisky bottle to him.*

HANSON. One of the very worst brands, old friend.

ARNIE (*wipes his hand, surprised, across his forehead*). I'm
  sweating.

JOAN. I told you he'd fall down.

MAUREEN. Perhaps we better put on the music and calm
  down.

ARNIE. An event of such gigantic proportions as to be
  virtually invisible to the naked human eye! It is . . . Do
  they wash up in this?

HANSON. Only one of the minor rituals of distillation.
  Why, I could tell you . . .

JOAN. We'll have that another time.

ARNIE. I want . . . *all* of you. I want all of you to be
  content. This evening I want you to remember . . . I want
  you to remember. I want you.

HANSON. What?

ARNIE. What?

HANSON. Well, if not 'what' then 'why'?

ARNIE. I don't want to know why. Any damn fool can give
  you reasons *why*. All I'm interested in is *how*. *Why* is a
  kind of sentimentality I heartily eschew. I *eschew* it. Why
  is of no more interest to me than *when*. You can put why
  and when into . . . wherever you'd like to put them, and
  blow them to smithereens, for me.

HANSON. God! A religious maniac!

ARNIE. I want an evening of . . . ease, of peace, of
  relaxation. The . . . *flow* of gentle laughter, conversation
  . . . the natural intimacy between friends.

JOAN. I'd like to recite a poem.

ARNIE. What?

HANSON. Oh, steady, Joan.

JOAN. I think I shall.

ARNIE (*pained*). You're being revolting . . . I said the *natural* flow of conversation not a poem.

JOAN. You said the flow.

MAUREEN. Yes. You did say the flow.

JOAN begins to recite.

HANSON. Have another drink, Sheila.

SHEILA. Oh, ta.

HANSON. You are enjoying yourself?

SHEILA. Oh, super!

JOAN has begun to recite, at first her fingers holding her cheeks, then, as she goes on, growing more confident.

JOAN.
I saw love passing by my window
Early one morning on a lightsome day . . .

ARNIE. Oh, no.

HANSON. Joan . . .

JOAN.
Its face was warm and its look so hopeful
And pleasure and happiness in its features lay.

ARNIE has covered his face with embarrassment.

ARNIE. Oh, no. (*Groaning.*) This can't go on.

HANSON. Joan: my dear, dear girl . . .

SHEILA. No. Sir, it's super!

MAUREEN. No, let her go on.

For a moment they argue over this, SHEILA and MAUREEN attempting to quieten the other two. Meanwhile JOAN carries on reciting.

JOAN.
I saw love hurrying in the meadow
Its steps so light over the leaden clay,
Its breath was quick and its voice beseeching,
And I heard its cries as I fled away.

I saw love sitting in a cottage
About its feet did children play,
Their sounds were loud, their voices lusty,
And I saw love smile to see them gay.

ARNIE *has continued to groan, gradually quietening,*
finally subsiding on a chair, holding his stomach and
leaning forwards as if in pain. The others too have
quietened, turning to listen to JOAN.

I saw love bending with the sickle
Though all the thorns were clustered in its way,
Its body aged and its head now shaking,
And with the wind it seemed to sway.

I saw love trudging by my window
Late one evening on a darksome day,
Its face was worn and its look despairing
And grief and sorrow on its features lay.

ARNIE *has now looked up to watch* JOAN.

I saw love carried to the graveside
The day was sunny and the month was May.
Across its brow was a wreath of laurel
And in its hands a clean white spray.

They're silent. No one moves for a moment. Then:

HANSON. Oh, I say. That's very good.
MAUREEN. Lovely.
SHEILA. It was super, Miss.
HANSON. No, I really do think that was very good.

They all seem a little awed. ARNIE, *however, has*
suddenly jumped up.

ARNIE.
  There was a young woman of Leeds
  Who swallowed a packet of seeds,
  She grew peas on her chest,
  Runner beans in her vest,
  And all round her kneecaps grew weeds.
HANSON.
  There was a young man of Bangkok
  Who swallowed a musical clock . . .
ARNIE. Oh, I say . . .
HANSON.
  . . . He could play a toccata,

Chopin's Moonlight Sonata,
By simply removing his sock.

ARNIE. Oh . . . This is the happiest day of my life. I want
you to know that . . . Revelations are simply pouring
from the skies! Sheila!

He goes to JOAN *and puts his arm warmly about her.*

HANSON. Sheila: what contribution could you make, my
dear?

ARNIE. A few handstands might cause a stir. Perhaps some
extraordinary gymnastic feats acquired at the hands of
Miss Wilkinson?

HANSON. You can commit poetry, my dear. We – we can
merely recite it.

SHEILA. You've forgotten to give sir his telegram, sir.

HANSON. Telegram? Telegram?

JOAN. Telegram?

HANSON. Ah . . .

ARNIE (*totally bemused, his arm still warmly about* JOAN).
I once read somewhere in a novel, perhaps . . .

HANSON. Scott!

ARNIE. Scott?

HANSON. That's his name! (*Points to the door.*)

MAUREEN. Whose?

HANSON. You remember Scott? A tall, lanky boy who
wore glasses and dirty teeth. Won the long jump one year,
I believe, by simply falling on his head.

ARNIE. Oh, Scott! . . . Wasn't he the boy . . .

HANSON. Could contain himself no longer during a
mathematics lesson and furtively urinated out of an upper
window when he presumed no one was looking.

JOAN giggles.

MAUREEN. Now that's enough!

ARNIE. Brought on a case of Thompson's disease. An
hitherto unknown medical syndrome characterised by a
sudden staring of the eyes, an energetic raising of the
arms, and a loud, screaming sound emitted from between
the teeth.

HANSON. It was first witnessed in an elderly caretaker of

that name who happened to be passing beneath the
window at the time.

JOAN *breaks out into laughter.* SHEILA *giggles.*

JOAN. Is he *here*?
SHEILA. He was. (*Attempting to conceal her laughter.*)
ARNIE. A remarkable youth, I seem to recollect. Went
through all the stages of puberty by the age of eleven.
Caused endless consternation amongst the younger boys.
HANSON. As we were emerging from the house a short
while ago, my young companion and I (*Holds* SHEILA
firmly about the shoulders.) our course set for the
hostelry, whom should we discover on the step but Scott
himself attired in dark uniform and peaked cap. 'Great
Heavens,' said I, 'the police.' Whereupon he indicated an
insignia on his arm which suggested he was in the employ
of the Post Office with special responsibility for the
delivery of urgent messages. Thrusting one such into my
hand he departed with an alacrity I can only assume was
inspired by our past acquaintance. So intoxicated was I by
the chatter of my companion that, until this moment, I'm
afraid I have quite overlooked it . . . (*Finally retrieving it
after a search of his pockets, reads.*) Greetings!
JOAN. Is that all it says?
HANSON (*tendentiously*). That's merely the envelope. (*He
tears it open.*) Ah! This is what Scott has written.
Greetings again! Here we are . . . Regret . . . Regret.
Regret mother unwell stop cutting holiday short. Stop
hope to make it some other time. Stop father.
JOAN. What's that? (*She takes the telegram.*)
HANSON (*to* MAUREEN *and* SHEILA). Another drink?

Having read the telegram, however, JOAN *now giggles.*
ARNIE, *his arm still about her shoulder, gazes bemusedly
into the distance.*

JOAN. I cleaned every rotten stick in this house. (*To the
others.*) I've even dusted every rotten piece of dust.
HANSON. Oh! Oh, Oh . . .
JOAN. There's not a mark not a sign of life anywhere and
now they've decided not to come!

JOAN *is very pleased, yet apparently, with her giggling, trying to hide her feelings from* ARNIE.

ARNIE. Now. We are about to dance.

ARNIE, *as if unaware of all this, goes to the gramophone.*

JOAN. Here. Have you read this? Isn't it marvellous! That really is the best news I've had all day.

Music begins.

ARNIE. Sheila. Would you escort me about the floor? A limb here, a limb there. One or two gesticulations in unexpected places . . . and there we are. Ups!

ARNIE *is unsteady, slow and mechanical, as he manoeuvres* SHEILA *about the room.*

HANSON. Shall we form a chorus? Surround the principal players with thrashing . . .

JOAN (*to* ARNIE). Loved one! Did you hear? Have you seen this? (*She is still giggling, despite herself; for her, now, the evening is a huge success.*)

HANSON. Arnie. Show us your armour.

JOAN. We can get rid of that too while we're at it.

HANSON. I know a secret!

MAUREEN. What?

HANSON. I know a secret!

SHEILA (*laughing*). What is it?

HANSON. Are you ready?

JOAN. No rowdy stuff, Hanson.

HANSON. Are you ready? (*Darts to the cupboard, and with a sudden gesture.*) Woman! Behold thy . . . Oh, it's locked.

JOAN. Don't look at me.

HANSON. Arnold. What is this?

SHEILA. Oh, Arnie. Can't we see it?

ARNIE. What?

ARNIE *has paused. He stares at* SHEILA *in consternation.*

SHEILA (*quietly*). Can't we see it, sir?

ARNIE. Who asked you in here?

HANSON. I did, Robin.

ARNIE (*glances at her, then moves away.*) Show her the aeroplane. There's a stuffed eagle over there.

HANSON. Aren't we going to see . . .

ARNIE. And above the mantelpiece you'll observe a Lee-Enfield rifle, a weapon of historical importance to the British nation.

HANSON. Arnold, if you'll just allow . . .

ARNIE. With that weapon we preserved . . . (*He gestures airily about him.*)

HANSON. Look, I don't wish to get impersonal, old boy.

ARNIE. And what are we now? Gropers in the debris of our . . .

HANSON. Arnold. Do I understand you are about to entertain us?

ARNIE. Tell us, Hanson. How does your mother keep her stockings up?

HANSON. Ooo! Ooo!

JOAN. I think that's enough.

MAUREEN. We better quieten down . . .

SHEILA. It's good, Miss!

JOAN. If you want something to shout about there's always this. (*She thrusts the telegram into his hand.*)

ARNIE. It's Hanson. He's an historical aberration.

HANSON. Ooo!

ARNIE. A turnip!

HANSON. Ooo!

SHEILA *has given way to giggles;* JOAN *also.*

ARNIE. A sod.

HANSON. Ooo! Ooo! You heard him! (*Writes across a large imaginary blackboard.*) Tries hard: a willing worker, but effort frequently suffocated in pompous supposition.

ARNIE *waves his arms about indecisively.*

Ooo! You heard! (*Writes.*) Self-indulgent and tends to melodrama when opposed. Suffers from affectations, not least of which a pretension to reality. (*Bows to the room.*) Thus write I across all my reports. (*Vaguely facetious.*) Loved one.

JOAN. That's enough! (*Attempts to turn* ARNIE *away.*)

ARNIE. It's him. He's a propagator of untruth.

HANSON. Untruth! Why, he's a lie himself. If you measured him by any reality he'd be invisible. (*He puts his tongue out triumphantly at* ARNIE.)

ARNIE. That rifle's *loaded*.

HANSON pauses, then looks up. He hesitates. Then:

HANSON. Liar!

MAUREEN (*to* JOAN). Is it loaded?

JOAN. I don't know. (*Giggling*.)

MAUREEN. I think we've had enough of this.

SHEILA. They're only playing, Miss!

HANSON lifts the rifle down.

ARNIE. May I?

He puts the telegram in his pocket, first one, then the other, as HANSON *fumbles with the rifle. Then* ARNIE *takes it from him, removes the safety-catch and draws back the bolt.*

All right. A pretension to reality. (*He raises the rifle and presses it to* HANSON's *temple. He's still unsteady with drink.*) It's loaded.

HANSON (*pauses. Then calls*). Rubbish. (*Giggles*.)

ARNIE. I'll fire it.

HANSON is silent.

Well?

HANSON. Troublemaker, and known disseminator of bad habits.

MAUREEN. That's far enough.

ARNIE. Are you ready?

HANSON. Yes.

ARNIE squeezes the trigger.

JOAN. No!

ARNIE. It's rusty. Hold your head still.

HANSON stands tensely, holding the table now, assuming some dignity. SHEILA *has covered her face up.* ARNIE *holds the rifle more awkwardly to gain further pressure on the trigger. He squeezes again. There's a click.* ARNIE *still holds the rifle there.* HANSON *laughs.*

JOAN. Oh, God. That's enough.

HANSON. Everything you see. False all the way through. (*Takes the rifle from* ARNIE, *laughing with real pleasure. He points it at* ARNIE, *ramming back the bolt.*) Arnold: you're a falsity! (*His laughter suddenly breaks. He looks down at the rifle – examines it.*) It is loaded.

ARNIE. Yes.

HANSON (*looking up in horror*). And you pulled the trigger?

ARNIE. Yes.

HANSON. Why . . . You madman! (*He throws the rifle down.*)

ARNIE. It was a choice you made on the evidence of your own senses, Jeffrey.

HANSON. You're mad!

ARNIE. That's not true.

HANSON (*to the women*). He could have killed me!

JOAN (*dismissive*). Fools! You're both fools.

HANSON. What? (*He suddenly stares at her, drunkenly distracted.*) He could have killed me!

ARNIE, *swayingly, has meanwhile picked up the rifle. He points it at* HANSON.

ARNIE. As a matter of fact I still can.

HANSON. No!

JOAN. Arnie!

MAUREEN. No!

SHEILA *screams.*

ARNIE *pulls the trigger, then gazes intrigued at* HANSON's *expression.*

ARNIE. The firing-pin's removed. There's no contact with the cartridge. (*He lowers the rifle.*) It can never go off.

HANSON *grabs the rifle from him.*

HANSON. You know what I think?

ARNIE. You take it too seriously, Big John.

HANSON *stares at him impotently, blind with rage.*

(*Slowly.*) It really is unforgivable, isn't it?

MAUREEN. You better go, Sheila. Did you bring a coat?

HANSON. She's not going.

SHEILA. I don't want to go.

MAUREEN. I think you better, girl, and do as you're told this once.

HANSON. I said she's not going! (*He takes* SHEILA's *arm. Then, to* ARNIE.) God. What a deceiver. It was false, bogus, all the way through. He even makes a virtue of it.

ARNIE (*to* MAUREEN). Shall we dance?

MAUREEN. You've gone too far, Arnold. I think we'd better go.

HANSON. Go! I think – with all due insolence to our host – that he should be compelled to open his bloody cupboard *door*!

ARNIE. Mockery ill-becomes you.

HANSON. I think he should . . .

ARNIE. *You* think? Your thoughts, Hanson . . . they're superfluous here. And your insolence undistinguished. You've been revealed as a pompous boor. Your otiose circumlocutions no longer sufficient to conceal the cringing, shivering coward within; your boldest gestures about as revelationary as a flea's. Do you really believe that I'm under any obligation to reveal *my* soul to you? My weaknesses stand higher than your greatest virtues.

MAUREEN. That's enough, for God's sake!

ARNIE. My only regret is, out of past charity, I have such weak substances on which to wreak my revenge.

HANSON (*applauding*). Oh, bravo. Bravo.

ARNIE. I regret it all. All this. It's too puny for contempt!

JOAN. Where are you going?

ARNIE *has gone stumbling towards the stairs.*

ARNIE. What?

JOAN. These people: you *invited* them.

ARNIE *comes back, takes the whisky bottle from the table and begins to go out.*

ARNIE. Assume they aren't here. It's an easier alternative to assuming that they are.

JOAN (*casually*). Have you read that telegram?

He pauses again.

In your pocket.
ARNIE. I heard!

Pause.

JOAN. They're not coming. As long as you realise that when you wake up. And it's just as well they aren't. You're blind drunk!
ARNIE. Do you know what you're saying? (*He snatches at his pockets, searching for then finding the telegram.*) I know what it says! I heard! (*To* HANSON.) Did you say that Scott wrote this? He wants firing! Did *he* write this? Then sack him! He's no good. Did I tell you what he did to Thompson?
JOAN. You better go to bed.
ARNIE. I am! I am! . . . (*He stares round at them, full of threat.*) I *am*! (*He goes to the stairs, stumbles, regains his balance, and goes.*)
HANSON.
So's friendship, if not love, repaid;
And by a graceless hand is trust betrayed.
MAUREEN. Stop it! I've had enough! All this *indulgence*.
HANSON (*going to cupboard*). Well, that comes out at least. (*He tries to wrench the cupboard door open, then kicks the thin wood open.*) Why it's empty! There's nothing here! (*He turns round, broken by his rage.*) He must have it up there with him.
JOAN. Just look what you've done . . . (*Giggles.*)
SHEILA. He's jealous.
JOAN. What?
SHEILA. It's because he's jealous. That's why he's gone . . .
MAUREEN. Sheila!
SHEILA. He is. He's jealous of Mr Hanson. Anybody can see.

JOAN *is more disillusioned than annoyed.*

JOAN (*tediously*). Oh, for goodness sake. Get her out.
SHEILA. He is!
JOAN (*almost indifferently*). Get out.
MAUREEN. Go on, Sheila. Go on. You better go now. (*To* HANSON.) Take her out.

SHEILA. He is! You're all jealous. All of you!
JOAN (*tediously*). Take her out for goodness sake.

MAUREEN *has taken* JOAN's *arm as her violence grows.*

MAUREEN (*to* HANSON). You'd better go.

HANSON *has taken her arm.*

HANSON. All right. All right. But don't blame her. That
camel up there. Now you just shout at him!

JOAN *stands tensely,* MAUREEN *holding her, until*
SHEILA *and* HANSON *have gone.*

Silence. Then:

JOAN (*quietly*). I'll have to wait for my mother. She should
have been back by now. That girl.
MAUREEN. I'll stay a little longer.
JOAN. Would you? Do you mind? It's very kind of you.
MAUREEN. We might as well sit down.

JOAN *turns out of her arms and wanders about the room.*
Then:

JOAN. That girl.
MAUREEN. I shouldn't worry.
JOAN. Isn't it quiet? It must be late. (*Pause.*) She can't be
long. Everything must be shut by now.
MAUREEN. Will Arnold have gone to bed?
JOAN. Oh . . . (*She listens.*) We won't see him again
tonight. (*Pause.*) I've been dreading having a scene with
my mother this evening while people were here. That's
why I asked her to go out.
MAUREEN. Asked her?
JOAN. I told her this evening that she would have to leave.
Go and live somewhere else . . . It sounds hard. But there
was no other way of doing it. Believe me.
MAUREEN. Is that what Arnold was in a mood about? I
mean, when we came.
JOAN. No. No. He doesn't know I've told her yet.

MAUREEN *watches* JOAN *moving listlessly about the*
room.

I had to tell her to go, you know. (*Pause.*) I've never seen her so hurt. Never. She . . . I've never seen her so hurt.

MAUREEN. Where will she go when she leaves?

JOAN. She's grown so attached to Arnie. (*Sinks into a chair opposite her.*)

They're silent. Then:

Don't you think it's strange? The way he's always surrounded by women?

MAUREEN. Women?

JOAN. I don't know. He can't bear to be in this house alone. Can you imagine that? Don't you think it's extraordinary? (*Pause.*) You should see the look of relief on his face when I come in. Or my mother comes in. And he's sitting here alone. I don't think he's even aware of it. (*She gets up, moves around the room again, restlessly. Then:*) I was like a wild animal when I first got married. Always smashing things. I couldn't put my hand down without knocking something over. I was never still for one minute. (*She sits down again in the same seat, facing MAUREEN.*) We were always fighting. You know, fists and things. (*She laughs into her hand.*) It's awful, isn't it? But we used to stand up, bashing each other.

MAUREEN *laughs.*

I think this drink's beginning to have an effect on me. (*She snorts into her hand.*) Have you heard of anybody carrying on like that? I'm glad, actually. That they're not coming tomorrow. (*She looks round at the room.*) It was all prepared. All ready. Actually, they're very nice. I don't know why. Will you have something else? I'm sure you'd like them.

MAUREEN. No. I don't think I will.

JOAN. Would you like a stuffed eagle?

MAUREEN. I don't think so. No.

JOAN. A ship?

MAUREEN. No thanks.

JOAN. It's all yours if you want it. S'all going out. Sweeping changes. Actually. You mustn't tell anybody about this, will you?

MAUREEN. No . . .

JOAN. You promise?

MAUREEN (*nods uncertainly*). Yes.

JOAN. The fact is, Arnie doesn't give a damn for anybody. I'm exactly the same. Do you know anything about children?

MAUREEN. Well, I teach them.

JOAN. Ah, yes. (*She looks at* MAUREEN *freshly*.) Are you religious? You don't mind me asking?

MAUREEN (*pause*). No. Well . . .

JOAN. Do you believe in God?

MAUREEN. Well, in a sort of . . .

JOAN (*lifting back her hair*). I honestly don't know what to believe in. Is that the time? You absolutely promise?

MAUREEN. Yes.

JOAN. Well, I'll tell you. (*Looks round*.) Arnold actually . . .

MAUREEN (*pause*). Yes?

JOAN. Is God.

MAUREEN. Oh.

JOAN. He's only assumed the identity of a schoolteacher in order to remain incognito. Inconspicuous. For a God, you see, who believes in modesty and self-effacement there are severe doctrinal problems in asserting that he's God at all. Do you understand what I mean?

She watches her for a moment with some satisfaction.
MAUREEN *gives no reply at all.*

It's an enormous privilege, of course. (*Pause*.) Being married to Him at all.

Slow footsteps have already started on the stairs. It's only now, however, that MAUREEN, *who is facing the stairs, actually looks up. She stands up immediately.*

MAUREEN. Oh!

JOAN *turns dreamily, slowly, as she sees* MAUREEN's *reaction.*

MRS ELLIS's *appearance is dreadful: dressed in men's pyjamas, she has a bottle in her hand. Her look is compounded of many feelings: possessiveness, triumph, greed. Her matronly breasts are scarcely concealed by the*

*jacket, and as she sways at the bottom of the stairs the
vision quickly changes to that of a besotted old lady.*

For a moment JOAN *fails to grasp what she sees. When
she does it's with a cry of denial like a child's.*

JOAN. Mam! (*She staggers to her feet.*) Mother!

MRS ELLIS. Do you know . . .

JOAN. Mam! . . . (*She glances frantically at the hall door
where she'd expected her mother to appear.*)

MRS ELLIS. It's not in there. Not in there – as we all
thought. (*She indicates the cupboard.*) It's not in there at
all. He's hidden it – would you believe it, the cunning
devil? – he's hidden it under the bed!

JOAN. No. No.

MRS ELLIS (*to* MAUREEN). Underneath! Well! Whoever
said he wasn't cunning!

JOAN. Mother.

MRS ELLIS. It's all lies. Everything. (*Violent.*) You said he
wanted me to go! You did! . . . In fact. He doesn't want
that at all.

JOAN. What?

MRS ELLIS. Arnie. (*She stands swaying, looking down at
her daughter with something between consternation and
triumph.*) You ask him.

JOAN. Oh, no . . . No.

MRS ELLIS. You . . . You. The things you told me.

JOAN. Oh, God. No. (*She sinks down, burying her face in
her hands.*)

MRS ELLIS. Well. Well, then . . . Who's sorry now? (*She
collapses slowly into a chair.*) Are we having a party?
Who's this, then? Another of Arnie's friends?

Lights fade.

ACT THREE

Scene One
Next morning.

The suit of armour stands to one side, around it the various 'pieces'.

JOAN *is tidying the room and preparing the table for breakfast. She's dressed neatly and tidily, and works briskly. Bottles from the party are stacked on the sideboard.*

After a while ARNIE *appears at the foot of the stairs, tousled, genial, his shirt unbuttoned. He stands at the foot of the stairs, yawns, stretches, smacks his lips and looks round.*

JOAN *goes on working.*

ARNIE. Well. Well. Shipshape. Someone has been up early, I can see.
JOAN. I've made coffee. Is that all right?
ARNIE. Ah, fine. Fine. (*He comes slowly into the room, looks at the armour but makes no comment.*)
JOAN. I haven't cooked anything. I didn't think anyone would feel like eating.
ARNIE. Quite true. Quite true. (*He comes to the table, looks round at the various objects on it*). Well, well, well. That was a very frivolous evening, Joan. All that booze. We shan't go through that again. Not for a very long time. No, we shan't. We certainly shan't. What? We shan't. (*He yawns. Snaps his mouth shut. Suddenly he shadow-boxes, briefly, quickly. Then he yawns again, stretches.*) I've got to get down to weight. This is getting embarrassing. Last fight I ever had I only weighed three stone ten. No, was it four? (*He sits down at the table.*)

JOAN *has poured his coffee.* ARNIE *gazes across at the armour, then, after a while, begins to sing softly.*

Come, ye thankful people come,
Raise the song of harvest home.
All is safely gathered in
Ere the winter storms begin;

God our Maker doth provide
For our wants to be supplied;
Come to God's own temple, come,
Raise the song of harvest home.

Where's Edie, then?

JOAN. She hasn't got up yet. (*She has rearranged the table and gone back to her cleaning.*)

ARNIE. The fact is, I feel in a very philosophic frame of mind. All my life I've looked for some positive reaction in people. Did you know that?

Pause. JOAN *goes on with her tasks.*

There are certain tribes in the Northern Province of Nigeria who use carrier bags for latrines. (*Abstracted, he now looks up at* JOAN *directly, waiting a moment, then:*) This man at school told me that. He worked out there once on famine relief. Saved thousands from starvation. His life was full of significance and meaning. (*Abstracted a moment.*) He said there's this enterprising man in Birmingham who sends them out regularly by post. To an agent. Who sells them at a fantastic profit. It cuts down the risk of malaria or dysentery or something. (*Pause.*) 'Hoyle's Supermarket' they've got printed on the side. (*Pause.*) It's amazing what human initiative will rise to once it sets itself to a particular task.

He has become quite abstracted. JOAN *continues with her work.*

ARNIE *gets up and goes on talking absently.*

When I was a boy we had a milkman who came in a horse and trap. He wore a little bowler hat and a striped apron and came in each morning from the country with cans of fresh milk and ladled it all out with little ladles. Beautiful. They went up from one the size of a thimble to one as big as his hat.

JOAN *has sat down casually on the arm of a chair, holding her face with her hand.*

He ran over a boy one day. The wheel of his cart went over his head. It wasn't his fault. But he offered the boy's mother free milk for a year; you know, for goodwill and neighbourliness. She was very poor. She had eleven children. I don't think he knew that at the time. (*Pause.*) He went out of business in six months. Bankrupt. (*Pause.*) You should have seen this woman's house. Milk, there was, everywhere. Nothing but milk. (*He suddenly looks round.*)

JOAN *gets up and resumes her tasks: taking the coffee pot to the kitchen.* ARNIE *talks through to her.*

You know, I've always had the ambition to be a writer. The things I'd write about would be fairly rhetorical in manner.

JOAN *re-emerges.*

Subjects . . . Well, it may even have caught your attention. The extraordinary mixture of hysteria and passivity one gets in society today. I mean . . .

While he's been talking MRS ELLIS *has appeared from the stairs. She's carrying a small suitcase and is dressed in a coat and hat, a small fur round her shoulders.*

MRS ELLIS. I'll send for my things when I've got an address.

JOAN. You'd better put the case down . . .

ARNIE. I thought there for a moment, you know, that we were going off on holiday. God, weather like this, too. It's incomprehensible.

JOAN (*ignoring him*). I'm heating up the coffee.

MRS ELLIS *stands gazing irresolutely around her.*

And do take that coat off. You'll be roasted alive. The tray's ready to fetch through. (*She busies herself now rearranging the table.*)

MRS ELLIS. Joan . . .

JOAN. All it requires is lifting.

ARNIE. This is quite extraordinary. I've forgotten his name now. But this boy fell off the school roof on . . . Friday, it must have been. Over forty feet in height. No. I'm wrong there. Nearer fifty. Fell like a stone. Bang. Right on his head. By every right it should have killed him. But no. This should interest you, Edie. He's scarcely hit the ground than he stands up and says, 'Sir, I didn't fall.

Sombebody pushed me.' So damned anxious, in
wandering near the parapet, to show he hadn't broken a
rule.

MRS ELLIS *has gone into the kitchen. She comes out
again now, almost immediately, lost.*

MRS ELLIS. I don't seem able to find it.

JOAN. Look for it, Mother. Put the light on. Open the
curtains.

MRS ELLIS. Yes . . .

JOAN. And do take your coat off.

MRS ELLIS. Yes . . . (*She starts back, falters.*) I don't know
how you can just sit there.

ARNIE. Sit?

MRS ELLIS. I can hardly stand!

ARNIE. Now, then. Now, then. There's no need to get
upset.

MRS ELLIS. Upset! (*She buries her face in her hands.*)

JOAN. It's all right, Mother.

MRS ELLIS (*moaning*). I don't know what to do.

JOAN. You'll stay here, Mother. It's all right.

MRS ELLIS. Oh, Joan . . . Joan.

JOAN. Now, you're all right. You're all right.

MRS ELLIS *cries into her hands.*

ARNIE (*brightly*). How about some coffee?

JOAN *has gone to take* MRS ELLIS *in her arms.*

JOAN. Come on. You better come upstairs. I'll help you up.

MRS ELLIS. Oh, God, Joan. What am I going to do?

JOAN. Oh, now. You come up. Come on, now. Come
on . . .

MRS ELLIS. I can't. I can't.

JOAN. I'll bring you something up. Now, come on. You'll
be all right.

She leads her mother to the stairs. They go out.

ARNIE *has stood up. He walks about. Puts his hands in
his pockets. Whistles.*

ARNIE. This is quite extraordinary. (*He touches the armour
confidingly.*) About two days ago the Director of
Education came up to me and said, 'Bancroft,' he said – I

mean it's not as if my name was Bancroft – 'Bancroft, I
don't know quite how to tell you this, and I should hate it
to get around. But the fact is, Bancroft, my wife has
recently begun to manufacture money. The thing is, that
periodically she lowers her knickers and from inside takes
a miscellaneous collection of coins. The process, as far as I
am aware, Bancroft, has completely taken over her
excretory organs. And it's mostly silver. The coins, I
mean.' You know – would you believe it – the only
comment he made after telling me all this was 'Pity it isn't
gold, Bancroft. Just like that rotten bitch to produce
second best.' (*He laughs.*) Anyway, I thought you'd like to
know.

JOAN *has come in as he finishes this.*

Oh, how is the old bird?

JOAN *begins her preparations of making a glass of warm
milk.*

You know, this unnerves me. I'm looking for some sort of
constructive attitude from you, Joan. Something a bit
bolder. To generalise about one's misfortune is invariably
a sign of moral recovery in my book. If you could work
something up on those lines I'd be immensely grateful.
JOAN. Yes. (*Goes on with her task.*)
ARNIE. I think I need to feel degenerate.
JOAN. I'm taking my mother up a glass of milk.
ARNIE. You see. Those are not the sort of remarks I'm
looking for, Joan.

JOAN *has now gone into the kitchen.* ARNIE *talks
through to her.*

The sort I'm looking for only you can provide. There's no
one else. My only other opportunity for being punished
lies immobilised, apparently, upstairs.

JOAN *returns to collect the sugar from the table.*

JOAN. There's an old woman up there, broken in two.
ARNIE. Well, at least she has that reassurance. What have I
got? Nothing. Nothing. I don't understand it. I don't. I get
no crumb of consolation from this at all. I feel I should

get something. I deserve to suffer something, Joan. Even if
it's only retribution.

JOAN *hasn't answered.*

These silences unnerve me. At any moment I'm going to
suffer a relapse. I think I should warn you, Joan. You
know what that might lead to.

JOAN *still offers no answer.*

(*Suddenly.*) I should also like it to be known that this
sudden and alarming capacity to behave like a frog . . . to
bespatter detachment on every side, to spawn ill humour,
to sit for hours on end on a pad of disaffection . . . that
all these qualities, while adding conviction to your image
as a woman, *in no way*, in no way, improve your image as
a man!

JOAN *still makes no sign. Silence. Then* ARNIE *indicates
the armour.*

I don't understand. Some blame for my predicament
attaches itself to you. I lie here, caught up in a million
abominations, attributes, some of them fed in long before
conception. And some of them, *some of them*, fed in by
you! In that clammy little hand lie parts of me I don't
think, in all honesty, you understand.

He follows JOAN *to the kitchen door.*

Guilt and austerity are not necessarily compatible, Joan, I
mean . . . effusiveness could make your message just as
clear.
JOAN. You've behaved like a dwarf. Everything in your life
is like that. Dwarfish.
ARNIE. Well. Yes. That's something. (*He talks through to
her in the kitchen.*) A dwarf. (*Pause; reflects.*) I don't like
that somehow. (*Half-laughs.*) You know I object to that,
Joan. I don't feel like a dwarf. (*He looks at his hands.*) I
wouldn't describe them particularly, for instance, as
dwarfish. (*Silence.*) Haven't you anything else to say?

JOAN *re-emerges with the glass of milk.*

JOAN. What are you going to do, Arnie?

ARNIE. I don't know. (*Pause.*) I'll do the only decent thing, I suppose.

JOAN. Yes.

ARNIE. That's all there is to do.

JOAN. Yes.

ARNIE. I'll marry her.

They're silent. Then:

JOAN. Why don't you leave, Arnie? And rid yourself of all this torment?

ARNIE (*abstracted*). I don't know. Life has no dignity, Joan. No, I do agree with that. (*Pause.*) And death hasn't a great deal to recommend it, either. (*Pause.*) Both of them, when you look at it: they're pretty anonymous affairs. I don't know. I feel I should be able to do something. I feel . . . the moment's come . . . it's actually arrived. (*He grasps the air.*) And yet it refuses to . . . emanate. (*Suddenly looks round at the room.*) Anyway, I couldn't leave all this. My own fireside. I've worked hard for all this. I have. It's mine. This is my situation in life.

JOAN, *after watching him with some attention, has turned away at this towards the stairs.*

Perhaps I could go mad. Insanity, you know, is the one refuge I've always felt I was able to afford. The insights that irrationality brings. Well, in the end, that's what we're looking for. Cleavages. Cracks. Fissures. Openings. Some little aperture of warmth and light.

JOAN, *after some hesitation, goes with her glass of milk.*

Look, this is a very poor arrangement. I haven't got your attention at all. (*He turns away.*) I don't know. I might as well be talking to the wall. (*He goes to the armour: examines it sadly. Then he goes to the wall. He moves from one patch to another on the wall as if carefully selecting the right one for his task, rubbing his hand over its surface, then finally choosing one spot and taking up a stance before it.*)

When I was young, my mother said to me:

'Never drown but in the sea –

Rivers, streams and other dilatory courses
Are not contingent with the elemental forces
Which govern you and me – and occasionally your
father –
So remember, even if the means are insufficient, rather
Than die in pieces subside by preference as a whole,
For disintegration is inimical to the soul
Which seeks the opportunity or the chances
To die in the circumstances
Of a prince, a saviour, or a messiah –
Or something, perhaps, even a little higher –
You and me and several of your aunties,
On my side, though working class, have destinies
Scarcely commensurate with our upbringing:
I hope in you we are instilling
This sense of secret dignities and rights
– Not like your father's side, the lights
Of which, I hope, we'll never see again,
Who have, I'm afraid, wet blotting-paper for a brain!'

Pause.

'Please, please my son,
Don't fail me like your father done.'

*He stands for a moment regarding the wall, expectantly,
tensed. Then slowly he relaxes. His head sinks, his
shoulders droop. His forehead leans against the wall.*

Oh. Oh. Oh.
When I was young, when I was young,
There were so many things I should have done.

Fade.

Scene Two
Evening, a few days later.

*The room has been cleared of all ARNIE's possessions. It's
clean and immaculate. A large vase of flowers stands on the
table and another on the sideboard.*

From the hall comes the sound of voices.

HANSON (*heard*). Arnie? (*Pause.*) Arnie? Arnie! (*Pause.*)
He can't be here. (*Whistles.*)

MAUREEN (*heard*). Arnie? (*Knocking on outer door.*) Can't
hear anybody.

*The calling has been tentative, apprehensive. Then, finally,
the door opens and HANSON puts his head round.*

HANSON. No. No one here. (*Whistles.*) No.

He and MAUREEN come in. HANSON carries a parcel.

MAUREEN. Goodness.

HANSON. I say. (*They look round at the changes.*) Drastic
renovations, what?

MAUREEN. Joan?

HANSON. I say . . . (*Whistles a tune to himself as he looks
round, tapping furniture and empty spaces with his stick.*)

MAUREEN. Joan? (*She has glanced in the kitchen.*) No: no
one. (*Shrugs.*)

HANSON. Well, then . . .

MAUREEN. I suppose we better wait.

HANSON (*looks at watch*). I don't know. What? Arnie!
(*Then distracted.*) I say. Cupboard restored. Would you
believe it? (*Goes to look, then, in the kitchen. Comes
back. Sets parcel he is carrying on the table.*) Ship
deserted, what? Oh . . .

*Sounds of the outer door opening etc. HANSON hastily
composes himself, tie, etc. MAUREEN, who has sat
down, gets up. MRS ELLIS comes in, carrying a basket.*

MRS ELLIS. Oh . . .

MAUREEN. Mrs Ellis . . .

HANSON. We . . . Oh, allow me . . . (*Offers to take her
basket.*)

MRS ELLIS. No . . . It's all right.

MAUREEN. We found the door open. We knocked, but
there was no one here.

MRS ELLIS. Oh . . .

MAUREEN. Is Joan out, too?

MRS ELLIS. Yes . . . I've just been . . . She . . . I'll just put
these in the kitchen.

HANSON. Please. Allow me. (*Offers to take basket.*)

MRS ELLIS. No. No, it's all right. (*She goes into the kitchen.*)

HANSON. Well, well . . . (*He whistles a tune again, glances at his watch, at* MAUREEN, *wanders round the room.*)

MAUREEN *goes to the kitchen door.*

MAUREEN. How is Arnie, Mrs Ellis?

After a moment MRS ELLIS *comes out.*

MRS ELLIS. Oh, he's . . . all right.

HANSON. Fine. Fine. We . . . popped round. He hasn't been to school: the past few days.

MRS ELLIS. No.

HANSON. We . . . ah . . . thought we'd pop round.

MRS ELLIS. Yes.

HANSON. Fine. Fine.

MRS ELLIS *has taken off her coat and goes through to the hallway to hang it up.* HANSON *and* MAUREEN *exchange glances.* HANSON *whistles a tune.*

Outside in the hall the sound of Joan's arrival: 'Oh, it's you.' 'Visitors.' 'What?' 'Mr Hanson . . . schoolteacher . . .'

HANSON *recomposes himself. A moment later* JOAN *comes in.*

JOAN. Oh, hello.

HANSON. Joan.

MAUREEN. And how are you?

JOAN. I'm well. Fine. And you?

MAUREEN. Yes. Fine.

HANSON. Fine. Fine.

JOAN. Isn't Arnie in?

MAUREEN. We knocked, and shouted.

HANSON. Found the door ajar. What? No answer.

MAUREEN. No.

JOAN (*taking off her coat*). If the door was open he can't be far away.

HANSON. Well, then . . . (*Silence.*) Everything in order, then?

JOAN. I think so. More or less.

HANSON. Well, then . . . (*Glances at watch.*) I suppose we better . . . be making tracks.

MRS ELLIS *has come in and gone through to the kitchen.*

JOAN. Stay and have some tea if you like.

HANSON. Yes. Fine. Well.

JOAN. My mother will be making some.

HANSON. Fine. Fine.

MAUREEN. How is Arnie, Joan?

JOAN. I don't know. All right. (*Shrugs.*)

HANSON. We were just remarking. Several days since he put in an appearance, what? At school.

JOAN. Yes.

HANSON. Nothing to worry about, then?

JOAN. No. I don't think so.

ARNIE *has appeared behind them, from the stairs. His head is done up, turban-fashion, in a towel. In his hand he carries the sword.*

HANSON. Good. Good. We were just remarking. Vast changes. What?

JOAN. What?

HANSON. The room.

JOAN. Ah, yes.

HANSON. Flowers! (*Smells them.*) Beautiful.

JOAN. Yes.

HANSON. Altogether. (*Indicates room.*) Lighter.

JOAN. Yes.

In glancing round they become slowly aware of ARNIE. Silence. Then:

ARNIE.
The King, though broken by his plight,
Shall rise again to set things right!

HANSON. Oh . . .

MAUREEN. Arnie . . .

ARNIE. Well, well, well. How are we all? Jeff?

HANSON. I'm fine. Fine.

ARNIE. And Maureen. How are you, my dear?

MAUREEN. I'm well, Arnie.

ARNIE. Just arrived, eh?

HANSON. Yes. Yes. Just about.

ARNIE. Thought I heard sounds. Couldn't be too sure. Got both my damned ears fastened up.

MAUREEN. And how are you, Arnie, yourself?

ARNIE. Oh, not so bad. Not so bad. Can't grumble. Can't complain.

HANSON. The Head sends his felicitations, Arnie . . .

ARNIE. Fine. Fine.

HANSON. And the staff and pupils likewise. Looking forward, needless to say, to your early return to duties.

ARNIE. Ah, yes.

HANSON. Brought a few essentials here, Arnie. (*Indicates the parcel.*) Keep the system mobile, mind alert.

ARNIE. Ah, yes!

Silence.

HANSON. We were just remarking.

ARNIE. Yes.

HANSON. Vast changes since we were last here.

ARNIE. Changes.

HANSON. The room . . .

ARNIE. Gave them all to the refuse-man, you know.

JOAN. I'll just see about the tea.

Goes to kitchen.

ARNIE (*to* MAUREEN). And how are you?

MAUREEN. I'm well, Arnie.

ARNIE. I suppose you've seen their lorry? They have a blade in the back which crushes them all up. (*Suddenly, hugely.*) Crush! Crush! Crush!

HANSON. What, all of them, old boy?

ARNIE. Absolutely. (*Gestures at the room.*) The lot. (*Then, after a moment, swinging the sword.*) 'Cept this, of course.

HANSON. Yes.

ARNIE. I kept it back. (*Whistles then between his teeth as, in demonstration, he slashes it about him.*)

HANSON. Ah, yes.

ARNIE. Bound to come in useful.

HANSON. Yes.

ARNIE. At least, so I thought.

HANSON. Ah, yes, old boy.

ARNIE. Arms, hands, feet, legs, abdomen. The lot. (*Mimes the lorry's blade.*) Head! (*Gurgles, hand across his throat.*)

HANSON. We spoke to Sheila, by the way.

ARNIE. Yes?

HANSON. Had a little word in her ear.

ARNIE. Ah, yes.

MAUREEN. I think she'll show a little discretion.

ARNIE. She will?

HANSON. I think so, old man.

ARNIE. Good, good. I could do with a little bit of that myself. (*Laughs.*) Joan? (*Looks round. Then he gestures towards the kitchen.*) She has a job.

MAUREEN. Oh.

ARNIE. Out to work each day.

HANSON. Yes?

ARNIE. Perhaps she mentioned it?

MAUREEN. No. (*Shakes her head.*)

ARNIE. She acquired her credentials, I'm glad to say, long before I married her. In a secretarial capacity, of course.

HANSON. Ah, yes.

ARNIE. Type. Type. Type. You should see her fingers. Flexing. Even in bed.

HANSON. Ah, yes, old boy.

ARNIE. On the other hand . . .

HANSON. Yes, old boy?

ARNIE. Absolutely nothing to worry about.

HANSON. No, no . . .

ARNIE. The doctor recommends a long sea-voyage.

MAUREEN. Sea-voyage?

ARNIE. And a complete change of air.

MAUREEN. I see.

ARNIE. I would have thought, myself, that the two of them were perfectly synonymous.

HANSON. Absolutely.

ARNIE. I'm overworked.

HANSON. My dear boy . . .

ARNIE. My nerves, Jeff, are stretched beyond endurance. (*Glances round with some exaggeration to see that he is not overheard.*) I'm afraid I should have warned you. Joan . . . (*Taps his head.*) You will find her, I'm afraid, considerably changed. Her work — the contingencies of high office, the flow, the rapid, reckless interchange of ideas which has been her lot now (*Dramatically consults his bare wrist.*) for the past six hours, leaves her — I'm very much afraid — *prostrate.*

HANSON. Ah, yes.

JOAN (*entering*). My mother's bringing in the tea.

HANSON. Oh, that's very kind of you, Joan.

MAUREEN. Shouting at the devils all afternoon. Just one of those days. When you want a bit of peace you can never get it.

ARNIE. What do you really think, Jeff?

HANSON. Think?

ARNIE. Feel, if you like. What do you really feel?

HANSON. I feel we're completely out of touch with one another, if you really want to know.

ARNIE. I'm not out of touch with you. I can see, for example, that you are embarrassed at being here, anxious to conceal it, and looking forward to the moment when you leave and can tell people outside how I am looking and behaving, and what things I say. And as for Maureen — I can see how my behaviour has licensed what was previously impossible. Does that sound like someone out of touch with you?

HANSON. You take to insanity, Arnold, like other men take to drink.

A silence. Then:

ARNIE. You have insufficient innocence to be a fool, Jeffrey.

ARNIE *watches him a moment. A pause, then:*

MAUREEN. We're still struggling along, by the way, Arnie, with rehearsals . . .

HANSON. Oh, yes. I'm afraid your absence, old man, has been severely felt. And, somewhat ineffectually I must confess, I have been obliged to take your place . . .

ARNIE. Robin Hood!

HANSON. Ah, yes!

ARNIE. Jeff. You must have discovered it for yourself.

HANSON. Yes?

ARNIE. A usurper. An outlaw!

HANSON. Ah, yes.

ARNIE. Always on the outside of things. Maureen! – cynical
of the established order: disenfranchised, dispossessed. A
refugee, if you like, from the proper world.

MAUREEN. Yes.

ARNIE. I hope you've kept them to it, Jeff!

HANSON. Well, as a matter of fact . . .

ARNIE. *Kings.* (*A dramatic self-gesture.*)

JOAN (*to* ARNIE). Why don't you sit down?

ARNIE. They're a sort of receptacle, if you like. Into which
flow all the goodness and intentions of mankind: and out
of which in turn flow benevolence – and decisions.
Authority. Rule. One becomes a king, not by chance – but
by right: attributes fed in long before conception.
Preordained.

HANSON. Well, we weren't making it that complicated.
(*To* JOAN.) Robin stood on his bow yesterday afternoon
and nearly guillotined his ear.

ARNIE. You think kingship's something foreign to me, Jeff?
Let me tell you – I've studied it all my life. It's my
profession. History! . . . You think I come from an age
sentimental about its motives. You're wrong. My ancestry
is rooted in action, in events, not causes. It's only fools
who worry *why* they are. (*Pause.*) Do you know what
goodness is?

HANSON. Goodness? (*Glances at the others.*)

ARNIE. Do you know what evil is? (*He looks round at
them; they don't answer.*) Look. A simple arithmetical
problem – set in all the schools. (*He pulls up a chair and
sits facing them.*) Take what we are from everything, and
what remains?

HANSON (*pause*). I don't know.

MAUREEN (*as* ARNIE *looks to her*). No.

ARNIE. Goodness and Kings. (*He studies* HANSON *a
moment. Then:*) Kings rise above themselves. They
become . . . inanimate. Formed. (*He shapes it with his
hands. Then he looks up at them; sees their looks.*) Do
you know what the greatest threat to the present century
is? (*Pause.*) The pygmies. (*He smiles at them.*)

HANSON. Yes.

JOAN. Arnie . . .

ARNIE. So small, so inconspicuous, they infiltrate everywhere. Not only out there, but into seats of government and power. And, of course, they're disguised. Not as men. Not even as small men. But as conditions of the soul. (*Relaxes.*) You think that's a conspiracy? No. We *choose* the lesser men.

HANSON. Yes.

ARNIE. Napoleons – they have their day. Usurpers, whether for good or ill. But the king rules not by revolution but by constitution. He is *born*: he is *bred*: he is created king *inside*. (*Pause.*) His *constitution* makes *the* constitution which makes him king. Joan, I don't like you standing behind me.

JOAN. It's my mother. She's bringing in the tea.

JOAN *has gone to hold the kitchen door:* MRS ELLIS *enters with a laden tray.*

HANSON. Ah, grand. Lovely.

MRS ELLIS *nods without looking up.*

ARNIE. Isn't that a miraculous sight? A tea-tray elevated through the air entirely by its own volition.

JOAN. Arnie, I'm afraid, has taken to assuming my mother doesn't exist.

MRS ELLIS *puts the tray on the table. She serves the tea according to instructions.*

Maureen. Milk and sugar?

MAUREEN. Thank you. We ought really to be leaving fairly soon. (*She looks to* HANSON.)

ARNIE. Oh, don't stay on my account, Maureen. I can perform miracles any time for your amusement. If you wish, I can make that tea-tray depart to where it came from entirely under its own resources.

JOAN. Milk and sugar, Jeff?

HANSON. No sugar. I've decided I must slim.

ARNIE. Or sugar transfer itself, unsolicited, from bowl to
cup.

MAUREEN (*to* HANSON). Ay, now . . .

HANSON. That's to say, someone has decided for me.

ARNIE *has been overlooked.*

ARNIE. What's that!

HANSON. My dear Arnold.

ARNIE. *What?*

HANSON. You don't have to play these games for *us.*

ARNIE. Oh?

HANSON (*taking the bull by the horns*). We're your friends.
Whatever you do, you're a friend, and we're concerned
for you. (*Looks to* JOAN *and* MRS ELLIS.) Look, I don't
wish to embarrass you, Joan. But you understand?

JOAN. Yes . . .

HANSON. So there's no need for this eccentricity, Arnie.

ARNIE. What are you trying to do, Jeff?

HANSON. I'm trying . . .

ARNIE. Hoping to *ingratiate* yourself with me?

HANSON. I hope there's no need for me to do that.

ARNIE. You're being very foolish. Do you know *anything*!

HANSON. It seems not.

ARNIE (*carried away*). Scars . . . (*He holds out the palms of
his hands, looking at them.*) They inhabit the skin. They
grow there after a while like natural features. Deformities
actually acquire that authority. (*Looks up bitterly at*
HANSON.) Did you know? (*Pause.*) Remove them – and
you remove life itself. Well?

HANSON. I don't know what you're talking about actually,
Arnold.

ARNIE. I'm talking about . . . alternatives.

HANSON. Alternatives. I see.

ARNIE. To kingship. (*Stares fixedly at* HANSON. *Then he
smiles. A moment later he relaxes completely.*) Oh, Jeff.
(*Laughs.*) You looked positively embarrassed. Didn't he?
Pompous, if I didn't know him better.

MAUREEN. Well . . .

ARNIE. Ah, come on, now, Jeff. Fair's fair. 'A friend.' You
old prigster!

I know a man with two left feet
Who'd rather be dead than be seen in the street:
Yet the fellow would hardly have seemed such a sight
If he hadn't have had two more on his right.

(*He laughs, spreading out his hands.*) I shall now tell you
a dirty history.

HANSON. I honestly think, Arnie, we've had enough.

ARNIE. History has always had a certain fascination for me.

MAUREEN. Joan. I really think we should go.

ARNIE. The raising of Lazarus as a permanent act of
restitution. Kings, queens, emperors. Saints! Inhabited by
one's own domestic soul!

They're silent.

(*Getting up.*) Everything has to be defined. Yet how can
you define anything except by its limitations? Why! – my
limitations are limitless!

MAUREEN. I really think we ought to be going, Joan, you
know. We can pop in again, later in the week – if that's
convenient.

JOAN. Yes. Any time you like.

HANSON. Well . . .

ARNIE. Do you remember Scott? . . . Scott!

HANSON. Arnie. I'd like . . .

ARNIE (*direct to* HANSON). Certain things can't be
destroyed, however much you try. Rifles rust, erode, and
fall apart. They become mechanically defunct. But swords
– while rusting too, preserve down to their last grain an
emblem of the truth. Instruments of honour, which the
world is a feebler place without! . . . Dignity. (*Draws
himself up.*) The past brought down to us in swords!

HANSON. Arnie, we have to be going.

ARNIE. Ah, yes.

HANSON (*to* JOAN). If there's anything we can do,
Joan . . . You will let us know?

JOAN. Yes. Thank you.

MAUREEN. Bye, Arnie.

HANSON. Goodbye, Arnold.

ARNIE (*cheerfully*). Goodbye. Goodbye. It's been very good
of you to come.

MAUREEN. Goodbye, Mrs Ellis.

MRS ELLIS *nods and, having collected the cups etc., carries the tray out to the kitchen.*

ARNIE *nods cheerfully, standing to one side as they leave. Left alone, he walks up and down a moment, then goes to the fire, gazing down. There are sounds of farewell from the hall, then* JOAN *enters.*

JOAN. Do you want some more tea?

ARNIE. What? I don't know.

JOAN. Soon, there'll be nobody coming here at all.

ARNIE. No. No. That's quite true.

JOAN. Where did you manage to find that?

ARNIE. I extracted it.

JOAN. Yes?

ARNIE. From the dustbin.

JOAN. My father had a sword.

ARNIE. Yes?

JOAN. When I was young. (*Pause.*) He could hold it at full stretch, in one hand, without the tip even quivering, and count slowly to a hundred.

ARNIE. I look behind me, Joan.

JOAN. What?

ARNIE. I live. I go along. I look behind . . . And I see . . . not achievements towering in my path.

JOAN. No . . .

ARNIE. Ruins. I can see . . . wonderful. (*A vision rises before his eyes. Finally, slowly, he sits down.*) If I raise you to the status of a queen, do you think you could be realistic?

JOAN *takes the remainder of the things into the kitchen.*

ARNIE *sits alone, abstracted, still, the sword in his hand.*

After some little while JOAN *comes out followed by* MRS ELLIS.

JOAN. Arnie . . . ? Is there anything else you want?

ARNIE (*pause*). What?

JOAN. My mother has something to tell you.

ARNIE. What?

MRS ELLIS. Arnie . . . (*Looks concernedly at* JOAN, *then*

clenches her own hands.) I . . . we've . . . I'll be leaving tomorrow.

ARNIE. What? What? Who said that? Who!

MRS ELLIS. Arnie. I'll be going tomorrow. I've found a room.

ARNIE. I could have sworn . . .

MRS ELLIS. It's a small flat, really.

ARNIE *looks up*.

The place I've found.

ARNIE. It's you! It's you!

MRS ELLIS. Joan helped me to find it. And . . .

ARNIE. Look. You are, or are you not, *positively speaking*?

MRS ELLIS. I . . . It's already furnished.

ARNIE. Well . . . at least that's clear. It would have been alarming, Joan, at this late hour, to have discovered . . . of all things . . . that I suffered from hallucinations.

MRS ELLIS. I think it's the best for all of us.

ARNIE. I'm sure. Yes. Yes. I'm sure. I'm sure. (*Suddenly.*) We've had a good time, Edie.

MRS ELLIS. Yes.

ARNIE (*taps side of his head*). I had something then on the tip of my tongue. No. No. It's gone. It's gone.

MRS ELLIS. It's not so far away . . . that I can't pop in from time to time.

ARNIE. No. No. I'm sure. We have, after all . . . what have we? . . . What? This is extraordinary. After all these years.

JOAN. Yes.

ARNIE. I'd say . . .

JOAN. Yes?

ARNIE. That that was a revolution.

JOAN. Yes.

ARNIE. Or a revelation. I'm not sure which. (*Pause.*) Ahem! (*Pause.*) I better make a speech. A moment like this . . . Can scarcely go by. Unacknowledged.

JOAN. I don't think it's necessary, Arnie.

ARNIE *has stood up*.

ARNIE. No? (*He puts down his sword.*) This is a very heavy sentence, Edie.

MRS ELLIS. I'm not sure . . .

ARNIE. On us. On us. I might well have to make
amendments. To the constitution. To accommodate that.
(*He holds the top of his head.*) It had been my intention
. . . to leucotomise my wife.

MRS ELLIS. Yes . . .

ARNIE. Amongst several other . . . As it is . . . (*Gazes up at
them from beneath his hands.*) We better have a party.

MRS ELLIS. After I've gone.

ARNIE. Yes. Yes. After you've gone.

MRS ELLIS. I'll . . . go up. I've still some things to finish.

ARNIE. Yes. Yes.

She goes.

Silence. Then:

Back to school. Monday!

JOAN. Yes.

ARNIE. Rest. Recuperation . . . Work!

JOAN. Yes.

Silence. Then, suddenly:

ARNIE. Oh! (*Cries out.*)

JOAN. Arnie!

ARNIE. Oh! There's something coming out!

JOAN. Arnie . . .

ARNIE. Oh, dear, Joan.

JOAN. Arnie . . . It's all right.

ARNIE. Oh, dear, Joan. There's something here . . . that's
very hard . . . Merciless.

JOAN. Arnie . . . It's all right.

ARNIE. Oh, dear, oh! (*He covers up his head.*)

JOAN. Arnie.

ARNIE. Oh, dear. Oh, dear. There's something. What? Oh,
dear. There's something coming out.

JOAN. Arnie.

He looks up, still holding his head.

Come on, now.

ARNIE. Oh. Oh. (*His hands are clasped to the top of his
head.*) What am I to do?

JOAN. Here. (*She holds out her hand.*)

ARNIE. Oh. *Now.* (*Screams, hugely. Then:*)

JOAN. It's all over.

ARNIE. Oh, dear. (*After a moment he lowers one hand.*) Oh I'm sure . . . I think.

JOAN. Yes.

ARNIE. In all sincerity. (*He calms. He looks slowly round.*) Nevertheless. I'm assuming that I can come out. The assumption is merely based, you understand, on a generality of feeling.

JOAN. Yes.

ARNIE. Oh.

> Oh, lovely woman . . . feel no obligation;
> Beauty is its own salvation.
> The rest is meant to burn.

> I can't hear a thing.

JOAN. Are you coming up?

ARNIE. Up?

JOAN. Yes.

ARNIE. Have I finished? (*He looks around.*)

JOAN. Yes.

ARNIE. I've finished?

JOAN. I think so.

ARNIE. Are you sure?

JOAN. Yes.

They stand facing one another, still some distance apart.

ARNIE. Oh. Joan. Thank God.

Fade.

In Celebration was first presented at the Royal Court Theatre, London, on 22 April 1969. The cast was as follows:

MR SHAW	Bill Owen
MRS SHAW	Constance Chapman
ANDREW	Alan Bates
COLIN	James Bolam
STEVEN	Brian Cox
MRS BURNETT	Gabrielle Daye
REARDON	Fulton Mackay

Directed by Lindsay Anderson

Characters

MR SHAW, a miner, aged 64
MRS SHAW, his wife, aged 60
ANDREW, aged 38 ⎤
COLIN,   aged 36 ⎬ their sons
STEVEN, aged 33 ⎦
MRS BURNETT, a neighbour, aged 60
REARDON, a neighbour, aged 68

IN CELEBRATION

To my mother and father

ACT ONE

Scene One

A solid, heavily furnished living-room: a door on one side
leads to the kitchen and the stairs, a door on the other side
to the front door and the road. There is also a window and a
fireplace. The furniture is heavy and provincial: a three-piece
suite, a table and four chairs, and a sideboard. There are
various cushions, photographs and pictures, as well as
several cowboy paperbacks. The atmosphere is one of
sobriety, with no particularly distinguishing features, either
of period or 'character'.

Mid-morning.

STEVEN comes in carrying a battered briefcase. He's
dressed in an overcoat: a man in his thirties.

STEVEN. Dad? . . . (Looks round.) Dad? (He hears a sound.
Puts his bag down. Rubs his hands against the cold.
Wanders round the room, examining old, familiar objects.
One or two he picks up, shakes his head, etc.)

SHAW comes in from the stairs: small and stocky, he's
just woken, and is dressed in trousers and shirt, the shirt
unfastened, the trousers held up by braces.

Dad . . .
SHAW. Steven . . . You're early. I've scarcely woken up.

They shake hands.

. . . What time . . . (Looks round dazedly.) . . . I thought
you weren't coming till this afternoon.
STEVEN. I got away early . . .
SHAW. Aye, well . . . How are you? You're looking all
right. (SHAW is a bit shy of his son.)
STEVEN (taking his coat off). So's yourself. A bit older . . .
a bit more weight to go with it.
SHAW. Oh, take no notice of me . . . I only got back from
work three or four hours ago. Nights. My age . . . You'd
think they'd give me summat else . . . Your mother's
out . . .

STEVEN. Yes . . . I met a woman down the road . . . she
told me . . .

SHAW. Nowt they don't know round here . . . Gone to buy
herself a hat.

STEVEN. A hat . . .

SHAW. For tonight. (*Looking round for his cigarettes.*) I
can't tell you . . . I've heard nothing else for the past
fortnight. You'd think we'd come up with a few
thousand . . .

Finds his cigarette packet on the mantelpiece: offers one to
STEVEN.

No, you don't, do you? Common sense. I'm choked up to
here . . . (*Coughs as he lights his own.*) Coal-dust. It's a
wonder I'm still alive.

STEVEN. I've heard that before.

SHAW. Aye. But you won't for much longer.

STEVEN. I've heard that before as well.

SHAW (*sighs*). Aye . . . Do you fancy a cup of tea? I'll just
make one. (*Going.*) How's the family, then? . . . Are they
keeping well? (*Goes to the kitchen.*)

STEVEN (*talking through*). All right . . . Up and down . . .
Look at this . . . I don't think ought's changed here since I
was last up . . .

SHAW (*reappearing*). Family, lad. Family. There's nothing
as important as that. A good wife: children. God's good
grace. (*Looks briefly up.*) If you have good health and
your family, you don't need anything else.

STEVEN. Aye . . .

SHAW. Sixty-four years next month. If I haven't learnt that
I've learnt nothing. (*Suddenly shows him his hand.*) Damn
near lost me hand last week. Seven stiches.

STEVEN. You'll have to watch out.

SHAW. Watch out? My age . . . You're joking. One more
year, you know, then I'm finished. Pension me off. Fifty
years, you know, I've been down that lot. That's what I've
got to show. (*Holds up his hands.*)

STEVEN. Oh, and a bit more . . .

SHAW. Nay, I can't grumble . . . And how's your lot?
How's Sheila? Best daughter-in-law I ever had.

STEVEN. She's all right.

SHAW. Four kiddies. There can't be ten months between them. I don't know how they do it. I thought I was impetuous. There was two or three years, you know, between you lot.

STEVEN. When are they getting up?

SHAW. I don't know. This afternoon. Colin's bringing Andrew up in his car. They'll get here sometime, I suppose. Your mother hasn't been able to sit down for two minutes. Up and down. You'll have to toss up for who's sleeping where. One down here, two up yonder. It'll be like old times. She's cleaned that floor a dozen times if she's cleaned it once. And them windows . . . it's a wonder there's any glass left in. Almost polished them right through . . . (*Looks out.*) Nothing changed out there either, you can see. Houses . . . houses . . . houses . . . as far as the eye can see . . . That's the kettle . . . Get your jacket off. Make yourself at home . . . Mind where you put yourself. She's puffed up every cushion, straightened every chair. It's like being in the army . . . (*He goes out to the kitchen. Off.*) How long are you staying?

STEVEN. I'll have to get back tomorrow.

SHAW (*off*). How's your work going?

STEVEN. All right.

SHAW (*popping in the door*). I wish I got half of what you got, I can tell you: and for doing twice as much. I wouldn't mind.

STEVEN. It's got its drawbacks.

SHAW. Drawbacks. It could draw back as far as it liked for me . . . Teaching. Good God . . . Ay up. Ay up. She's here. Look out. Look out. (*He goes back in the kitchen.*)

MRS BURNETT *comes in; a neighbour, in her early sixties.*

MRS BURNETT. Thought I saw you, Steven . . . How are you keeping, love?

STEVEN. Hello, Mrs Burnett . . . Well enough . . .

MRS BURNETT. And how's your wife?

STEVEN. Oh, surviving.

MRS BURNETT. I know. I've heard . . . They've shown me photographs, you know . . .

SHAW (*off*). Pretend she's not there. She'll go away. Just take no notice.

MRS BURNETT. Doesn't mind me popping in. Always the same . . . And your kiddies?

STEVEN. Fine.

MRS BURNETT. Your mother never mentions them. But I know. It all goes on inside. She's that sort of woman.

STEVEN. She's out shopping.

MRS BURNETT. I saw her go. New hat. She's very excited about tonight. Where are you taking them?

STEVEN. Into town . . . Colin's arranged something.

MRS BURNETT. Your Andrew and Colin not here, then, yet?

STEVEN. They're coming up by car.

MRS BURNETT. Eh. It's a lovely treat for them.

STEVEN. I hope so.

MRS BURNETT. Forty years. They'll not forget . . .

SHAW (*coming with a tray and two pots*). Yakking. Yakking. Yakking.

MRS BURNETT (*to* STEVEN). He never lets you get a word in. Don't worry.

SHAW. Word in? I can hardly open me mouth . . . (*To* STEVEN.) Smells tea, you know, a mile off. The 'uman blood 'ound. She's never out of this house.

MRS BURNETT. He hasn't forgotten me, don't worry, after all these years.

SHAW. No. That's true.

MRS BURNETT. He doesn't let you forget, don't worry. He's out showing it across the backs whenever he has any news. You get tired of hearing it, I can tell you . . .

SHAW. Tired? They spend all their day flat on their backs round here. They don't know what work is. As soon as their husband's gone off, out it comes: teapot, cushion behind their backs, feet up . . .

MRS BURNETT. I know. I know. That's why you never have anything to eat and your houses are full up to the chimney with last week's washing.

SHAW. Last week's. Last bloody year's more likely. (*To* STEVEN.) We've to bolt the door you know at times just to get a bit of peace.

MRS BURNETT (*to* STEVEN). Never changes. All the years

I've known him . . . Last week he gave your mother a
shock. (*Looking at* SHAW *concernedly.*) Came in. White
as a sheet. He was.

SHAW. Jumping up and down.

MRS BURNETT. They had me fetch the doctor.

SHAW (*to* STEVEN). Heart . . . (*Taps his chest.*)

MRS BURNETT (*to* STEVEN). Don't worry. He didn't treat
it lightly.

SHAW. 'Better take it easy. More rest.' I said: 'You must be
joking. How would you take it easy if you had a ten-ton
rock coming down on top of your head?'

STEVEN. What did he say?

SHAW. He laughed. They don't give a damn. Why should
they? An old man. It's a wonder I wasn't dead years ago.
She'll tell you . . .

MRS BURNETT. Go on . . .

SHAW. And that's what he thought, an' all. You can see it
in his eyes when he examines you.

STEVEN. I don't think that's right, somehow.

SHAW. Nay. I've no illusions. None . . . I've had a good
life. With a lovely woman. Can't ask for anything more
. . . Still . . .

MRS BURNETT. Aye . . . Well . . . (*Gazes at* SHAW
fondly.)

SHAW. Go on. Go on . . . Get shut. (*To* STEVEN.) Waiting
for a cup of tea. Be here all day if she has the chance.

MRS BURNETT (*to* STEVEN). I'll pop in later, love.
Remember . . . (*Gesturing at* SHAW *behind his back.*)
Pinch of salt. (*Goes.*)

SHAW. Pinch of bloody salt . . . I'll pinch her bloody salt.
Noses ten miles long round here . . . She'll be out yakking
it across the backs.

STEVEN. Aye. (*Laughs.*)

SHAW. We had a letter from Colin the other week. First one
I can tell you for some time. He's moved his job. Works'
liaison. A factory that big it'd take you a fortnight to walk
right round it . . . Cars . . .

STEVEN. So I heard . . .

SHAW. Offered to get us one. Brand new. Cut price.

STEVEN. You ought to take it.

SHAW. Nay, what would I do with a car? If you can't shove

it, pedal it, or hang it on a wall, it's no use to me . . . He has to argue, you know . . .

STEVEN. Yes . . .

SHAW. Whenever the workers – that's us – are going on strike, or feel they ought to, Colin's the one the management calls out to negotiate. He can charm the horns off a bloody cow, that lad. Been like it since I've known him. Industrial relations . . . When he was lying on that rug I little thought that that's where he'd end up. Industrial relations. A family with relatives like ours, an' all.

STEVEN. Aye . . .

They laugh.

SHAW. Offered to buy us a house, you know. Probably will when we retire. If I'm daft enough to let him . . .

STEVEN. It sounds like a good idea.

SHAW. If you're used to having money. As it is, I'm used to nowt. Still, times change. And people with it. Told me I ought to get out, you know. Retire now. He'd put up all the cash.

STEVEN. Why don't you?

SHAW. What? . . . (*Gets up, wanders round.*) Andrew's another one, you know. Chucked up his job to be an artist! He's only forty, with two children to support, one of them nearly old enough to go to university. It takes some reckoning. A career as a solicitor, that he's worked at . . . that *I* worked at. I've spent some hours, you know, working at that table with him: fractions, decimals, Latin . . . Do you know I'd go down that pit some nights declining or declensing, I've forgotten which, Latin verbs . . . I could have set up as a schoolmaster any time. Greek, algebra, physics, chemistry: the lot. It's a wonder I haven't taken a university degree myself.

STEVEN. I seem to remember . . .

SHAW. Nay. You were the last, Steve, but by God, the best. There wasn't much I had to teach you. As for them: I had to shove it down their throats. Like trying to eat burnt porridge.

STEVEN. How's Andrew making his money, then?

SHAW. Don't ask me. One of the reasons he's coming up, I

shouldn't wonder, is to see if he can borrow a bit. He's never been one to refuse a back-hander: that's why he was so good at law. He could make it fit any set of facts he wanted . . . I remember him coming home when he was about thirteen and proving to me that God no longer existed. He's never looked back since then.

STEVEN. Why don't you take up Colin's offer? We could all chip in a bit.

SHAW. Aye, well . . . (*Moves away.*)

STEVEN. What difference does one year make?

SHAW. I first went down the pit when I was fifteen, lad.

STEVEN. Yes.

SHAW. Forty-nine years. Half a century. One more now and it'll make it a round number.

STEVEN. Not worth risking your health for.

SHAW. No. Well . . . (*Gazes out of the window.*) Do you remember the war? I used to take one of you, out yonder . . .

STEVEN. Me.

SHAW. You? I believe it was. They hardly bombed here. Must have flown over and not thought we were worth it.

STEVEN. Made a mistake there.

SHAW. What? They made no mistakes about that. Miles of nothing, this place. Always has been, always will be. The only thing that ever came out of here was coal. And when that's gone, as it will be, there'll be even less. Row after row of empty houses, as far as the eye can see . . . It's starting . . . I pass them on the way to work. I stop sometimes and look in – holes in the roof, doors gone, windows . . . I knew the people who lived there . . . All this was moorland a hundred years ago. Sheep. And a bit of wood . . . When they come in a thousand years and dig it up they'll wonder what we made such a mess of it for . . . (*Gestures at the walls.*) Look at these foundations and think we all lived in little cells. Like goats.

STEVEN. We did. (*He laughs, gets up and pours himself some more tea.*)

SHAW. Aye . . . Here. Have a drop of something stronger. I got a bit in, in case . . .

STEVEN (*looks at the clock*). A bit early.

SHAW. Save it till later. Don't worry. We'll have a grand

time tonight. They'll have seen nothing like it round here for years . . . (*Watches him.*) How's your book going, then?

STEVEN. All right . . .

SHAW. If one of them was going to be famous, you know . . . I always thought it would be you.

STEVEN. Why's that? (*Laughs.*)

SHAW. Nay. I don't know. I suppose because you were so clever. (*Shy.*) Don't tell me it's something you forget . . .

STEVEN. I think I must have done.

SHAW. Aye . . .

STEVEN *glances away, across the room.*

Here. Do you want a wash? . . . I'll forget my own head one of these days.

STEVEN. I'll go up . . . Have a look around . . .

SHAW. Not much to see . . . I can tell you that. Two rooms, back and front. (*Laughs.*)

STEVEN *goes to the door.*

If the water's not hot enough, give us a shout and I'll heat some up for you . . . Won't take a minute.

STEVEN. Right . . . (*He goes.*)

SHAW *looks a little aimlessly about the room: picks up STEVEN's overcoat then his briefcase: looks round for somewhere to put them, then puts them down together in a chair. Looks at the fire, puts on a piece of coal, picks up bucket to take outside to fill . . . There's the sound of the outer door shutting. He looks up, puts the bucket down quickly, and sits down in a chair.*

MRS SHAW *comes in, dressed from shopping: sixty years old, matronly, circumspect: some authority and composure.*

MRS SHAW. There you are . . . (*Puts her bag on the table.*)

SHAW (*pleasant*). Nay, and where else would I be?

MRS SHAW. Have you had some tea, then? . . . (*Looks at the tray on the table.*)

SHAW. Aye . . . Aye . . .

MRS SHAW. Two of you.

SHAW. Aye . . . Mrs Burnett came in.

MRS SHAW. Did she? And you gave her some tea, then? (*Matter-of-fact, taking off her gloves and coat.*)

SHAW. Well, I thought I better . . .

MRS SHAW. Oh, yes. And what's going on, then?

SHAW. Going on? . . . Oh. Aye . . . Steven's here. I forgot.

MRS SHAW. Forgot.

SHAW. Slipped me mind . . . He's upstairs. Having a wash.

MRS SHAW. Having . . . Did you give him a clean towel?

SHAW. Towel . . . I forgot.

MRS SHAW. Honestly . . .

SHAW. It's a wonder the entire street didn't tell you.

MRS SHAW. Well, they didn't. I suppose I've got to ask to find out. (*Picks up tray to take out.*)

Sounds of STEVEN *returning.* MRS SHAW *looks quickly round the room.*

SHAW. Don't worry. Nothing moved. Nothing shifted.

MRS SHAW. We could do with some more coal.

SHAW. Aye . . . (*Gets up slowly.*)

MRS SHAW has put the tray down again and goes to the curtains, pulling them back slightly, adjusting them needlessly until she knows STEVEN is in the room.

MRS SHAW. Well, then. And where have you been all this time?

STEVEN. Oh. About . . .

He comes to her and embraces her, rather shyly.

MRS SHAW. You're not looking too good, love.

STEVEN. The climate. I'm not used to it up here.

MRS SHAW. Aren't they looking after you?

STEVEN. They are. All right.

SHAW has gone to the bucket, picked it up, watching them, smiling, then goes out.

MRS SHAW. Here. Let's have a look at you. You've put on a lot of weight. Or taken a lot off. I can't remember . . . (*She laughs.*)

STEVEN. I forget myself.

MRS SHAW. Have you had some tea? I'll get you something to eat . . .

STEVEN. There's no hurry . . .

MRS SHAW. How's the family?

STEVEN. Oh. Well.

MRS SHAW. They'll need a lot of upkeep. How old's Roger? Three months? Patrick scarcely one and a quarter . . .

STEVEN. I don't know. I've lost count.

MRS SHAW. Well, I don't know. There seems to be a lot of them. (*Collects tray again.*) I'll just put this away . . . I hope your Dad hasn't been on too much.

STEVEN. No . . . We were talking.

MRS SHAW. I think you'd do a lot of good, you know, while you're up there, if you persuaded him to come out of that pit. He's only another year . . .

STEVEN. He's told me.

MRS SHAW. Pride. You've never seen anything like it. (*Hears him coming.*) I'll just take this out.

SHAW (*coming in with the bucket of coal*). Now, then, my old china . . . (*Puts it down in the hearth.*) I'm good for lifting if I'm good for nowt else. When I come again I think they'll make me into a donkey. Reincarnation. It's stamped all over me from head to foot . . .

STEVEN. You better be careful. Somebody might hear you.

SHAW. Oh, she knows me. Ought to. Well enough.

STEVEN. I meant up there. (*Points up.*)

SHAW. Oh . . . He goes His own way. Nothing I say'll alter that. Don't you think she's looking well?

STEVEN. Yes. I think so . . .

SHAW. Forty years of married bliss . . . It's left its mark. When she walks down that street they step back, you know, to bow to her. If I come back as a donkey she'll come back as a queen.

MRS SHAW *comes back in.*

We were just saying, love. You look a picture.

MRS SHAW. I know. And what of?

SHAW. Nay. You don't need me to tell you. She spends that

long at the mirror that when I go to look at it I still find
her there – looking out.

STEVEN *laughs*.

MRS SHAW. He doesn't change, does he? You should see
him skip in the back and comb his hair when Mrs Burnett
comes around.

SHAW. Mrs Burnett? I'd need to be down to the last woman
on earth to consider that . . . As it is, love, I'm still up
with the first.

*He puts his arm round her shoulder, kissing her cheek: she
moves her head back slightly and moves away.*

MRS SHAW. I tell you. He hasn't known where to put
himself since he's known you were coming . . . I don't
think, ever since you went to university, he's known what
to do with himself. And that's how long ago?

SHAW. Fifteen years.

STEVEN. Longer . . .

SHAW. Education, lad: you can't get anywhere without . . .
Look at your mother. She left school at sixteen. Sixteen.
That was almost retiring age in those days. She's still got
her certificate upstairs . . .

STEVEN. I remember . . .

SHAW. 'Proficiency in Domestic Science, Nature Study, and
the English Language.' All done out in copperplate script.
'Miss Helen Swanson.' Her father was a pig-breeder, you
know. Just outside town.

MRS SHAW. A smallholder . . .

SHAW. A pig-breeder! He kept pigs. By go, you had to be in
love to step in that house, I can tell you. (*He laughs.*)

MRS SHAW. Well. I've heard some things . . .

SHAW. And she ends up marrying me. Never forgiven me,
have you, love? . . . Nay, lass, you know I love you. I
married you all the same. (*He laughs and kisses her
cheek.*)

MRS SHAW (*stepping back*). I'll see about some food. (*To
STEVEN.*) Colin and Andrew are driving up together.
They won't get here until this afternoon. I'll show you my
hat later, love.

STEVEN. Ah . . . Yes.

SHAW. Won't frighten us all, then, will it? Remember, we've got to walk down that street beside you. In public. I don't mind being seen with a woman . . .

MRS SHAW. Well, then, in that case you needn't be ashamed.

SHAW. Ashamed? I've never been ashamed, love. Whatever you wear, my darling, I've never been – and I never will be – ashamed.

MRS SHAW. Well, then, in that case, we'll be all right.

She goes, smiling at STEVEN.

SHAW (*to* STEVEN). Embarrassed, now. I might be a bit embarrassed. But I wouldn't be ashamed.

They laugh.

She's a good woman. A lady . . . One of the very best. You know, no one's ever got the better of her.

STEVEN. I can imagine.

SHAW. Bit of a let-down, marrying me.

STEVEN. Oh, now. I wouldn't have thought so.

SHAW. Nay, lad. Never one to grumble . . . (*Brightly.*) Well, then . . . What's it like to be back home, Steve?

STEVEN. Home . . .

SHAW. After all this time.

STEVEN. Well, I don't know, Dad . . . Very much the same.

They laugh.

Fade.

Scene Two
Afternoon.

MRS SHAW *is straightening the room, putting chairs more certainly in their places, straightening ornaments, mirror, pictures.*

There's a knock, then a banging on the outside door: whistles, etc.

MRS SHAW. Oh . . . (*Looks at herself in the mirror, goes off to the kitchen.*)

Bolts are drawn, locks turned.

(*Off.*) Andrew . . . There you are, then, love . . .
ANDREW (*off*). Been whistling half an hour . . .

Sounds of embrace.

On the lav, then, were you?
MRS SHAW (*off*). I was not!
ANDREW (*off*). By go . . . There's a lot been put on round here . . .
MRS SHAW (*off*). Get on. Go on . . .

ANDREW *enters: a fierce, compelling-looking figure dressed in a fairly dishevelled raincoat.*

ANDREW. Where is he? Where's he hiding? (*Calls.*) I'll be up there, old lad! (*To* MRS SHAW.) Snoring off his head . . . I'll go up and tip him out . . .
MRS SHAW. You won't . . .
ANDREW. What . . . ?
MRS SHAW. He's out . . . Went down to the pub. With Steven . . .
ANDREW. Steven . . .
MRS SHAW. After dinner . . . I've been expecting them any minute . . . Isn't Colin with you, then?
ANDREW. He's coming on behind. Don't worry . . . (*Going round, inspecting room.*) Steven's here, then, is he? Might have known . . . First in. Last out.
MRS SHAW. Go on. Get on . . .
ANDREW. Like a museum is this. Hasn't changed in five thousand years.
MRS SHAW. We've just had it decorated. A few months ago.
ANDREW. What with, then . . . soot? (*Runs his hand over the wall.*)
MRS SHAW. I can see somebody hasn't changed. I can.
ANDREW (*picks up paperback*). *Battle at Bloodstone Creek.* I used to marvel at that. My Dad's reading age hasn't risen beyond when he was ten years old.

MRS SHAW. We can't all be educated, you know.

ANDREW. No. No. Thank God for that.

MRS SHAW. Where is Colin, anyway?

ANDREW. Parking his car. Got moved on by a policeman.

MRS SHAW. Not here?

ANDREW. No. No. In town. Never seen anything like it.
Bigger than a bus. Antagonised them, I believe, no end.
Dropped off to buy a packet of cigarettes. 'Can't park that
here.' . . . Police.

MRS SHAW. Police . . .

ANDREW. Got to watch my step . . . These days in
particular.

MRS SHAW. I thought you were a lawyer.

ANDREW. Was, my dear. Was. Am no longer.

MRS SHAW. I don't know what Peggy thinks. She must be
out of her mind, worrying. What are you living on?

ANDREW. On love, my dear. Love. Like everybody else.
We've been married now, you know, for seventeen years.
If we haven't got a bit of that in stock then we might as
well not try.

MRS SHAW (glances out). I've heard of living on love
before. With Steven. Going to be a writer. And now look
at him: four kiddies in as many years, and he looks older
than any of you.

ANDREW. Ah well. Steven always was a difficult boy. An
infant prodigy, if I remember rightly. What we did under
duress he did by nature . . .

MRS SHAW. At school they said they'd never seen anything
like it.

ANDREW *looks across at her: she's gone to the window
again, glancing out.*

Where is he, then? It's not outside.

ANDREW. End of the road. Gone to find a garage. Didn't
want to risk it: leaving it outside.

MRS SHAW. I'm not surprised . . . Nowadays . . . I don't
know . . . (*Comes back.*) How are you living? . . . What
sort of pictures do you paint?

ANDREW. I know . . . (*Prompting her, goading.*)

MRS SHAW. What . . . ?

ANDREW. You think I paint young ladies.

MRS SHAW. What? (*Retreats*).

ANDREW. Or better still – young men.

MRS SHAW. What . . . ?

ANDREW (*pursuing her*). Come on. Admit it . . . You think I'm painting young ladies with no clothes on . . . She thinks I gave up my career as one of the greatest solicitors in the land in order to peruse certain ladies without their clothes on.

MRS SHAW. I thought nothing of the sort.

ANDREW. Come on. Come on. (*Stalking her round the furniture.*) You're as bad as Peggy. She thought the same.

MRS SHAW. I'm not surprised.

ANDREW. You see. I'm right . . . Just see what it is I'm up against . . . I really puzzled her.

MRS SHAW. What?

ANDREW. Puzzled. Abstract. Not a sign of human life.

MRS SHAW. What . . . ? (*Looking around.*)

ANDREW. Me picture . . . Peggy . . . Came home from me studio with it tucked underneath my arm. Thought she was going to see . . . Well, I don't know what she thought she was going to see. She was half-blushing before I'd even put it down. She knew, you see, I'd had me eye on the wife of the chap, from whom I rent my studio, for some considerable time . . . but . . . lo and behold. Triangles.

MRS SHAW. Triangles?

ANDREW. Or very nearly. The fact is, I'm not very good . . . Subtle indentations on either side. Bit here . . . Bit there . . . Each one a different colour . . . the variations in which would almost deceive the eye . . . beautiful. If you like triangles, that is . . . Abstract.

MRS SHAW. Abstract?

ANDREW. Not a sign of human life.

MRS SHAW. Oh.

ANDREW. Just the first. After that: squares.

MRS SHAW. Squares . . .

ANDREW. Rectangles. *Rhomboids*. Sometimes, even – nothing.

MRS SHAW. Nothing?

ANDREW. Well, I say nothing . . . there'd be a little . . . spot . . . of something, here and there. A little red (*Paints it for her.*) . . . cerulean . . . touch of viridian . . . trickle here . . . lovely. Still . . . old-fashioned.

MRS SHAW. Old-fashioned?

ANDREW. Absolutely. Don't use paint now, you know.

MRS SHAW. Oh, well . . . (*Dismissing it, turning away.*)

ANDREW. Plastic compounds. Plus: miscellaneous bric-a-brac picked up from the refuse dump outside the town. Got arrested once. Loitering with intent. Ran rings round them at the station. 'You better get a solicitor,' they said. 'I am a solicitor,' I said. 'Why, Mr Shaw,' they said, 'we didn't recognise you.' 'Artist now, mate,' I said. 'Don't you forget it.'

MRS SHAW. I can't understand why you gave it up. After all the years you spent studying. It seems a terrible waste. You were never interested in art before.

ANDREW. No . . . I'm not now, either.

MRS SHAW. Well, then . . . It's not as if you were independent. There's Peter and Jack. It'll be years before they're financially independent.

ANDREW. I don't know so much. I'm thinking of sending them out to support me. I don't think, paradoxical as it may seem, Mother, that I can, any longer, afford to educate my children.

MRS SHAW. Well . . . I . . . (*Gestures about her.*)

ANDREW. What is it?

MRS SHAW. I've said enough. You must know what you're doing. (*Goes to window again.*)

ANDREW (*picks up another paperback*). *Phoenix Showdown*. He must get through these faster than he does a cigarette.

MRS SHAW. He brings them home from work. I don't know where he gets them from.

ANDREW. I hope you fumigate them before they come into the house?

MRS SHAW. Well. I've thought about it a time or two, I can tell you.

ANDREW. I bet . . . No alien bodies in this house. That's always been our motto . . . What was that subject . . . ?

MRS SHAW. Subject?

ANDREW. You were always top in at school.

MRS SHAW. Domestic science.

ANDREW. No . . . no . . .

MRS SHAW. Human hygiene.

ANDREW. Human hygiene . . . I remember you telling us
when we were lads . . . human hygiene . . . the sort of
vision those words created . . .

MRS SHAW. It was an experimental class . . . It was the
first time it was ever taught in a school . . .

ANDREW. And never looked back since . . . No wonder we
were so clean . . . Came top, eh?

MRS SHAW. Well . . .

ANDREW. Used to tell me friends about it at school . . .
human hygiene . . . frightened them all to death. They
thought . . . well, I don't know what they thought . . .
Anyway. Never had any trouble with them after that.

They laugh.

MRS SHAW (*looking out*). Now, look . . . There he is. You
see . . . he must have walked for miles . . . I don't know.

She goes to the kitchen. ANDREW *picks up another
book, drops it, looks round.*

COLIN (*calls*). Hello . . . ? (*Comes in the other door: a
professional man in his middle thirties, not smooth, firm,
a bit rough. He's dressed in a Crombie overcoat.*)

ANDREW. Hello.

COLIN. What . . . ?

ANDREW. I say: 'hello'.

COLIN. Oh . . .

ANDREW. She thinks you're coming in the back.

COLIN. Mother . . . (*Crossing to the kitchen.*)

ANDREW. Did you park the car?

COLIN. Yes . . .

MRS SHAW (*coming in*). There you are! I thought . . .

They embrace.

Well, love. It's been a long time . . .

ANDREW. Trust him to come in the front. Only for royalty
is that. Workers, you know, have to use the rear.

MRS SHAW (*to* COLIN). Take no notice of him, Colin.
He's in one of his moods.

ANDREW. Iconoclastic.

COLIN. What?

ANDREW. I'm iconoclastic . . . I remember her looking it up when I was how old . . . eleven or twelve . . . 'I've got just the word for you, my lad,' she said, and got out her dictionary . . . you know, her first prize for . . .

COLIN. Hygiene.

ANDREW. You see! He remembers that . . .

MRS SHAW. I don't remember looking . . .

ANDREW. I didn't dare mention it for years. I went round, all that time, thinking it was some sort of sexual deviation.

MRS SHAW. Well, I don't remember that.

ANDREW. Iconoclastic . . . The first girl I ever went out with. When I took her home and we'd got to her gate, moonshining, I said, 'I better warn you, before you start anything, I'm iconoclastic.' 'Oh,' she said, 'well, I better go in, then.' 'Yes,' I said, 'I think you should.'

COLIN. Three hours of that I've had in the car. You've heard about his painting?

ANDREW has picked up another paperback, reading it, still standing.

MRS SHAW. I have.

COLIN. The only reason he took it up was because they couldn't stand his conversation in his office any longer. There was nobody – no clients, no staff, no nothing – to listen to him at all.

MRS SHAW. He's got his father's nature right enough.

ANDREW. I think I must have. (*Indicating book.*) I might take a few of these back with me.

Holds it out to COLIN.

Massacre in Wolf Canyon.

COLIN. Where is he, by the way? In bed?

ANDREW. At the pub.

MRS SHAW. He went with Steven for a drink. After lunch.

ANDREW. Lunch. (*Winks at COLIN.*) Used to be dinner in my day . . .

MRS SHAW (*to COLIN*). Is there anything I can get you?

COLIN. I could do with a cup of tea. I've walked for miles.

Did he tell you about being stopped in town? Five
minutes: it couldn't have been any longer.

MRS SHAW. I don't know. It makes your blood boil . . . I
don't know what it's coming to . . . I don't. Not any
more.

ANDREW. A police state.

COLIN. It is . . . I've parked it down at Sugden's. Not safe
to leave it parked out here.

MRS SHAW. Here. I'll make some tea, love . . . There's
your Dad, now. And Steven. I won't be a minute. (*Goes.*)

There are sounds of arrival from the kitchen.

ANDREW. All right . . . ? (*Nods amicably at* COLIN.)

COLIN. All right?

ANDREW. Tie straight . . . buttons . . . Little over to the
left . . . Smashing.

He straightens COLIN's *tie, coat, etc.*

MRS SHAW (*off*). You're back, then.

STEVEN (*off*). In one piece.

SHAW (*off*). Haven't been too long, I hope, my dear? (*Kiss.*)

MRS SHAW (*off*). Colin and Andrew are here.

SHAW (*off*). Are they? Are they? So we heard. (*Entering.*)
There you are, then . . . Heard about your commotion.
How are you, lad? How are you? (*He shakes their hands
in turn.*)

COLIN. You're looking pretty well yourself.

ANDREW. Damned old wreck. How many have you had?

SHAW. Ay, now. I go down there for social reasons. Not for
anything else.

ANDREW. Aye. We know . . .

SHAW. Nay, I'm not the drinker in the house. She's in there,
stoking up. (*Thumbs at the kitchen.*)

MRS SHAW (*off*). Oh, don't worry. They know you of old.

SHAW (*calls*). Are you making us some tea, then, love?

MRS SHAW (*off*). I am. I won't be a minute.

SHAW. Heart of gold. Never stops working . . . Was that
your car that Mrs Burnett told us about? We've just come
up with her. She saw it down the road.

ANDREW. They'll bury that woman in a glass coffin.

SHAW. Aye. If she couldn't look out she'd never step inside.

COLIN. Well then, Steve. How's your writing going?

STEVEN. Oh, all right.

COLIN. Me mother said in her last letter you were going to publish a book.

STEVEN. I was. Sort of.

COLIN. Well, then. I'll look forward to seeing it.

SHAW. Aye. He's got all the brains, has Steven.

ANDREW. And all the kiddies too.

SHAW. Aye! (*He laughs.*) Are you all right in there, love? (*Winks.*)

MRS SHAW (*off*). I'm all right. Don't you worry.

SHAW. They ought to run tea in pipes round here. Instead of water.

COLIN. They'd make a fortune.

SHAW. Round here they would. (*Coughs.*) Slakes your throat, you know. Dust.

ANDREW. Sounds as though you've got half a ton of best nugget down there, Dad.

SHAW. I have. Don't worry. I shouldn't be surprised.

STEVEN. My mother keeps telling him. He ought to come out.

SHAW. Come out. When I come out of that pit they can't tell the difference between me and a lump of muck. Never get out of that. Don't worry.

COLIN. I'll go and see if my mother needs some help. (*Goes into kitchen.*)

ANDREW (*gestures grandly after him*). Executive.

STEVEN. Nice bit of coat. (*Fingers it over a chair.*)

SHAW. You won't find one of them where I work, I can tell you.

ANDREW. I don't know. They tell me miners earn as much as dentists these days.

SHAW. What? At the bloody dogs they might. That's the only place they can.

ANDREW. I've even thought of going down myself.

SHAW. You've got a career you have. I spent half my life making sure none of you went down that pit.

ANDREW. I've always thought, you know, coal-mining was one of the few things I could really do. (*Looks at his hands.*) One of the few things, in reality, for which I'm

ideally equipped. And yet, the one thing in life from which
I'm actually excluded.

SHAW. You're ideally equipped to be a professional man.
Or ought you want. But that place: an animal could do
what I do. And I can tell you, most of them are.

ANDREW. Aye. You're right. (*Snarls at* STEVEN, *then
picks up one of the paperbacks.*) Been studying your
library.

STEVEN. One of the first things I ever remember was a
picture in one of them. A cowboy with a hat out here and
trousers flapping like wings, mounted on the back of a
rearing horse. Somehow, it still sums it all up.

ANDREW. What?

STEVEN. Dunno . . . Freedom.

Pause.

SHAW. They're nowt. They pass the time.

ANDREW. I bet you can't remember a single one . . . What
happens . . . (*Consults the book.*) . . . at Bloodstone Creek
when Barry Hogan rides up and sees a light glinting from
among the rocks?

SHAW. I couldn't tell you.

ANDREW. You're stunted. That's what you are.

SHAW. I am. It's a wonder I've grown one foot at all.

They laugh.

MRS SHAW (*returning*). Here we are . . . Colin's bringing it
in . . .

COLIN *follows her with the tray.*

ANDREW. He'd make a lovely mother.

SHAW. You want to watch him. Or he'll shove it right over
your head.

ANDREW. Couldn't knock a fly off a rice pudding.

COLIN. Don't be too sure.

ANDREW. He'd negotiate with it first.

MRS SHAW (*to* STEVEN). You're a quiet one, love. I hope
you didn't let your Dad persuade you to have too much to
drink.

STEVEN. No . . .

SHAW. He doesn't say so much, but he doesn't miss ought do you, lad?

COLIN. How's your book going, then, Steve?

COLIN *has put the tray on the table and* MRS SHAW *is pouring out the tea.*

STEVEN. Oh, all right . . . Well, not really. I've packed it in.

COLIN. Packed it in? Why, it's years . . .

STEVEN. Aye.

SHAW. Why have you given it up, then, lad?

STEVEN. Not my cup of tea. (*Laughs.*) Stick to what I've got, I suppose.

SHAW. Aye . . . (SHAW *watches him.*)

MRS SHAW. He's better off looking after his wife and family, not writing books . . .

COLIN. What was it all about, then, Steve?

STEVEN. Oh . . . (*Shrugs.*)

ANDREW. Modern society. To put it into words.

STEVEN. I don't know. (*Shrugs.*)

ANDREW. Indicating, without being too aggressive, how we'd all succumbed to the passivity of modern life, industrial discipline, and moral turpitude.

MRS SHAW. Don't mock him.

ANDREW. I'm not mocking him. (*Spreads out his hands.*) He let me read a bit of it once. What? Four years ago. He's been writing it nearly seven. I don't know why he's packed it in. I agree with every word.

SHAW. Agree with what?

ANDREW. I don't know . . . his view of society. The modern world . . .

SHAW. Nay, I can't make head nor tail of it . . .

MRS SHAW. Here you are, love . . . Come and get your tea.

MRS BURNETT (*popping in*). Are you in, love? Or are you out?

SHAW. We're out . . . Don't worry. We've had her in here afore.

MRS SHAW. We're in, love. Don't take any notice.

MRS BURNETT. He never changes, does he? (*To* COLIN, *putting out her hand.*) We hear all about you, now, you know.

COLIN. Not too much, I hope.

MRS BURNETT. No, no. Just the right things. What your father wants to tell us.

SHAW. Nay. Don't worry. I tell her nowt.

MRS BURNETT (*turning*). How are you, Andrew? I hear you've given up your job.

ANDREW. Aye. That's right. If you've aught going round here, just let me know.

MRS BURNETT. Get on with you. (*Laughs, digs him with her elbow.*) That'll be the day, when he comes looking for a job round here.

ANDREW. It'll be sooner than you think. Don't worry. We're thinking of setting up in business.

MRS BURNETT. Business? What sort of business, then, is that?

ANDREW. Glass coffins.

MRS BURNETT. Glass coffins?

ANDREW. Or wooden ones. With little windows in. (*Shapes one.*)

MRS SHAW. Would you like a cup of tea, then, love?

MRS BURNETT. I wouldn't mind. I wouldn't say no . . .

SHAW (*to himself*). Like asking a dog if it wants a pittle.

MRS BURNETT. I remember Colin. Mischief Night . . .

ANDREW. Mischief Night? What mischief then has Colin ever got into?

MRS BURNETT. He's shoved some crackers through my back door a time or two. I can tell you that.

COLIN. I think I did. She's right. (*Laughs.*)

MRS BURNETT. And drainpipes. Right along this street . . . And Steven.

MRS SHAW. Steven?

STEVEN. Aye. I think I must.

ANDREW. It's coming out. Good God! I wouldn't believe it.

COLIN (*to STEVEN*). Rafts on the canal. I remember that.

STEVEN. Aye . . .

COLIN. We shoved our Steven in a time or two. It's a wonder he wasn't drowned.

STEVEN. Aye . . .

SHAW. What about them kites, then, eh? Six foot. Fly for

miles. You'd see them floating across the town when you went out shopping. Me. Reardon . . . We used to give the lads half a crown to go climbing for them when they broke away . . . It took two men to hold them. The string . . . It could cut clean through your hand.

MRS BURNETT. Aye. I remember those days right enough . . . And now look at you. Children of your own. (*To* MRS SHAW.) It must be a proud day, love, for both of you . . . Forty years.

MRS SHAW. Aye . . .

SHAW. We'd have waited until we'd been married fifty, only I didn't think either of us would have lasted that long.

MRS SHAW. Oh, now . . .

SHAW. At least, I didn't think I would . . . We thought we'd better get it in while we had the chance.

MRS SHAW. Nay, I don't think it's as bad as that, love.

SHAW. Forty years. A round number . . . I'm near retiring – God willing . . . what with one thing and another . . . Their mother's going to be . . . well, I won't say, now, exactly . . . but a *certain age* next week.

MRS SHAW. I'll be sixty. I don't mind them knowing.

SHAW. She was a young lass of twenty when I married her. And in my eyes, she's been the same age ever since.

MRS SHAW. Oh, now. Don't let's exaggerate too much.

SHAW. You're as old as you feel, and that's how I'll always see you, love. (*Kisses her cheek*.)

MRS SHAW. Nay, I don't know. He says some funny things . . .

MRS BURNETT. Did you get your new hat, then?

MRS SHAW. I did.

SHAW. We'll have to go without food for a fortnight, I can tell you that.

MRS BURNETT. Oh, you'll look lovely, love.

SHAW. She'll look a picture. And for me she can dress up in rags.

MRS SHAW. I could as well. He wouldn't know the difference.

SHAW. Nay, we've gone without, I know. Getting these three into the world, setting them up in life.

MRS BURNETT. They're a credit to you, love. They are.

SHAW. Aye. Moments like this you begin to think it was all worth while.

They laugh.

MRS SHAW. Oh, now . . . Just look at the time.

SHAW. Aye. We shall have to be getting ready.

MRS BURNETT. 'The Excelsior Hotel'.

SHAW. That's the one.

MRS BURNETT (*to* COLIN). They only finished it last year. Twelve storeys high.

SHAW. It costs you a pound just to take your coat off. If you sneeze it costs you a fiver. And if you ask for a glass of water you've to tip ten bob just to pour it out. I tell you, I'm in the wrong bloody business.

They laugh.

MRS BURNETT. Aye . . . Well . . . I'm only sorry your Jamey never lived to see it.

SHAW. Aye. Yes.

MRS BURNETT. He was a lovely lad. He was.

SHAW. We'd have been all right with four of them. We would.

MRS BURNETT. They wouldn't remember him.

SHAW. Aye. Well. You have your tribulations.

MRS BURNETT (*to* STEVEN). Missed him, you did, by about three months . . . And Colin here . . .

MRS SHAW. He'd be almost two. Andrew here was nearly five . . .

MRS BURNETT (*to* ANDREW). Now, he could have been an artist. He could draw like a little angel. How old was he?

MRS SHAW. Seven when he died.

SHAW. He had a little book. His teacher sent it home. Drawings . . . You wouldn't have known they hadn't been done by an artist. Shapes and colours . . . There was one of three apples on a plate. You could almost pick them up . . . Pneumonia . . . They didn't have the protection against it, not in those days. Not like they have now . . . I'd have cut off my right arm. I bloody would . . . (*Sees*

MRS SHAW's *expression*.) Aye . . . Well . . . (*Brightly*.)
Right, then . . . (*Claps his hands*.) Let's be ready. On with
the dance.

MRS BURNETT. Aye. Well, I better be getting back.

ANDREW. How are your lads, then, Mrs Burnett?

MRS BURNETT. Oh, well enough. Half a dozen kiddies.
Not two minutes to come up and see their mother . . .
Still. That's how it is. (*To* MRS SHAW.) That's where
you're lucky, love. Your lads come home. Don't disown
you. Don't forget you as you're getting old.

SHAW. Aye. We've been damn lucky.

MRS BURNETT (*to* MRS SHAW). If you drop your key off,
love, I'll make sure your fire's in when you get back home.

MRS SHAW. Right, love . . .

MRS BURNETT. Don't do anything I wouldn't do.

SHAW. That doesn't leave us with so bloody much.

MRS BURNETT (*to the others*). Tara, love. I'm off before
he starts. (*Goes*.)

COLIN. One of the best. She is.

ANDREW. One of the best what?

COLIN. Forget it . . .

ANDREW. You should have heard him in the car. Talk
about the Two Nations. The dignity of the manual
labourer.

SHAW. Labourer?

COLIN. I should forget it.

ANDREW. Never ask an expatriate working-class man
about his views on his former class. Do you know, when
he left school and went to university, Colin was a card-
carrying member of the C.P.

MRS SHAW (*clearing cups*). C.P.? What's that?

STEVEN. A communist.

MRS SHAW. A communist!

ANDREW. To my mother, communist is synonymous with
sex deviate, pervert, luster after young girls, defiler of
young men.

MRS SHAW. I never said that . . . I never knew you were a
communist, Colin.

ANDREW. Neither did he. It only lasted a year. It gives him
an aura of respectability now when he's negotiating with
'the men'.

COLIN. You'd go down well, I can tell you.

ANDREW. Down well what? I've gone down. You can't get much lower than where I am, mate.

SHAW. We're here to celebrate, not to have arguments. (*To* MRS SHAW.) I remember when they were all at home. Arguments! It was like a debating palace. Your head got dizzy following each one.

MRS SHAW. Well, I'll get up and get changed. I suppose all you are ready?

COLIN. Yes . . . Here, I'll take that. (*Indicating tray.*)

MRS SHAW. No, no. I've got it, love . . . Harry? (*Goes.*)

SHAW. Aye. I better put on my suit. They might throw me out if I go as I am. 'The Excelsior'. Do you know, the man on the door, dressed up like an admiral – that much braid and epaulettes on that he knocks your eye out whenever he turns round – he used to work for me. Swore like a trooper and never washed his face from one Sunday to the next. There he is now, dressed up for a coronation, with a spot of scent behind his ears. 'Why!' I said to him when I last went past, 'You're like a bloody woman, Alf. Get off home and get some clothes on.' Do you know what he said? 'If you don't move on, my man, I'll have you physically removed.' 'Physically removed'!

ANDREW. Did you sock him one?

SHAW. Sock him? I wouldn't have muckied my hands.

They laugh.

Ay, look, you know. About Jamey . . . I shouldn't talk about him too much. I know you didn't bring it up, but your mother, you know . . . as you get older you start thinking about these things.

COLIN. What about them?

SHAW. Nay, look . . . I've said enough. (*Listens. Then, loudly.*) Right, then, lads. I'll go and get polished up.

ANDREW. Leave a bit of muck on, Dad. We won't know you without.

SHAW. Aye. Some hopes of that. (*Gestures up.*) I'll be given a thorough inspection . . .

ANDREW. Hygiene . . .

SHAW. Hygiene. You're right. (*Laughs.*) Right, then. I'll get up . . . Think on . . . (*Goes.*)

ANDREW (*cheerful*). Well, then: this time tomorrow we'll all be back home.

COLIN. I should just lay off, you know. Just once. Give it a rest.

ANDREW. Are you going to negotiate with me or something, Colin?

COLIN. We're here to give them a good time. Something they'll remember. God alone knows they deserve it.

ANDREW. Aye. He's right. How about you, Steve? What're you so quiet about?

STEVEN *shrugs*.

Silent Steven. (*To* COLIN.) They called him that at school.

COLIN. I've just thought. I'll have all that way to walk back to get the car.

STEVEN. Ring for a taxi.

COLIN. It's the same distance to the phone box, the other way.

ANDREW. You forget, don't you, what a primitive place this really is. Do you know, the other morning, we ran out of toothpaste at home, and there was all hell let loose with Pete – he's courting his head-girl at school – and I suddenly remembered: we never had toothpaste at home. Do you remember? We all used to clean our teeth with salt. (*Laughs.*) Three little piles on the draining-board every morning, when we came down.

STEVEN. We never had any cakes either. Do you remember that? There was a jam tart, or one piece of a sponge roll, for tea on Sunday.

COLIN. And old Steve there used to stand at table because we only had four chairs.

ANDREW. I remember. Would you believe it.

They look round at the room.

Do you remember when old Shuffler came to see my Dad about my going to university?

STEVEN. Shuffler?

COLIN. He'd left by the time you'd got there.

ANDREW. Sixth form. Careers. Came here one night to talk to my Dad about 'the pros and cons' of going to

university. Sat in a chair: we had it there. Put his hands
out like this and . . . ping! Bloody springs shot out.

COLIN. Nearly dislocated his elbow!

They laugh.

ANDREW (*laughing*). And my Dad . . . my Dad said to him
. . . 'Would you mind not putting your hands on the arms,
Mr Rushton? . . . The springs are coming out!'

They laugh.

COLIN. Bare floors. We had a piece of lino which my
mother moved round each week, trying to fit the chairs
over the holes and spaces.

STEVEN. Newspaper on the table for dinner . . .

ANDREW. Breakfast, supper and tea.

STEVEN. 'Don't read when you're eating.'

They laugh.

COLIN. Do you remember my mother cutting up
newspapers into lengths and trying to roll them together
like a proper toilet roll?

They laugh.

ANDREW. Obsessive man.

COLIN. After he came here Shuffler never talked to us
again. Whenever we met in the school corridor he used to
gaze at some point exactly six inches above your head.
Talk about the pain of poverty. I still dream about that
look. I do . . . I often wake up trying to convince him that
we're not as poor as that any longer.

Pause.

ANDREW. That comes of going to a good school.

COLIN. Full of drapers' sons, minor bureaucrats, and the
children of the professional classes.

ANDREW. My dear old Col: your children are the children
of the professional classes.

COLIN. I have no children.

ANDREW. Good God. You haven't. I'd forgot.

STEVEN. Why have you never married, Colin?

COLIN. Don't know. Haven't had the time.

ANDREW. You're not . . . er . . . ? (*Quivers his hand.*)

COLIN. Don't think so.

ANDREW. I mean, if you are, for my mother's sake, I'd keep it under your hat.

COLIN. Oh, sure.

ANDREW (*to* STEVEN). It's one thing my mother cannot stand. 'I don't mind a man being as promiscuous as he likes' – within reason, of course, and with the sole exception of my Dad – 'but the thought of one man going with another . . .'

COLIN. I don't think we've quite come to that . . . In any case, as far as marriage is concerned, I probably might have to.

ANDREW. You don't mean . . . there's not some unfortunate lassie carrying an embryonic Colin in her tum . . .

COLIN. No. It's just less embarrassing to *be* married than not to be.

ANDREW. I see. Well. As long as it's only that.

COLIN. Yes.

ANDREW. You know the real reason he's never married.

COLIN. No, I don't think he does.

ANDREW. Well. Never mind . . . Forget it . . .

STEVEN. In any case . . .

ANDREW. Yes?

STEVEN. With all that money lying around, Colin, you ought to make some woman happy.

COLIN. Aye! (*Laughs.*)

ANDREW *watches* STEVEN *a moment. Then*:

ANDREW. What's gone wrong, then, Steve?

STEVEN. I don't know what you mean there, Andy. (*Moves about the room, casual.*)

ANDREW. I mean . . . I don't know what I mean.

COLIN (*to* STEVEN). He's not sure what he means.

ANDREW. For one thing . . . in your youth . . . you were so contemptuous of the proven way.

COLIN. The proven way . . .

ANDREW. Admittedly you were – for ever – silent. But even when at school – the school we have only a moment before described, fit only for the sons of Christ – and then only after the most rigorous scrutiny – your arrogance,

your disdain . . . your *contempt* – were there for everyone
to see . . . I know. I know. Actually I respected you – very
much – because of that. Misplaced it may have been –
contempt . . . God knows: the educated sons of that
school, Steve, deserved all the pity they could get. But you
– just look at you. Where oh where has all that venom
gone to? Where, for Christ's sake, Steve, is the spirit of
revenge?

STEVEN *shrugs*.

COLIN. Four hours of that I've had inside that car . . . You
should have heard him . . . If you ever have a car don't
ever let him in it. Two miles with him in the passenger
seat and you'll drive it into the nearest wall.

ANDREW. Though in his case, of course, he's more
appreciative of the cost.

COLIN. You know, your one grievous disability, Andy – if
you don't mind me mentioning this – is not only have you
never grown up, but you've never even put in the first
preliminary effort.

ANDREW (*to* STEVEN). 'Management' talk. His 'men's'
talk is both more subtly obscene and more overtly
gratuitous.

COLIN. I must say, it's come to a sorry bloody pitch. (*To*
STEVEN.) I could have got him a job years ago if he'd
wanted. I could have even got him on the board; what
with his gifts, his tongue, his golden sense of opportunity.
He might even have done him a bit of good.

ANDREW. You are listening to a man whose life – believe it
or not – is measured out in motor cars.

COLIN. In blood! In men! In progress!

ANDREW. Do you know what he told me on the way up
here? Cigar in mouth. Gloved hands firmly on the wheel.
'The well-being of this nation is largely – if not wholly –
dependent on maintaining a satisfactory level of exports
from the motor industry.' The *nation*! . . . If my bloody
nation is largely dependent on that I'd rather crawl
around on all fours with a pigskin on my back and a bow
and arrow in my bloody hand. I would.

COLIN. You probably might have to. (*Laughs pleasantly.*)
Sooner than he thinks.

ANDREW. May God speed that day. (*Looks up.*) May God speed it.

COLIN. And that mind you after witnessing my poor old father's life. Crawling around – in pitch black, on his belly, his life hanging on the fall of a piece of rock – for fifty bloody years!

ANDREW. My father – *old friend* – has more dignity in his little finger than all you and your automated bloody factories could conjure up in a thousand years.

COLIN. Yes?

ANDREW. You know, I weep for you. To think you once lived here, under this roof. My brother. And you end up . . . Just look at you . . . Like this.

COLIN (*goes to the stairs*). Are you ready, then, up there?

SHAW (*off*). Nay, damn it all. We're trying to fasten your mother's dress.

MRS SHAW (*off*). Don't worry, love. We won't be long.

COLIN *goes to the kitchen: starts to wash as:*

ANDREW. I'm not trying to disparage, Steve . . . your work. Your ideas . . . It's simply: I do not understand.

STEVEN. No.

ANDREW. What's happened to that revitalising spirit? To the iconoclast, to use my mother's word.

STEVEN. I don't know.

ANDREW. Steve!

STEVEN. Look. There's no hard and fast rule. The world's as real as anything else: you don't . . . compromise yourself by taking a part in it.

ANDREW. No? . . . Not even with *this* world, Steve? (*Gestures through at* COLIN.)

STEVEN. No. It's not essential.

ANDREW. And that's why you look as sick as you do, because that's something you believe?

STEVEN. I look as sick as I do – if I do look sick – because I'm not a moralist like you. In the end, attitudes like you've described are easily adopted. All you have to do is throw over what's already there. You're like an evangelist. You both are. You forget there's another kind of temperament.

ANDREW. Well . . .

STEVEN. I don't know what the word for it is. (*Turns away*.)

ANDREW. Have you ever thought of taking up welfare work?

STEVEN. What?

ANDREW. The *all-surveying eye* – inherited – I haven't a shadow of a doubt – from my mother, but used, also I have no doubt, with greater circumspection – isn't this something you could put to better use than . . . advising on – what is it? – suitable post-graduate, post-everything pursuits?

STEVEN. I don't know.

ANDREW. But for the fact that I almost witnessed the event, I would find it difficult to believe that you came, as it were, of man and woman, Steve. Dearly as I would like, myself, to be an intellectual . . .

STEVEN (*to* COLIN). Intellectual . . . (*Laughs*.)

ANDREW (*through to* COLIN). Whenever one such passes me in the street, whenever I meet a man who describes himself as a humanist, a rationalist, a man of reason, something in my soul, something deep inside me, calls out – in pain, in protest. 'This man,' it tells me, 'is *obscene*.'

COLIN (*coming in, drying face*). It seems there's an awful lot of obscenity in your life, Andy.

ANDREW (*to* STEVEN). When you see a cancer it's no commendation of your powers of loving to fall on your knees and give it a damn great kiss.

COLIN (*to* STEVEN). He'll kill us all off. He will. He really will.

ANDREW. We already are.

COLIN. What?

ANDREW. Dead. Zombies. Killed by good intentions, administered by the ones above. (*Gestures up*.) Corpses.

COLIN (*lightly*). Good God . . . What's he on about, then, Steve?

STEVEN. I don't know . . . It's not worth arguing about. I remember, when he first started grammar school . . .

ANDREW. Minor public. It said that in the brochure . . . (*To* COLIN.) My dad underlined it with black, colliery crayon.

STEVEN. He came home and devastated all of us – me

certainly, without a shadow of a doubt – with all the reasons why it was no longer tenable – a belief in God. As if belief itself were a kind of property, like a limb, which you could put on or take off at will . . . Believe me: remove any part and all the rest goes with it. I don't even understand . . . You've lived here half your life – Reardon – Mrs Burnett – even Shuffler . . . What sort of vengeance do you have in mind?

ANDREW. Are you *listening* to what I said?

STEVEN *nods.*

. . . God knows, you were always the most serious of the three – and God knows, there were sufficient reasons for it . . .

COLIN. What *is* all this? What reasons? What God knows? . . . I must say, for somebody who doesn't believe in God he invokes Him an awful bloody lot . . . you know . . . Formative traits have always been an obsession with our Andrew: as if he were a function of them and nothing else . . .

ANDREW. All right . . . (*Turns away.*)

COLIN. Good God. (*Takes his tie from his pocket and starts to put it on.*) Amazing.

ANDREW. When poor old Jamey died . . .

COLIN. I knew it!

ANDREW. When poor old Jamey died . . .

COLIN (*to STEVEN*). Do we have to go through all this again?

STEVEN. Andrew has a new theory about his origins.

ANDREW. Not new. And not theoretical, either.

STEVEN. He's discovered . . . I told him. A little time ago now . . . that Jamey was born only three months after my mother got married.

COLIN (*putting on tie*). Good Lord. (*Feels walls.*) No. No. Upright . . . Standing.

ANDREW. Can you imagine, for one moment, what went on during those six months' negotiations? Prior to the event.

COLIN. . . . Let me see.

ANDREW. This is something you should be particularly good at . . . I mean: first in human hygiene . . .

COLIN. Why does he go *on* about that?

ANDREW. English language, domestic science: didn't leave
school until she was sixteen . . . religious . . . raised up by
a petty farmer to higher things . . . ends up being laid – in
a farm field – by a bloody collier . . . hygiene . . . never
forgiven him, she hasn't . . . Dig coal he will till kingdom
come. Never dig enough . . . Retribution.

COLIN. Do you know what I'd say to you?

ANDREW. What?

COLIN. Mind your own bleeding business.

ANDREW. Oh . . . All right. (*Turns away.*)

COLIN *goes off.*

Poor old Jamey.

COLIN (*off*). Poor old Jamey . . .

ANDREW. Poor old Dad.

COLIN. Poor old Dad. (*Reappearing with waistcoat: and
jacket – which he puts on a chair.*)

ANDREW. Well, that's it exactly.

COLIN. What?

ANDREW. Guilt. Subsequent moral rectitude. They
fashioned Jamey – as a consequence – in the image of
Jesus Christ.

COLIN. I can think of worse examples. (*Goes to mirror to
check tie.*)

ANDREW. Yes?

COLIN. Well – I wouldn't wish to get too personal.
(*Laughs.*)

ANDREW. No. No. On the other hand?

COLIN. On the other hand . . .

ANDREW. Christ didn't take too kindly to Jamey. His was
not, after all, a Messianic role.

COLIN (*to* STEVEN). 'When Mary said, "We have a son,"
her husband said, "Tell me another one." '

STEVEN. Andrew thinks Jamey died because he could never
atone . . .

COLIN. Atone? For what?

STEVEN. I don't know . . . Whatever my mother felt . . .

COLIN. He died of pneumonia, according to the certificate.
I remember seeing it myself, years ago. (*Looks round for
his jacket.*)

ANDREW. He died from a bout of galloping perfection.

COLIN. Did he?

ANDREW. Do you remember Jamey?

COLIN (*to* STEVEN). Not really . . . I was only two or three at the time . . . (*Picks up his jacket and puts it on.*)

ANDREW. I was nearly five. I remember him very well. Sitting there . . . drawing . . . Or upstairs. Crying. They never beat us, you know. But him . . . he was black and blue . . . And like Steven there – but for his little bloody pictures – *silent as the tomb*. (*To* STEVEN.) . . . Come on.

COLIN. Come on? Come on what? Honestly, the way he dramatises the slightest inflection. Black and blue. I don't remember that. And I remember my Dad landing *me* one once or twice, I do . . . (*To* STEVEN.) And you.

STEVEN *doesn't answer.*

Well?

STEVEN *shrugs.*

ANDREW. Come on. Fair's fair. If Colin's going to whitewash everything, why not give him every chance?

STEVEN. It's nothing . . .

ANDREW. Nothing . . . ?

STEVEN (*shrugs*). It's nothing.

ANDREW (*to* COLIN). Years ago . . .

STEVEN. Years ago . . .

ANDREW. My Dad . . .

STEVEN. My father . . . it's really nothing . . . (*Sees* ANDREW's *look.*) . . . He told me – shortly after Jamey died – my mother tried . . .

COLIN. What?

ANDREW. To kill herself.

STEVEN *turns away.*

ANDREW. Oh, no. Fair's fair. Look . . . She was already six months gone with Steve . . . sitting here . . . on the floor . . . hugging a knife . . . when the old man staggers in through that very door . . .

COLIN. Not drunk . . . ?

ANDREW. From work . . . You see, this doesn't interest him at all.

COLIN. Do you think, in all honesty, that it should? All right . . . she tried to kill herself.

ANDREW. You already knew.

COLIN. Yes. That's right. I already knew . . . She told me . . . Years ago. I can't remember.

ANDREW. Well, then. That's that.

COLIN. All right. She tried to kill herself.

ANDREW. And Steve.

COLIN. And Steve . . . He wasn't even born.

ANDREW. No. No. He wasn't . . . Waiting there, that's all . . . *To be delivered* . . . Just look at him . . . Still waiting. Solemn . . . Silent.

COLIN. All right. All right . . . I mean . . . poor bloody soul . . . is it something I should bear with me, every second, every day? . . . I mean . . . are we supposed to be endlessly, perpetually measured by our bloody imperfections, by our more unfortunate bloody actions? . . . Just what precisely are you after, Andy? Do you want somebody to hold your hand throughout your entire bloody life?

ANDREW. Ask Steve.

COLIN. What about 'ask Steve'? He's more bloody common sense. For Christ's sake. You really take the can.

ANDREW. Ask Steve . . . (*To* STEVEN.) Tell him . . . Go on . . . I mean, giving up his book isn't really what you'd think . . . a sign of his growing up . . . maturity. He actually has been having nightmares . . . In true, I might add, evangelical style.

COLIN. Nightmares? What about?

ANDREW. Jamey . . . He sees him – crying out . . . trying to appease the immaculate conception. Trying to tell them it *wasn't his fault* . . . Jamey in the wilderness, Jamey on a mountain top, Jamey at the window . . . saying . . . 'Even if you were first in human hygiene, and intended marrying someone smarter than my Dad, it wasn't my fault. Please God, forgive me . . . Please . . . God forgive me, Ma! It's not my fault.'

COLIN *looks at* STEVEN *who shakes his head.*

COLIN. What's he on about?

ANDREW. He wrote me a letter recently, Steven. I say recently. Some months ago – and I apologise for taking over . . . appropriating, his pre-natal, post-natal, pre-genetive feelings of contempt – I'm sorry, in fact if I appear to sit in judgement on his suffering, on his perpetual psychic silences . . . but that sickness, I should add, is a disease of mine. His affliction, I can assure him, is not endemic to his solemn, silent nature, atrophied while inside my mother's remorseful tum . . . Jamey's cry, I can assure him, comes from the family! . . . not just from his own, sleeping, nocturnal soul . . .

COLIN. What's he . . . ?

ANDREW. Colin's trouble is that he can't put an engine inside his consternation and drive it off . . . *Good old Col!* Something has actually struck home at last.

COLIN. Look . . . I've had enough. Just pack it in. For Christ's sake . . . Steve.

STEVEN. It's nothing. I wrote Andy a letter a few months back. A year . . . Asking what he thought. Revenge, I'm afraid, is his only answer. And I understand his motives well enough . . .

COLIN. Revenge? On what?

STEVEN. On them.

COLIN. On them . . . For what?

STEVEN. I don't know . . . Everything.

COLIN. I see . . . Nothing less than that.

ANDREW. Projecting him into a world they didn't understand. Educating him for a society which existed wholly in their imaginations . . . philistine, parasitic, opportunistic . . . bred in ignorance, fed in ignorance . . . dead – in ignorance.

STEVEN. Only, of course, his common sense – perhaps even his compassion – forbids him to say anything of the sort . . . The most tedious thing about his social attitudes, his moral insights, is the perversity of their motives – that's something I've always felt before about these screaming revolutionaries . . . but now . . . I see more clearly what they're intended to appease.

ANDREW (*to* STEVEN). We'll build a bloody statue to you yet. I'm warning you. We shall . . . He thinks by some

superb gesture of self-exorcism, powered and engendered
by God knows what, he'll rid himself of all this. His
dreams and nightmares . . .

STEVEN (*quietly*). No . . .

ANDREW. Transcend it. Become . . . manifest.

STEVEN. No . . .

ANDREW. I think, you know, some suitable post should be
found for Steven. (*To* COLIN.) He'll do you out of a job,
if you're not careful. Don't let him near your factory.
He'll have everybody, unless you're very careful, consoling
one another.

STEVEN. Yes. Well . . .

ANDREW. You're like a man with one foot on either side of
an ever-widening chasm. The kind of detachment – or
even the kind of *involvement* – you're telling me about:
very soon, as your looks suggest . . . is going to rip you
wide apart. You can't be *for* this crummy world and at
the same time be for your own psychic . . . spiritual . . .
moral autonomy, any longer. It is now the season of the
locusts, and if you have anything to save then save it.
Grab it in both hands and run.

STEVEN. Yes . . . well.

ANDREW. Well? Well, what?

STEVEN. Let's hope there aren't too many of you.

ANDREW. Too many?

STEVEN. Someone has to stay behind.

ANDREW. Behind? You're not behind. You're nowhere.
You're *overrun*.

SHAW (*off*). Well then . . . Well, then . . . Here I come . . .

COLIN (*to* ANDREW). Forget it. (*Calling.*) Do you want a
hand, or can you manage?

SHAW (*off*). I don't damn well know . . . ooh! (*Groans.*)

COLIN (*to* ANDREW). Look. Just lay off . . .

ANDREW *begins to whistle a tune, wandering round the
room, his hands in his pockets.*

SHAW *comes in, in his best suit, dark blue, and a little
old-fashioned in cut. He carries his shoes in his hand.*

SHAW. By go. These braces. They're like a straitjacket on
your back . . . Your mother won't be a minute. I had to
hang around to give her a hand. Can't reach any of her

buttons these days, you know. Oooh! (*Sits down to put on his shoes.*) Just look at that. (*Holds up a shoe.*) She's had me polishing that since a week last Sunday. If you shone a light on it it'd burn your eyes.

They laugh, looking at one another.

COLIN. Look . . . I better fetch the car.

SHAW. Aye. I was thinking of that . . . Can you wait till she comes down? She wants to make 'an entry'. She'll be another half an hour after that, doing her gloves up, getting her hair right. So you'll be all right.

COLIN. Aye. Well. There's no great hurry. We'll have a drive around.

SHAW. She'd like that. She's been on at me to get a car. At my age. I can't bloody see a lamppost till it hits me in the face . . . She's had a hard life. She's worked very hard. Kept this like a palace . . . One woman in a house of men. She'd have given aught, you know, to have had a daughter. You know, somebody to talk to . . . Ay up. Here. She's coming. (*He gets up to take up a casual pose by the fireplace, winking at the others.*)

MRS SHAW (*off*). Are you ready?

SHAW. Aye. We're ready, love. We've been waiting here for hours.

MRS SHAW (*off*). Ups! Won't be a minute.

SHAW (*to the others*). Last-minute hitch.

They're standing now in their respective places round the room, facing the door.

MRS SHAW (*off*). Are you ready, then?

COLIN. We're ready.

SHAW. Here she comes . . .

Pause. Then MRS SHAW appears at the door. She wears a dignified blue costume, her coat folded neatly over her arm. In one hand is a pair of white gloves and a handbag. On her head is a matching blue hat, not ostentatious.

COLIN. Wow!

ANDREW. Lovely.

SHAW. Beautiful.

MRS SHAW. Do you like it?

STEVEN. It's very nice. I couldn't have done better myself. (*He embraces her.*)

COLIN. Super . . . smashing. (*Embraces her.*)

SHAW. Here . . . better give her a kiss an' all. (*Kisses her modestly on the cheek.*)

ANDREW. Well, then. Are we ready?

COLIN. I'll go fetch the car.

MRS SHAW. Nay, well, look . . . Let's all walk down. It's only half a mile.

COLIN. Well . . .

ANDREW. Do you feel up to it?

SHAW *and* COLIN *laugh.*

MRS SHAW. We've walked down that road together often enough in the past. Once more won't do us any hurt.

COLIN *holds the coat and she puts it on.*

(*To* SHAW.) Can you lock the door?

SHAW. Aye. Aye . . . I'll just get my coat. (*Goes.*)

COLIN. Have we to go in front, or do we follow on behind? (*Pulling on his own coat.*)

MRS SHAW. Well, I don't know.

COLIN. Here you are, then. (*Offers her his arm.*) We'll go in front. Show the flag.

MRS SHAW. Have you all got your coats?

STEVEN (*pulling his on*). That's an old familiar question.

COLIN. Cleaned your shoes? Washed your faces? Ties straight? Got your handkerchief? Right, then: have you all got your coats?

They laugh.

SHAW (*returning, his coat on*). All locked up. Ready.

COLIN (*leading* MRS SHAW *the other way*). Nay, out of the front door today, Mother. Dad – bring up the rear.

COLIN *goes with* MRS SHAW *on his arm.*

SHAW. Bring up the rear, he says. Who's boss here, I'm thinking.

ANDREW. You and me, old lad. (*Puts his arm round* SHAW's *shoulder.*) Come on, Steve . . . We're not leaving you at home.

ANDREW *and* SHAW *go.* STEVEN *remains a moment, buttoning his coat.*

He pauses: looks round.

MRS SHAW (*off*). Steven?

He looks round the room once more.

Then, slowly, he moves to the door and goes, closing it behind him.

Curtain.

ACT TWO

Scene One
Late evening.

MRS BURNETT *comes in. She puts on the light, draws the curtains, looks in the kitchen, puts coal on the fire.*

Unseen by her, REARDON puts his head round the door: an elderly man dressed in a neat suit, dark, a handkerchief in the top pocket, with gloves and a walking-cane: an Irish accent, dandyish but by no means effete. He watches MRS BURNETT a moment. Then:

REARDON. *Aha!*

MRS BURNETT. Ooh! (*Jumps, startled.*)

REARDON. Thought I saw a light. Burglars!

MRS BURNETT. Burglars. They'll be catching you one of these nights.

REARDON. Reardon? The one-man vigilante? . . . (*Hastily looks round.*) They haven't left a drop, have they, by any chance?

MRS BURNETT. They have not. And the key's in my possession for safe keeping. Not for letting strangers in and out.

REARDON (*with dignity*). Harry Shaw and I have been the closest friends for over thirty-five years.

MRS BURNETT. I know. And never closer than when he's standing at a bar.

REARDON. One man, one round. That has always been my motto. And what little secrets have you been prying out? (*He is moving round the room inspecting.*)

MRS BURNETT. None. Not any. I have more respect for people's privacy than that. (*Shifts chairs etc. as she talks.*) I've been building up the fire. They'll be back soon, unless they're going to make a morning of it as well as half a night . . . Now . . . (*Gestures at him to stop prying.*)

REARDON. It's all right. It's all right. Didn't I meet them on the way down the street this evening? 'Good day,' says I, 'but that's a sight for sore eyes. Three famous sons taking out their mother and dad.' Are you sure . . . ? (*Gestures at the sideboard.*)

MRS BURNETT. If there was I wouldn't touch it. In all the years they've left me with the key I've never once touched anything in here, and I never shall.

REARDON. Harry Shaw and I have never allowed the perversity of private property to come between us. 'What is mine is yours, and what is yours is mine' has always been our motto.

MRS BURNETT. Well, the same doesn't go for Mrs Shaw, and she's the one you have to make account to.

REARDON. That's true. There goes a woman before whom I shall always remove my hat.

MRS BURNETT. I should think so, too.

REARDON. Behind every great man, now, you find a promising woman.

MRS BURNETT. You do. Don't you forget it.

REARDON. Am I likely? The one deficiency in an otherwise phenomenal life. Your respect for the privileged classes does you credit, Mrs Burnett.

MRS BURNETT. Privileged?

REARDON. When the aspirations of the working classes are to join the lower middle, what do the Shaws do, but jump over a couple and land right up there, at the very top.

MRS BURNETT. The top?

REARDON. I wouldn't pretend, now, that they'd be aristocrats, within the one generation. But it wouldn't surprise me if one day, in the not too distant future, a Shaw is found sitting in the House of Lords, breathing down enlightenment on every side, a mind nurtured . . . formed, inspired, within these four walls. So is a beacon lit, Mrs Burnett. And so are the great allowed to shed their light . . . One of gin, one of sherry, one of soda water, and unless I am very much mistaken, a damn great one of Scotch. (Has opened the sideboard cupboard door.)

MRS BURNETT. I don't care whether there's a crateful. You're not touching a single drop. (She steps in and shuts the cupboard door.) I would have thought Mrs Reardon would have wanted you home in bed hours ago.

REARDON. Mrs Reardon, alas, Mrs Burnett, has not wanted me home in bed, or anywhere else for that matter, for more years than you and I could count together.

MRS BURNETT. Well, I'm sure . . .

REARDON. If my father had given me the opportunities that Mr Shaw has given to his sons, do you know where I would be now?

MRS BURNETT. I've no idea. It'd have a bar in it, I know that for sure.

REARDON. You're right. I would accumulate what little wealth my golden opportunities had provided and, splitting everything in half, I would retire . . .

MRS BURNETT. Retire?

REARDON. To the west coast of my native land, the wildness of which is past description. And from where, so many years ago I've lost count, my old father, God rest his soul, first brought me, a mewling infant in my mother's impoverished arms.

MRS BURNETT. And half would be for what?

REARDON. Half would be for building a modest little cottage, hewn from the rock from which my forebears sprang, the homeland of my fathers – stretching back into the very mists of time, before Christ, before the great dynasties of Egypt and Crete and Persia . . . those mist-shrouded, northern shores . . . where the sun rises like a holy fire . . .

MRS BURNETT. Well . . .

REARDON stands for a moment, gazing out, abstracted, one arm raised.

And the other half for what?

REARDON. The other half . . . ? The other half, my dear. With that I shall build a deep, concrete, lead-lined, bomb-proof, a-tomic shelter.

MRS BURNETT. A shelter.

REARDON. Unlike Mr Shaw, I am past retiring age. Certain irregularities in the local office of the National Coal Board have allowed me to spend rather longer than legally I am entitled to in the colliery office, checking pay, attempting, in my own small way, to settle amicably the various disputes – soothing the manager's sorrow, the deputy's rage, appeasing whenever I could the miner's consternation . . . I have seen two world wars and several minor ones, and not a little of my life's energies have been expended in avoiding each and every one: I have lived through the most calamitous half-century since time began and my instinct for war, for rivalry and destruction, is unparalleled, I would imagine, by almost anyone. I have a vision, Mrs Burnett, a presentiment . . . of a holocaust so gigantic, so monumental in its proportions, that beside it all our little dreams and hopes, our sorrows, and our little aims and fears . . . must count as nothing. Whether these are the sort of visions endemic to a man very close to retiring age – and to a pension it can only humiliate him to receive – or whether they are a definitive view of reality as we and our children shall eventually come to know it – I cannot say. All I can see before me, I must confess, are flames – flames, pillage, burning, terror.

MRS BURNETT. You've been drinking. That's what you've seen: the bottom of too many glasses.

REARDON. When I retire to my bomb-proof shelter, Mrs Burnett, I will – if you'll grant me the privilege – take you with me. While the flames roar around our pathetic heads I shall take comfort from your good-natured incomprehension and – who knows? – recognise in it maybe some hope and reassurance for the future. Only those who cannot – through their own intrinsic stupidity – appreciate that something calamitous is happening: only among those will I feel really safe.

MRS BURNETT. There they are. You see. (*Lifts curtains to look out.*) I don't know what they're going to think to find somebody else in here . . .

REARDON. I shall retire, Mrs Burnett. And who knows? A few moments later I might quite easily pop in my head as if I were, in a manner of speaking, passing by, on my way home, to my dear wife . . . In all my life I have never been an embarrassment to anyone . . . No. No . . . and, if I can only manage it now, I never shall. (*He goes off with a little bow, through the kitchen.*)

Noises of Shaws off: MRS BURNETT *makes a last quick inspection.*

The door from the front opens. ANDREW *comes in.*

ANDREW (*calling back*). No, no. It's Mrs Burnett. All safe. Come in . . . (*To* MRS BURNETT.) They thought they were being raided.

SHAW (*entering*). What did I tell you? . . . By, that's lovely and warm.

MRS BURNETT. I thought it might be going out . . .

SHAW. Aye . . . aye.

MRS BURNETT. Have you had a nice time?

SHAW. Grand! Grand! Lovely . . . Couldn't have been better.

MRS SHAW *comes in on* STEVEN's *arm.*

We have to hold her up. Got us nearly arrested.

MRS SHAW. Hold me up! I'm quite all right . . . (*To* MRS BURNETT.) It was very good of you, love. I appreciate it. That's a lovely fire.

MRS BURNETT. I've put the key on the sideboard.

SHAW. Nay, don't rush off yet. We're having a celebration, you know. Still got a drop put by.

MRS BURNETT. Well . . .

SHAW (*to* MRS BURNETT). Best night of my life! 'Excelsior'! Seen nothing like it. We had that many waiters running round the table you couldn't see the food . . . (*Belches.*)

MRS SHAW. Oh, now . . .

SHAW. That's right, love. You sit down.

MRS SHAW *is helped to a chair.*

MRS SHAW. Oh . . . (*To* MRS BURNETT.) It's been lovely.

MRS BURNETT. Ey, I'm glad . . .

MRS SHAW. The view . . . All the walls are made of glass. On the top floor, the restaurant. You can see right over the town.

SHAW. From the muck-heap at one end to the muck-heap at the other.

MRS SHAW. It wasn't like that at all . . . You can see the moors from up there. Miles. Sweeping away. And rocks . . . When the sun set you could see the light – glinting on a stream . . . well, it must have been miles away.

STEVEN. Yes. That's right.

MRS SHAW. Beautiful. You'd have liked it . . . When it got dark all the lights came on. You could see right up the valley . . . Lines of lights. Little clusters . . . And a train. Just like a snake . . . winding in and out . . . I don't know.

We've lived here all our lives and I've never seen it like
   that.

SHAW. We've skint our Colin. (*To* ANDREW.) Isn't that
   right?

ANDREW. Aye! (*Laughs.*)

SHAW. He won't come up here again in a hurry, I can tell
   you. Champagne? He's even got a bottle in the car. (*Takes*
   MRS BURNETT'*s arm.*) We tipped the doorman. Should
   have seen his face. Remember Alf Dyson? He worked with
   me. Face as black as a Christmas pudding. Never washed.
   'Here you are, my man,' I said, and doffed him a five-
   pound note. Our Colin's. You should have seen him.
   Nearly dropped his medals in the road.

They laugh.

I bet there isn't a bottle left in the place. What's he up to?

ANDREW *has been looking in the cupboards.*

ANDREW. Trying to find it.

SHAW. Here. In here, old lad. A bit of space left for a drop
   more.

MRS SHAW. Not for me, thanks.

SHAW. Mrs Burnett. You'll have the first. We'll have
   another toast.

MRS BURNETT. Oh, well . . .

REARDON *puts his head in from the door leading to the
   front.*

REARDON. Did I hear . . . 'Toast'?

SHAW. Why! . . . Look what's here! Look what's here!

REARDON *comes in, followed by* COLIN.

COLIN. Found him skulking about outside . . .

REARDON. Just passing by. Saw a light. Thought: by jove,
   burglars! Apprehend . . .

SHAW. Nothing of the kind. (*To the others.*) He can smell a
   drop of Scotch a mile off. We once went walking on the
   moors . . . this is just after I was married . . .

ANDREW. Already running off . . .

SHAW. Nay. Nay. I was always going for walks . . .

REARDON. He was.

SHAW. Got lost . . . Should have seen us. Moorland
   stretching round on every side.

REARDON. It was. Those were the great days of our life.

SHAW (*indicating* REARDON). 'Reardon. Which way is it
   to the nearest pub?'

They laugh.

He turns this way . . . (*Turns.*) Then that. (*Turns.*) Then
he says, 'Harry. This is the road we want.'

They laugh.

REARDON. I did.

SHAW. And it was. Over the next rise and there we were.

REARDON. 'The Flying Horse'.

SHAW. 'The Flying Horse'! You're right!

REARDON. Never forget a name like that.

SHAW. No. No. Me neither. Not them sort, any road.

*They've been pouring out the drinks and passing them
round.*

Should have seen our Andrew.

REARDON. What's that?

MRS SHAW. Oh, better not . . .

SHAW. Halfway through the meal – restaurant full of
   people.

REARDON. Captains of industry, Harry.

SHAW. They were. They were. You're right. Mill-owners.
   Engineering managers. Leaders of our imports . . .
   exports. Never done a day's work in their bloody lives . . .
   He gets up and goes round to every table.

MRS BURNETT. What?

SHAW. 'I'd like you to know,' he says, 'that *that* lady and
   that gentleman, sitting over there, is – my mother and –
   my Dad. The finest mother and the finest father you ever
   saw.'

MRS BURNETT. He said that?

SHAW. At every table. Went round the entire place.

MRS SHAW. He did. I didn't know where to put myself.

SHAW. 'If you'd like to do something which, in years to
   come, you'll be able to recount to your grandchildren,
   with pride, with a feeling of achievement, then get up, off

your backsides, go over there, and shake them by the hand.'

MRS BURNETT. He did that?

MRS SHAW. I thought they'd throw us out.

SHAW. Throw us out? . . . They couldn't afford it. (*Indicating* COLIN.) Tipped the waiter two fivers when we went in . . .

MRS SHAW. Head-waiter . . .

SHAW. Head-waiter. 'Keep an eye on us, will you?' An eye! For that I'd have kept both bloody feet and a half a dozen hands.

They laugh.

MRS SHAW. Now, now. Just go careful. (*To* MRS BURNETT.) He hasn't been very discreet with some of his jokes.

SHAW. Nay, when I have a good time I have one. No shilly-shallying about. I know how to enjoy myself, I do.

REARDON. That's right. I can vouch for it now. As long as I care to remember.

ANDREW. A toast then . . .

COLIN. A toast . . .

ANDREW. Are you totted up, Steve?

STEVEN. Yes. I'm fine.

ANDREW. To the finest mother and the finest Dad that these three sons have ever had.

They laugh.

To the finest mother and the finest Dad.

ALL (*but* MRS SHAW). To the finest mother and the finest Dad.

They drink.

ANDREW (*to* SHAW). Nay, you don't say it, you daft nut.

SHAW. What . . . ?

They laugh.

COLIN. It's you we're toasting.

REARDON. Never lost the opportunity to take a glass.

SHAW. No. He's right. I never have . . . To the best wife, my darling, in the land.

REARDON. Aye.

SHAW. The best wife that any man could have.

ALL. The best wife!

They drink.

REARDON. To the best family in the land.

ALL. The best family in the land.

They drink.

SHAW. To the best neighbours that a man could wish to have.

ALL. The best neighbours!

They drink.

SHAW. I've damn well run out.

REARDON. Now, then. Allow me, if you don't mind, to put that immediately to rights. (*Offers bottle round.*)

MRS BURNETT. No, no. I think I've had enough.

STEVEN. No, no. I'm all right.

The others take a refill. MRS SHAW shakes her head.

SHAW. We'll soon get through this. Come this time tomorrow . . .

REARDON. Plenty more where this came from, I'm thinking.

SHAW. Aye. Aye. The sky's the limit!

REARDON. Like the old days, Harry.

SHAW. Like the old days, Jim. You're right. There wasn't a bar we didn't turn upside down in those days.

MRS SHAW. The terror of the town.

SHAW. We were. We were . . . Didn't know Jim here was once a professional fighter.

STEVEN. No.

ANDREW. I don't believe I did.

REARDON. For four consecutive weeks it lasted.

They laugh.

SHAW. Jim's trouble – shall I tell you? . . . Never done a day's hard work in all his bloody life. Licking envelopes, filling in forms, wage-packets: dangling round the manager's back pocket.

REARDON. Ah, now, any damn fool can wield a pick and

shovel. Takes a man with brains to get paid for sitting on his backside. Ask your sons, Harry.

SHAW. He's right. He's right. I'll tell you something now . . . Do you know how high it is where I work? (*He looks round.*)

They shake their heads.

Thirteen inches.

COLIN. It can't be.

SHAW. Thirteen inches. (*Stoops and measures it off the floor with his hand.*)

REARDON. He's right. The Rawcliffe seam.

SHAW. Thirteen inches. If I as much as cough, the whole damn roof'll come down on top of me. Two hundred yards of rock above, and the centre of the earth beneath. Why, you're nothing but a piece of stone yourself, propped up between one bit and the next. You lie with your belly shoved up against your throat.

MRS SHAW. Oh, now. We've just had our dinner . . .

SHAW. They don't believe me, you know. I've often thought I ought to take her down, just once, in all these years, for her to see what it's like.

MRS SHAW. I've heard enough, without having to find out.

SHAW. Nay, you can't know what it's like unless you've been down . . . And not even then. It takes a few years of going down before you get a glimmer . . . You get a view of life you don't get anywhere else. You really get a feeling of what God's good protection means. (*Coughs.*) I tell you, if you stuck a pin in me you wouldn't get any blood: a little pile of coal-dust'd be all you'd see run out.

They laugh.

MRS SHAW. He ought to come out. While he's got two arms, and two legs. And a head to go with it.

SHAW. Nay, they don't understand. You have some pride. Damn it all. You can't just come out and leave it. What's it all add up to?

MRS SHAW. Fifty years of good fortune. How many men have you seen maimed? And killed.

SHAW. Aye. Well. I shan't get morbid. Not at this hour of the night. Mrs Burnett: another drop!

MRS BURNETT. I ought to be going . . . One last one,
    then.

REARDON. She has a great gift for it, I saw it at a glance.

MRS BURNETT. Once at Christmas. That's the only time I
    try . . . and on an occasion like this, of course.

REARDON. My dear lady . . . (*Fills her glass.*) Steven: your
    father tells me you have a learned text on the way as well.

STEVEN. Had. It's on the way, I'm afraid, no longer.

REARDON. Ah, now, artistic endeavour. It's open to a
    great many disappointments.

STEVEN. Well, it was nothing as ambitious as that.

REARDON. And what was your subject, Steven? If you
    don't mind me asking.

STEVEN. I'm not sure myself.

ANDREW. It was a summing-up, Mr Reardon, of society as
    it is today.

REARDON. Society today? And is society today any
    different from society yesterday?

STEVEN. I suspect not. In any case . . .

REARDON (*encouraging*). No, no. Despite appearances to
    the contrary, I have a student's curiosity about the world.
    How it came to be; what it is; and in what manner it will
    die out.

MRS BURNETT. Believes we're going to be bombed to
    death. Going to build himself a shelter.

REARDON. Well, well. A figure of speech.

MRS BURNETT. No, no. He said a shelter. Wanted me to
    come in it with him.

ANDREW. Mr Reardon!

MRS SHAW. Where? Not round here, I hope.

REARDON. No. No. A figure of speech. A figure of speech
    entirely.

SHAW. Do you remember the shelters during the war, then,
    Jim?

REARDON. Do I not? . . . A certain one I recollect of a
    remarkable construction. (*To the others.*) The largest hole
    you ever saw.

SHAW. These lads: they won't remember it.

ANDREW. Remember it? We dug the bloody thing.

SHAW. Went down . . . what was it? Fourteen feet. (*To*
    MRS BURNETT.) Should have seen it.

ANDREW. You're forgetting, now. She did.

SHAW. 'Course. 'Course. Forgetting. Opened it first night of bombing to let her in . . . Swam around, then, didn't you, love?

MRS BURNETT. I nearly drowned! Calls himself a miner . . .

SHAW. Nay, ladies first. Alus been my motto . . . (*Laughs.*) Whole place was full of water . . . By go . . . Freetened of being bombed to death and you end up being drowned. (*Laughs.*)

MRS SHAW *has begun to hum the hymn tune 'Aberystwyth' quietly to herself.*

REARDON. It was truly a miner's work of art. But for the fact that it was always full of water, it would have been of incalculable benefit to us all. As it was . . .

MRS BURNETT. Spent all the time in the cupboard underneath the stairs.

REARDON. We did. Many a happy hour have I spent playing cards by the light of a single candle while the drone of German bombers came, hour after hour, from overhead.

SHAW. I used to carry Steven out. To watch the rockets. They came over sometimes in threes.

REARDON. I remember.

SHAW. You could see the flames from their exhausts . . . used to rattle . . . (*Indicating* STEVEN.) He took it all to heart. Tried to tell him – you could tell when they were going to land . . . Engines cut out. Silent . . . Hell of an explosion.

REARDON (*to* MRS BURNETT). No warning, now, the next time. Liquefaction will be the order of the day.

SHAW. Aye. It doesn't bear thinking of.

REARDON. No. No. Thank God we've reached the twilight.

SHAW. In one piece.

REARDON. In one piece. You're right.

They're silent.

MRS SHAW *humming, then at the third line:*

MRS SHAW (*sings quietly*).
    While the tempest still is high:
    Hide me, O my Saviour, hide,
    Till the storm of life is past;
    Safe into the haven guide,
    O receive my soul at last.

COLIN, ANDREW *and* STEVEN *exchange looks,*
ANDREW *turning away to hide his laugh.*

Other refuge have I none . . .

REARDON *starts, then* SHAW, *to sing too.*

Hangs my helpless soul on Thee;
Leave, ah! Leave me not alone,
Still support and comfort me . . .

MRS BURNETT *has started to sing too, they sing*
strongly. At the last ANDREW, *then* COLIN *and*
STEVEN, *join in.*

All my trust on Thee is stay'd,
All my help from Thee I bring;
Cover my defenceless head
With the shadow of Thy wing.

MRS SHAW *carries on humming the tune.*

COLIN (*to* ANDREW). Remember Sunday School?
ANDREW. 'Crusaders'. I was in 'St Andrew's',
    appropriately enough . . . He was in 'St Peter's' . . . each
    saint, you see, had a different pew.
COLIN. A different banner to each group.
ANDREW. St Peter was a fish. Eyeballs like damn great
    saucers.
COLIN. St Francis a bird . . .
ANDREW. One leg, and a beak like a damn great parrot.
COLIN. He was no artist, that's for sure, who painted those.
ANDREW. No . . . Jamey, now. He'd have gone down like
    a bomb.
COLIN. Jamey . . .
MRS BURNETT. He would. (*To* REARDON.) We were just
    saying earlier on . . .

SHAW (*to* REARDON). Do you remember the night he died?

REARDON. I do. I shall never forget . . .

SHAW (*indicating* REARDON). Woke him up . . . knocking at his door.

REARDON. Aye . . . he did.

SHAW. We were just lying there in bed . . . couldn't sleep . . . could we, love? . . . then suddenly on the wall, just above the bed, three damn great crashes . . . Like a fist . . .

MRS SHAW. Bigger . . .

SHAW. Bigger. Like a damn great giant . . . Shook the house . . . Tell you, frightened us to bloody death. Went to Jim's . . . he sat with us . . .

REARDON. The rest of the night.

SHAW. I've never been able to make that out. There were you two . . . (*Indicating* COLIN *and* ANDREW.) Never heard it . . .

MRS SHAW. Slept right through . . .

SHAW. I could never make that out. Three blows. Just like that . . . The only two who heard it. (*Indicating himself and* MRS SHAW. *To* ANDREW.) He died, you know, without any warning . . . caught a chill one night . . . dead by the next morning. Couldn't believe it . . . I'd have given aught to have saved that lad . . . Asked Him a time or two to take me in his place . . . willed them rocks, I have, to fall on my bloody head . . . He was a lovely lad . . . I'd have given bloody aught. Still. (*Sees* MRS SHAW's *look.*) Aye. Well, then . . .

MRS SHAW. I shall have to go to bed. I'm sorry. But I'm nearly asleep sitting here . . . All this excitement.

MRS BURNETT. Aye. Look at the time . . . I only came across to make up the fire. I've left the light on, the door open.

SHAW. Never mind, love. A damn good job you made of it.

REARDON. Shall I escort you across the way?

MRS BURNETT. No, no, I'll manage on my own, if you don't mind. I'll see you all tomorrow. (*To* MRS SHAW.) I'm glad you've had a good night, love.

MRS SHAW. Yes. Thanks, love. I'll see you tomorrow . . . all being well.

MRS BURNETT. All being well. Sleep tight . . . I'll let myself out. (*She goes.*)

REARDON. Ah, well. I better be off, too. My wife will be thinking I've run away at last. After all these years, now, I don't wish to raise her hopes unduly.

MRS SHAW. Oh, now. Get on . . .

He goes to the door.

REARDON. I shall pop in, if I may, in the morning, and say my farewells.

ANDREW. Aye. We'll have one more before we go.

REARDON. Now there's a promise I'll not forget . . . Good night. And may sweet dreams illuminate your slumbers.

They laugh, call 'good night', and he goes.

MRS SHAW (*cheerful*). It's been a lovely night. It has . . . But if I stay up any longer . . . Do you know where you're all sleeping?

COLIN. Don't worry. We'll toss up . . . Good night, Mother. God bless . . . (*Embracing her.*)

MRS SHAW. Good night, love . . . it's been a lovely night, it has . . . (*To* STEVEN.) Good night, love . . . (*To* ANDREW.) Good night, love . . .

They kiss her cheek in turn.

See you in the morning . . . You don't mind me going off?

COLIN. No. No. You get your rest.

SHAW. I'll be up in a jiffy, love. Shan't be long.

MRS SHAW. Good night, then. And thank you all again.

COLIN *and* ANDREW. Good night . . .

She goes.

SHAW. Aye . . . She's enjoyed tonight. She has . . . Wouldn't have sung that hymn if she hadn't!

They laugh.

(*To* COLIN.) Nay, you take it from me, lad. That's the best night she's ever had . . .

ANDREW (*to* COLIN). Heads I sleep upstairs, tails you sleep down here.

COLIN. Right . . .

ANDREW *tosses a coin.*

ANDREW. Tails . . . You sleep down here . . . (*To* STEVEN.) Heads I sleep up, tails you sleep down . . .

COLIN. Ay . . . wait a minute!

They laugh.

ANDREW. The destiny of fifteen thousand men rests in his hands, and you can fiddle him with a penny.

They laugh, SHAW *turning to the mantelpiece, and taking down a box of matches.*

COLIN. It's late. That's the only reason.

ANDREW. God bless our motor industry, and all who crucify themselves inside her.

SHAW. Here. Shortest match sleeps down. (*Holds three between his fingers, the ends concealed.*) . . . Steve . . .

STEVEN (*takes one*). Not me.

COLIN (*takes one*). . . . Me.

They laugh.

STEVEN. Ah, bad luck.

ANDREW. I hope, for the nation's sake, you have better luck at work.

COLIN. Oh, it won't be so bad. (*Trying the settee.*) Fine.

SHAW. Ah, well. A damn fine night. You can have it all. A car, money, a big house . . . They're nowt. A family like this. That's all that counts.

ANDREW. You can tell he's enjoyed himself.

SHAW. I have. I have. Tonight's meant more to me than ought.

COLIN *yawns, stretches.*

Ah, well. I'll leave you to it . . . this time tomorrow I'll be back down. Nights . . . It's one I'll remember. I want you to know that. You've made me and your mother very proud.

COLIN. . . . Nothing of it. We'll be back again this time next year, don't worry.

SHAW. Nay, I might damn well hold you to that as well . . . Good night. And God bless you . . . (*To* STEVEN *as he passes* SHAW *on the way to the stairs.*) You're coming up?

STEVEN. Aye . . . (*Goes.*)

SHAW (*watches him, then*). Is Steve all right?

COLIN. What?

SHAW. I don't know . . . He's not looked very well.

COLIN. Oh, he's all right . . . (*Looks to* ANDREW.)

ANDREW. Aye.

SHAW. He works too hard. He's always put too much into whatever he did.

COLIN. He'll be all right.

SHAW. Aye. Right. Well . . . I'll get off. Good night again.

COLIN. Good night, Dad.

ANDREW. Good night.

SHAW. Don't make a noise, will you? Your mother sleeps very light . . . Good night. (*Goes.*)

ANDREW. A fiver.

COLIN (*pause*). What?

ANDREW. Me bed.

COLIN. You're joking.

ANDREW. I'm not. (*Feels the sofa.*) Ugh. Iron. They've had this twenty years.

COLIN. They haven't. I bought it for them only last year.

ANDREW. Terrible taste.

COLIN. It was their taste. My money. I'm not going to tell them what to buy.

ANDREW. Rest of the furniture, too?

COLIN. Just about.

ANDREW. What about it?

COLIN. Not likely.

ANDREW. You stingy sod. The money you earn, no dependants. And you won't give up five quid for a decent bed.

COLIN. It's not that. It's just a feeling of repugnance.

ANDREW. Repugnance?

COLIN. My brother selling me his bed – well, not even his – for five pounds.

ANDREW. Course, you could go in the car. But then . . . you might get run over.

COLIN. Or back to 'The Excelsior'. Don't worry. I know your mentality. The fact is, for me, it's a privilege sleeping in this house.

ANDREW. A privilege? Here . . . are you all right?

COLIN. Look. I honour what my mother and father have

done. And I don't give a sod for your bloody family anlaysis . . .

ANDREW. Four pounds ten.

COLIN. No.

ANDREW. All right. A sacrifice. Four.

COLIN. Nothing. I'm sleeping here.

ANDREW (*watching him*). High-pressure meetings tomorrow morning.

COLIN. I have, as a matter of fact. Tomorrow afternoon.

ANDREW. I don't know how they've managed without you. (*Looks at the clock.*) Must be what? . . . ten hours since they last saw you . . . You're not getting undressed, are you?

COLIN. Not entirely. No. (*Begins to take off his shoes, jacket and waistcoat.*)

ANDREW. You know. I just can't make this out . . . Only two years ago, it seems, you were running in through the door with little short trousers and a snotty nose.

COLIN. I'm tired. I've got to drive back and work tomorrow.

ANDREW. Yes, well. You're a busy man . . . I suppose you have a secretarial assistant.

COLIN. Yes . . .

ANDREW. Don't you ever . . . you know, feel you could make some progress with her?

COLIN. She happens to be a man.

ANDREW. A man!

COLIN. The assistance I require is not the kind that you imagine. There are any amount of women pushing typewriters.

ANDREW. I see . . . On second thoughts, I might be safer upstairs.

COLIN. Good. I'm glad. Good night.

ANDREW. Shall I put out the light?

COLIN. If you don't mind. I'll be very grateful.

ANDREW. And . . . er . . . I won't say anything to Mum.

COLIN. Look. Hop it. Scarper. Knock off.

ANDREW. I'm going . . . (*Puts out the light; goes.*)

COLIN *settles on the settee beneath a blanket.*

A moment later ANDREW *reappears.*

COLIN. Is anything the matter?

ANDREW. Forgot to say good night.

COLIN. *Good night*!

ANDREW. Three quid.

COLIN. *Good night*!

ANDREW. Two.

COLIN. *Good night*!

ANDREW. Ah, well. I hope it kills you . . . (*Goes: comes back in.*) I hope, when you come to negotiate tomorrow afternoon, you can't even *sit down*!

COLIN. Good.

ANDREW. One pound ten.

COLIN. For Christ's sake!

ANDREW. Right . . . I'm going. (*Goes.*)

COLIN *settles down again, turns one way then another, settles down.*

After a while ANDREW *comes back, in shirtsleeves.*

ANDREW. Psst . . .

COLIN. Wha . . .

ANDREW. Are you asleep?

COLIN. For Christ's sake.

ANDREW *puts on the light.*

Oh! . . . God! (*Shields his eyes, half rising.*)

ANDREW. It's Steven.

COLIN. What . . . ?

ANDREW. He's at it again.

COLIN. What . . . ?

ANDREW. Crying.

COLIN. Oh, Christ.

ANDREW. In his sleep.

COLIN. Oh, God . . . (*Gets up.*) What's the matter with him.

ANDREW. How do I know?

COLIN. Can't you wake him?

ANDREW. I don't know . . . All right. I suppose I'll have to.

COLIN. Look . . . He may have drunk too much.

ANDREW. You must be joking.

COLIN. It could be anything. Indigestion . . .

ANDREW. Indigestion?

COLIN. Anything . . .

ANDREW. All right. You go. If you're so bloody efficient. (*Sits down on settee.*) Perhaps you can negotiate some suitable compromise . . . Let's say . . . a whimper.

COLIN (*goes to stair*). I can't hear anything . . .

ANDREW. No. Probably not.

COLIN. Look. Is this something you've just . . . What're you doing?

ANDREW. Well, I can't sleep up there with that row going on. (*He's taken* COLIN's *place on the settee, lying down.*) It's yours. For nothing.

COLIN. Look here . . . God. There's somebody getting up. (*Listens at the door.*)

ANDREW. It'll be Steven . . .

COLIN. No . . . (*Listens.*) My Dad . . . Oh, Christ.

ANDREW. Better go up.

COLIN *listens at the door leading to the stairs.*

It's not so bad here after all. I was wrong . . . (*Eases himself, covering himself more surely with the blanket.*) . . . Bit more on the fire, and we'll be all right.

COLIN. Oh, Christ.

ANDREW. What?

COLIN (*coming across*). He's coming down.

ANDREW. Better get the cards out. Be here all night . . . Where's that Scotch?

COLIN. Look, you better get up off there . . .

SHAW (*coming in, blindly, in trousers and shirt*). What's going on, then?

ANDREW. What . . . Colin's just off to bed. I've swapped him. Need a spot of oil. Hear those springs? Christ . . .

SHAW. There's Steven . . .

ANDREW. Steven? (*Looks around.*)

SHAW. Upstairs, in bed.

ANDREW. What . . . ?

SHAW. I've just been in.

ANDREW. Sleeping. Wind . . .

SHAW. Well . . . I've never heard a noise like it . . .

ANDREW (*matter of fact*). Look here, Col. You better go up and have a look.

COLIN. What . . . ?

ANDREW (*getting up*). All right. I'll go. (*To* SHAW.) What did he say?

SHAW. Nothing . . .

ANDREW. Right . . . Well. (*Nods at* COLIN.) Soon settle that. Can't have him saying nothing . . . Right . . . Well . . . Off we go. (*Looks round then goes.*)

COLIN. Do you fancy another drink?

SHAW. I couldn't touch another. I couldn't . . . I was . . . look. I was fast asleep and I thought it was a cat. Then I thought it was in here . . . then . . . (*Listens.*) I don't know . . . If your mother hears . . . I've shut her door.

COLIN. He could be just dreaming.

SHAW. He was awake. His eyes were open. When I leaned over him he shook his head. (*Looks up. Listens.*) He never cried as a baby . . . Did you know that? . . . The only time he ever cried was once . . . I better go up.

COLIN. Right . . . look . . . All right. No. Look . . . We'll both go up . . .

SHAW. Don't make a noise . . .

SHAW *has gone to the door: as he goes out, and* COLIN *makes to follow him, he pauses.*

Oh . . . He's coming . . . (*Comes back in.*) He's coming . . .

COLIN. Who?

ANDREW *comes in.*

SHAW. What's he say?

ANDREW. Dreaming . . . nothing . . . right as rain. (*Looks round.*) Better have another drop. Knock us all out together.

SHAW. He's been working too damned hard. I know. I could see it when he first came. He's always been so conscientious.

ANDREW. He's coming down . . . Dressing-gown. Would you believe it? Brought it in his little bag . . . Show you he's all right. Dreaming. Wind. Nothing to worry about. (*To* COLIN.) That *steak Diane* . . . I almost made a complaint when I first saw it. Did you see him put it in the pan?

COLIN. No . . .
ANDREW. Damn faded colour. Set light to it before you could have a proper look. Chopped onions and mushrooms on top of it . . . I bet they'd had that in for weeks waiting for somebody like us . . . uneducated. Inexperienced.

SHAW *is looking towards the stairs.*

What was yours?
COLIN. Tartare . . . Steak.
ANDREW. I'd have thought that was very fresh . . . Going by the colour. Blood red.
COLIN. Yes . . .

STEVEN *has appeared. He's wearing a dressing-gown, his trousers underneath.*

ANDREW. Steve's was the rump, wasn't it?
COLIN. Sirloin . . .
ANDREW. Sirloin . . . Could easily have been that. I wouldn't have minded having another look at those carrots. The way he served them from the pot . . .
COLIN (*holding his stomach*). All right . . .

STEVEN *has sat down.*

SHAW. Are you all right, Steve?
STEVEN. Yes.
SHAW. I mean, nay lad . . . if there's anything the matter.
STEVEN. No.
SHAW. It's not Sheila is it?
STEVEN. No. No. (*Shakes his head.*)
ANDREW. Sirloin . . . If we'd all had *steak tartare* like Colin . . . trust him to have all the luck.
SHAW. Nay, look . . . I don't know . . . Your mother'd be that unhappy to see you upset . . .
ANDREW. She would.
SHAW. You're not ill? . . . I mean . . .
STEVEN. No . . . (*He shakes his head.*)
SHAW. Well . . . It could be tonight . . . All that excitement. I mean, well, it's been a very emotional evening for all of us.
COLIN. It has . . . What with that.

ANDREW. . . . And the *steak Diane*.

COLIN (*to* ANDREW). Look. I think we've had enough.

ANDREW. Yes. (*Walks about, hands in pockets, whistling quietly to himself.*)

STEVEN *sits as if abstracted.*

(*To* COLIN.) Better watch it.

COLIN. What?

ANDREW. Watch it.

COLIN. Look. I've just about had enough . . . His systematic . . . bloody . . . disparagement . . . of every . . . bleeding thing . . . inside this house . . .

SHAW. I don't know what's going on, you know, but you better keep your voices down. I'm not having your mother woken up. If you have any arguments you can save them till tomorrow . . . outside, any time. But not down here. I've asked you that.

ANDREW. Why not? What's she to be protected from?

SHAW. What?

ANDREW. I mean . . . that . . . Goddess, we have up there.

SHAW. What?

COLIN (*to* SHAW). Take no notice of him. He's drunk. He doesn't know what he's saying.

ANDREW. He'd know of course. The supreme bloody sycophant. The professional bloody paster-over-er. The smoother-downer. The shoddy, fifth-rate, sycophantic whore . . .

SHAW. Look . . . look . . . you better get out . . .

ANDREW. Get out? I've never been in.

SHAW. What . . . ?

ANDREW. This family.

COLIN. Oh God.

SHAW. What . . . ?

ANDREW. Look. (*Points to* STEVEN.) Tears! What the hell is he crying for?

COLIN. You better get out. Go on. I'll bloody turn you out myself.

ANDREW. Dad. Wise up. You've enshrined that woman in so much adoration that she's wellnigh invisible to you as well as to everybody else.

SHAW. What . . . ?

ANDREW. You owe her *nothing*. What're you trying to pay off?

SHAW. What . . . ? (*Stands, blinded, in the centre of the room.*)

COLIN (*to* ANDREW). I think you better go. Go on. I'll give you the keys. You can drive to the hotel.

ANDREW. I've no money on me.

COLIN. . . . (*Hunts round for his coat.*)

ANDREW. Aye . . . Aye . . . (*Watches* COLIN *get the notes out. Then, as he offers them.*) Are you actually aware . . . I mean, of what you're doing?

COLIN. I am.

ANDREW. I mean, can you actually detach yourself a moment – perverse as such an action well might be – and actually see what it is you're doing?

COLIN. I'm protecting . . .

ANDREW. Protecting? You're protecting nothing. (*To* SHAW.) He's the one you ought to kick out. And that one with him, up yonder . . . The one that's made us so bloody clean and whole.

SHAW. What . . . ?

COLIN (*to* SHAW). Leave him. It's envy. It's jealousy. Listen to nothing he has to say.

ANDREW. No, no. He's right. Listen to nothing that I have to say. Instead . . . (*Gestures at* STEVEN.) Fasten your eyes on that.

SHAW. If . . . What . . . ? (*Holds his head.*)

COLIN. Dad . . . (*Takes* SHAW's *shoulder.*)

ANDREW. Come on, Steve. You're not deaf. You've heard it. What is it, seething around inside that head, that causes you and . . . *look* . . . my Dad, to cry?

STEVEN *stands up. He gazes before him a moment, distracted.*

No, no. No rush. No hurry. Come on . . . What's eating out your mind?

COLIN. Shut up.

STEVEN. I've . . . (*Shakes his head.*)

SHAW. Look . . . Steve . . .

SHAW *goes to* STEVEN. *He puts his arm round him, as much for his own support as* STEVEN's.

You mustn't lad . . . You mustn't . . . Nay. All I ever had . . .

COLIN (*to* ANDREW). God. I'll bloody kill you for this.

SHAW. Nay . . . every night . . . Look, Steve . . .

ANDREW. I hope she's listening. (*Looks up.*) I hope you're listening . . . I hope in all sincerity she can hear . . . Her sons, her abject bloody lover . . . commend their bloody souls to thee.

COLIN. For Christ's sake.

SHAW *has turned away, lost.*

ANDREW. Dad. Dad. Forty years . . . what chance have we ever had with *that*! . . . *Steve* . . . *Steve* . . . Tell him.

COLIN. I'll bloody kill you for this! I will! I'll bloody kill you!

ANDREW. Let's negotiate a settlement, Col . . . Forty years of my father's life for a lady like my mother, conscientious, devout of temperament, overtly religious . . . sincere . . . for getting her with child at the age of eighteen, nineteen, twenty . . . I've forgotten which . . . on the back of which imprudence we have been borne all our lives, labouring to atone for her sexuality . . . labouring to atone for . . . what? Labouring to atone . . . When I think of all the books I've had to read. When I think of all the facts I've had to learn. The texts I've had to study. The exams I've had to . . . with that vision held perpetually before me; a home, a car, a wife . . . a child . . . a rug that didn't have holes in, a pocket that never leaked . . . I even married a Rector's daughter! For Christ's sake: how *good* could I become? The edifice of my life – of *his* life – built up on that . . . We – *we* – are the inheritors of nothing . . . totems . . . while all the time the Godhead . . . slumbers overhead.

STEVEN. My mother . . .

ANDREW. What?

STEVEN *has shaken his head.*

COLIN. You blame them for that . . . ?

ANDREW. Blame? Blame? . . . Blame . . . Good God. No blame. No bloody nothing.

STEVEN. No . . . (*He shakes his head.*) No.

ANDREW. . . . . What is it, Dad? What image did you have . . . crawling around down there at night . . . panting, bleeding, blackened . . . What world was it you were hoping we'd inherit?

COLIN. Shurrup. For Christ's sake, shurrup.

ANDREW. These aren't your sons, old man . . . I don't know what you see here . . . But these are nothing . . . less than nothing . . . has-beens, wash-outs, semblances . . . a pathetic vision of a better life . . .

COLIN. I think you've said enough.

ANDREW. Enough? Life measured out in motor cars . . . I'll put one on your tomb . . . I hope tomorrow you have a damn great strike. And I hope they come along and ask you to negotiate. I hope they make you Chancellor, or Prime Minister. And I hope it gives you something to do, fills in your time, infects your life with a certain feeling of significance and meaning . . . for if it doesn't, I hold out for you, Colin, *brother*, no hope of any kind at all. Steve! . . .

No answer.

Dad? . . . Fast asleep . . .

SHAW *sits dazed across the room.*

Why not . . . Steve? Nothing. I'll go on up, then. Cheerio. (*He goes to the stairs, and goes.*)

COLIN. My God . . .

They're silent for a moment.

Dad? . . . It's all right . . . (*He goes across to him.*) Dad?

SHAW. Aye . . .

COLIN. It's all right . . . It's all right.

SHAW. Aye . . .

COLIN. Are you listening? . . . Dad!

SHAW. Aye . . . It's . . . (*Shakes his head.*)

COLIN. Look. It's okay . . . Are you listening?

SHAW. Nay . . . whatever's happened? . . . I don't know.

STEVEN. Dad?

SHAW. I'd do ought for you lads. You know that.

COLIN. Aye. We do.

SHAW. I don't know . . .

COLIN. Trust the Shaws . . . Not two minutes together –
and out it comes . . . Fists all over the place.

SHAW. I'll never forgive him for that. You know. I
won't . . .

STEVEN. Dad . . . Don't.

SHAW. Nay, lad. He took advantage of us . . . If your
mother ever got to hear, it'd tear her in two.

STEVEN. Dad . . . Leave it.

SHAW. Aye . . . I know. You do too much, Steven. You've
got to live your life as well as work. There's Sheila. Your
family . . . I can tell you, I know what too much work
does to a man.

STEVEN. Yes . . . Well, Dad . . . You go to bed.

SHAW. I could sleep down here . . .

STEVEN. Now what for? . . . You go up. Go on . . . No.
Look. I'm all right . . .

SHAW. Nay . . . I don't know . . . Are you going up?

STEVEN. I am. In a minute . . . Go on . . .

SHAW. I shouldn't sleep with him up yonder.

STEVEN. Dad: he was upset as well . . .

SHAW. I should stay with Colin. Let him lie up there alone.

STEVEN. Go on, now . . . you get off.

COLIN. Aye . . . Go on, Dad. We'll be all right.

SHAW. I hope to God she's not awake . . .

COLIN. She won't be. Don't worry.

SHAW. In the morning . . .

COLIN. Don't worry. We'll have that troublemaker out.

SHAW. Aye . . . Right . . . He said some things . . .

COLIN. Go on, now . . .

SHAW. Aye. Well . . . Good night, lads.

COLIN. Good night, Dad.

SHAW. Aye . . . Well . . . Good night . . . (*He turns and
goes.*)

COLIN (*sighs; then, to* STEVEN). Do you want a drink?

STEVEN. No . . . (*Shakes his head.*)

COLIN. I'll have one. I'll have two, I think. (*He's gone to
pour it out.*) Christ. Thanks for small mercies . . .

STEVEN *looks up.*

My Dad. Didn't understand a word.

STEVEN. No . . . He's like a child.

COLIN. Andrew? . . . Say that again.

COLIN *watches* STEVEN *for a while, uncertain of his mood. Then*:

STEVEN The funny thing is . . . (*He laughs.*) The funny thing is that he (*Gestures up.*) raised us to better things which, in his heart – my Dad – he despises even more than Andrew . . . I mean, his work actually has significance for him . . . while the work he's educated us to do . . . is nothing . . . at the best a pastime, at the worst a sort of soulless stirring of the pot . . . Honestly, what hope have any of us got?

COLIN. I think I'll have another.

STEVEN. What actually do you do with it, Colin?

COLIN. What . . .

STEVEN. I mean, this feeling of disfigurement.

COLIN. Disfigurement?

STEVEN. I mean . . . this crushing, bloody sense of injury . . . inflicted, as he says, by wholly innocent hands.

COLIN. Well, I don't . . .

STEVEN. No. Well . . . I better get up.

COLIN. Do you . . . I mean, have you had any medical advice?

STEVEN. Advice?

COLIN. About your . . .

STEVEN. No . . . Well . . .

COLIN. Shouldn't you get some sort of guidance? I mean, Christ, there's any amount of stuff nowadays.

STEVEN. Yep . . .

COLIN. Christ, if we all thought like that maniac up yonder – we'd all be what?

STEVEN. Artists, most likely.

COLIN. Sure. (*Laughs.*) And I can just see the sort of art . . .

STEVEN. Aye. Well, I better get up.

COLIN. First thing in the morning – we must get him out.

STEVEN. Yep . . . Right . . . I'll say good night.

COLIN. Are you okay, then . . . ?

STEVEN. Sure . . . Right . . . I'll see you.

COLIN. Good night, Steve, then . . .

STEVEN. Aye . . . Good night (*Goes.*)

> COLIN *gazes after him a moment; then he glances round.*
> *He picks up the blanket, the glass, puts out the light. He*
> *goes to sit in a chair by the fire, wraps the blanket about*
> *him. He drinks from the glass, empties it, then sits gazing*
> *at the fire.*

> *Slow fade.*

Scene Two
Morning.

> COLIN *is sleeping in the chair, his head fallen on one side.*
> *There's the sound of activity in the kitchen, plates, cups, etc.*

> *After a moment* MRS SHAW *comes in, dressed, from the*
> *kitchen. She goes to the window, opens the curtains.*

COLIN. Oh . . . Oh! . . . (*Eases himself stiffly in the chair,*
   wakening.)

MRS SHAW. Did I wake you, love? I've made the breakfast
   . . . If we don't eat it it'll all get cold.

COLIN. Yes . . . Aye. (*Stretches.*)

MRS SHAW. Did you sleep all right?

COLIN. Yes. Fine . . .

MRS SHAW. What was the matter with the couch?

COLIN. Oh . . . I . . . dropped off here.

MRS SHAW. I thought it'd be either you or Steven. Trust
   Andrew. Snoring his head off in bed.

COLIN. Aye. (*Rubs his hair. Gets up. Stretches his stiff*
   body.)

MRS SHAW. Fire's still going from last night. We were up
   that late. What time do you have to be leaving?

COLIN. Oh, pretty soon. Straight after breakfast . . . Sleep
   all right?

MRS SHAW. Like a top. It was a lovely night. Thank you.
   (*Kisses his cheek in passing.*) I'll just fetch it through.
   (*Goes.*)

COLIN (*looks out of the window*). Rain . . . Looks like it.

MRS SHAW (*off*). We don't get much else this time of the year.

COLIN (*talking through*). You know, you ought to get my Dad to retire. He'll listen to you. Not to us . . . I can get you a house on the coast, a cottage or a bungalow. You'd have no extra work to do.

MRS SHAW (*re-entering with the tray*). Nay, I've tried. Work for your father, well, it's something he doesn't seem able to do without.

COLIN. Even then, I think you could persuade him. There must be some inducement he'll listen to.

MRS SHAW. He's not going to come out of that pit until they carry him out, and then he'd go back at the first chance. I don't know . . . He's been a good man. But I don't know: in some things he's been very simple.

COLIN. Aye . . . (*Turns away and starts to get dressed, i.e. tie, waistcoat, shoes, jacket.*)

MRS SHAW. I'll go and call them down. Andrew'll sleep all day, if I remember.

COLIN. Aye . . .

She goes.

MRS SHAW (*off*). Dad . . . Steven!

SHAW (*off*). I'm coming.

MRS SHAW (*off*). Can you knock up the others? Tell them it's getting cold.

SHAW (*off*). Aye . . . Aye . . . I will.

MRS SHAW (*reappearing*). Well, then. That's that . . . What time do you want to be off by?

COLIN. Oh, as soon as that one up there is ready.

MRS SHAW. Are you taking him back with you?

COLIN. I suppose I'll have to.

MRS SHAW. He's wrecking his career. I suppose you realise that? . . . Still. They're old enough to look after their own affairs at his age . . . He was always wild.

COLIN. Yes . . .

MRS SHAW. I don't know. He took it very badly . . .

COLIN. What? . . .

MRS SHAW. When Jamey died. He was five years old –

Andrew. We put him out with Mr Reardon, you know, when Steven was born.

COLIN. Why was that?

MRS SHAW. Nay, love. To save me the work . . . Saved my life, you did, you know. We kept you at home. You were only two. (*Kisses his head.*) I don't know where we'd have been without . . . I don't think he's ever forgiven me.

COLIN. What? . . .

MRS SHAW. Andrew . . . He was away six weeks. He used to come to the door, crying, you know. I don't know . . . I tried to tell him. If he'd have been here we'd have had a terrible time. What with your Dad at work, Steven . . . Jamey . . .

COLIN. Aye, well. We all have our problems, love.

MRS SHAW. We have . . . As you get older you find more and more that these things somehow work out.

COLIN. Aye. That's right . . .

MRS SHAW (*she goes to the stairs. Calls*). Dad! It's getting cold . . . I'll have to tip it away in a minute.

SHAW (*off*). Aye . . . We're coming.

MRS SHAW (*to* COLIN). Well, we better be getting ours.

COLIN. Yes.

MRS SHAW. And how's your work going?

COLIN. Oh. Very well . . . As a matter of fact . . .

MRS SHAW. Yes . . .

COLIN. Well, I didn't want to tell you about it . . . until I was more certain . . .

MRS SHAW. Now . . . you'll have to. Come on . . .

COLIN. Nay, well . . . (*Scratches his head.*)

MRS SHAW. Come on. We'll have it out of you . . .

COLIN. Well, it's not finally settled . . . But fairly soon, now . . .

MRS SHAW. Come on!

COLIN. I might be getting married.

MRS SHAW. Well!

COLIN. It's not all been agreed yet. But it's . . . sort of on the cards.

MRS SHAW. Well!

COLIN. So . . .

MRS SHAW. Here. Let me give you a kiss, love. (*She comes*

round the table and kisses his cheek.) Well, then . . .
Congratulations . . . I knew something was up!
COLIN. Up?
MRS SHAW. Oh, your mood. I could tell. On top of things
. . . Well, then. And what's she do?
COLIN. A dentist.
MRS SHAW. A dentist!
COLIN. I'll bring her up . . . You can have a look. Better
still – you can come down. Show you round the factory.
MRS SHAW. Well, then . . . (*Watches him, pleased*.) Have
you told your Dad?
COLIN. No . . . No one yet.
MRS SHAW. Honestly. If you'd have told us last night! I am
pleased . . . After all these years.
COLIN. Yep.
MRS SHAW. Going to take the plunge . . . I thought you'd
never get to it. (*She laughs*.) . . . Oh!

SHAW *appears*.

I thought you'd gone to work or something.
SHAW. No, no. Just waking them lot upstairs.
MRS SHAW. We've just got some news to tell you . . . Are
you feeling all right?
SHAW. Yes. What news?
MRS SHAW. Nay. You've to be in a proper mood to hear
it. (*To* COLIN.) I told you he'd drunk too much last
night.
SHAW. I am in a proper mood . . . (*Looking at* COLIN.)
COLIN. I was telling my mother . . . I might be getting
married. Fairly soon.
MRS SHAW (*to* COLIN). Fairly soon . . .
SHAW. Aye. Well. That's very good.

Pause.

MRS SHAW. Aren't you going to say more than that?
SHAW. Nay, well. I'm very pleased.
MRS SHAW. Well, if that's all you have to say.
SHAW. No. Well . . . Congratulations, lad. (*Shakes his hand
formally*.) It's a grand thing, I can see that.

MRS SHAW. Well, you don't have to tell us . . . Here . . . there's your breakfast . . . (*Pleasant.*)

SHAW. Nay . . . I didn't sleep too well last night . . . Nay, I'm pleased, Colin . . . When are we going to see her?

COLIN. I was just saying . . . I might bring her up. Or you could come down . . .

SHAW. Aye . . .

ANDREW's *cheerful whistling off.*

MRS SHAW. Wait till the others hear . . . That'll wake them up. (*Laughs.*)

ANDREW *comes in.*

ANDREW   Morning. Morning. Morning. And a lovely day it is.

MRS SHAW. It is. He's right for once.

ANDREW. I am . . . And how's my old mater this morning? Apple of my eye.

MRS SHAW. I'm very well, thank you.

ANDREW *kisses her cheek with a loud embrace.*

ANDREW. Been dreaming about you, I have.

MRS SHAW. I hope something pleasant for a change.

ANDREW. Oh, very pleasant. Very. (*To* COLIN.) And how are you, old chap, today?

COLIN. All right.

MRS SHAW. He's just given us some very wonderful news. That's how well he's feeling.

ANDREW. He's not . . . Good God . . . he can't be . . . For one minute there I thought he might be pregnant.

MRS SHAW. He's getting married. Fairly soon. That's all he's got to say.

ANDREW. Oh . . . Look at this. Dried up . . . Tea cold. (*Examines the breakfast.*)

MRS SHAW. Is that all you've got to say?

ANDREW. Well done. Poor sod. Oh, dear. Whatever it is that's recommended.

MRS SHAW. Well, I must say.

SHAW. Nay, mother. Just leave them to it.

ANDREW. That's right. Settle it up among ourselves.

MRS SHAW *starts to take the teapot to the kitchen.*

No, no. It's hot enough. No, no. Really, I assure . . . I was merely pulling your leg. And . . . er . . . (*To* COLIN.) When's this happy event going to take place, Col?

COLIN. It hasn't been announced yet.

ANDREW. She hasn't started suing you yet?

COLIN. No: merely that it hasn't been announced.

ANDREW. I hope she's one of us, Col. I mean, not one of them . . .

MRS SHAW. A dentist.

ANDREW. A dentist! By God. (*To* SHAW.) I knew he'd marry a sadist. Formative experience: can't beat it. Every time . . . this tastes very nice . . . Good job you came up with the goods, Col. My mother was beginning to get worried. (*To* SHAW.) Thought he might be one of those . . . (*Quivers his hand.*)

MRS SHAW. I thought nothing of the kind.

ANDREW. Must have thought something . . . I mean, all that time, you couldn't have thought nothing.

MRS SHAW (*reasonably.*) I thought he was taking his time.

ANDREW. Taking his time. He's been through half a dozen motor cars while we've been waiting . . . thought he'd given up the human race . . . look well if he'd fathered a string of shooting brakes, or a line of two-tone limousines, as it is . . . well done. Come up to scratch.

MRS SHAW (*to* COLIN). What did I tell you? Same as usual.

ANDREW (*to* MRS SHAW). What did you tell him?

MRS SHAW. Well, nothing, exactly. Except we might have expected something like that.

ANDREW. Oh, might you? I'm as predictable as that?

SHAW. Now look. Let's just have our breakfast . . . I'll just give Steven another shout.

MRS SHAW. Nay, you don't have to defend him. He's always been old enough to look after himself.

ANDREW. I have. She's right. Ever since I was turned out I've been able to look after myself.

MRS SHAW. You weren't turned out.

ANDREW. No. No. Brought back into the fold, now. I remember. (*Embraces her.*) Here's Steve, now, looking as bright as a Christmas penny . . .

STEVEN *has come in from the stairs.*

MRS SHAW. Good morning, love. How are you?

STEVEN. Well . . . thanks.

ANDREW. Aren't you going to give your mother a birthday kiss? Forty-first year of marital bliss we're moving into.

MRS SHAW. He's got out of the bed the wrong side this morning.

ANDREW. I have. Same every day. Without exception.

STEVEN *embraces* MRS SHAW.

Well, then. That's that. Colin's got an announcement to make.

STEVEN. What's that?

ANDREW. Nothing calamitous. Don't worry . . . Not for us at least, it isn't.

MRS SHAW. He's trying to say – I don't know whether you can tell – that Colin is going to get married.

STEVEN. Oh.

ANDREW. Galvanised him into action. Look.

STEVEN (*to* COLIN). Congratulations.

COLIN. Thanks.

MRS SHAW. Well, I don't know. What's got into you this morning?

ANDREW. I think it's the atmosphere up here . . . Industrial pollution. It's noticeable the moment you step off that train.

SHAW (*to* ANDREW). Look . . . what . . . when . . . ?

COLIN. We'll be going in a few minutes.

MRS SHAW. Oh, now. As quickly as that?

ANDREW. That's all right . . . Important meetings. The destiny of the nation . . . Steve and I can prop our feet up a little longer. Keep things ticking over.

COLIN. I thought you were coming back with me.

ANDREW. Well, I am. But I'm not leaving at this hour. Damn it all. I've only just got up. If you were an artist you'd understand these things.

COLIN (*looking at his watch*). Well, I'm going pretty soon. If you want a lift you better hurry.

ANDREW. The arrogance of the man. S'what comes with property and position. No, no . . . I'll probably hitch one instead. Haven't done it, I must confess, for some considerable time, and it is some distance. Nevertheless, I think – speaking, of course, entirely as an artist – the insecurity might do me good.

COLIN. Yes . . . well.

MRS SHAW. For me you can stay all day. You know that. We see so little of you . . .

ANDREW. You're very kind. And we appreciate it, don't we, lads?

No answer.

MRS SHAW. Well, I don't know. You've all got up all right . . . Next time we have one of these I'll see you don't drink as much, for one thing . . . Aren't you going to have anything, Steve?

STEVEN. No . . . I . . . This tea is fine.

MRS SHAW. Well, if that's all you're eating, then, I can start clearing this away.

ANDREW. Yes. Yes. I think that might be in order.

MRS SHAW *waits.*

STEVEN. Oh . . . Sorry, I'll give you a hand.

MRS SHAW. Thanks, love.

COLIN. Here . . . I'll take that.

ANDREW (*to* COLIN). Give 'em a good wash will you, while you're at it. You never know, the experience might come in handy. A dentist . . . (*To* SHAW.) You know, I always thought that they were men.

COLIN *and* STEVEN *clear the table into the kitchen.*

SHAW. Well, I better be getting my work things out.

MRS SHAW. Work things! What on earth's the matter? You're not going to work for . . . what? Ten hours.

SHAW. Aye . . . Well . . .

MRS SHAW. The way you're looking I think you ought to stay home another day. In bed. I've told you. Once you start, you just don't know how much you're drinking.

SHAW. Aye, well, I've played one night. I can't play
  another.
ANDREW. I think it'd be better, Dad, if you retired
  altogether.
SHAW. What?
ANDREW. My mother was saying before. It doesn't do
  anyone any good, this endless digging, digging, digging
  . . . What're you trying to dig out anyway?
SHAW. What . . . ?
COLIN (*reappearing*). Look . . .
ANDREW. No, no. I was just asking. For his own good,
  Colin, as it were.
SHAW. I'm not trying to dig out anything.
ANDREW. No, no. I mean, you'd be silly if you were,
  wouldn't you? I mean, there's nothing down there, is
  there, but lumps of bloody coal.
SHAW (*to* MRS SHAW). Look . . . I'll go up and get
  dressed.
ANDREW. You are dressed.
COLIN. It's time I was leaving . . .
MRS SHAW. What on earth . . . ?
ANDREW. The trouble is, Mother, you see . . .
SHAW. That's enough!
ANDREW. We had an argument last night. After you'd
  gone to bed. One of the usual Shaw domestic tourneys:
  nothing to get excited about. You were probably too
  replenished to hear our little contretemps, but one or two
  people here, unless I'm severely mistaken, got very worked
  up indeed.

  STEVEN *has come to stand in the door from the kitchen.*

MRS SHAW. Oh. And what was all that about?
COLIN. ⎱ You needn't . . .
SHAW. ⎰ It wasn't . . .
ANDREW. Well, you'll be very pleased to hear, Ma . . .
  (*Waits, looking round.*) . . . politics.
MRS SHAW. Well, I know he gets very worked up about
  that.
ANDREW. Oh, he does. I mean, I suppose, with all our
  years of experience, we ought to be ready for it. But no:
  stick a pig. We'll never change.

MRS SHAW. It's a good job I wasn't there . . . I'd have fallen asleep.

ANDREW. You would. You would. It's true. Nid-nod.

MRS SHAW. I would have thought, in any case, you were all on the same side. Your background, and the experience you've had . . . (*She's finishing off the table, putting the cloth away, etc.*)

ANDREW. Oh, it's true. We are. It's just that Steven, unbeknown to us, as it were, had some very unusual opinions to express . . . I mean, that caught us unprepared.

MRS SHAW (*laughs*). Oh, and what opinions were those, then, Steve?

STEVEN stands in the doorway and shakes his head.

Well, if you don't want me to know . . .

ANDREW. No, no. Come on, Steve. I mean, it's all over. We've settled, as it were, the issues out of hand . . . What opinions were they?

MRS SHAW. Nay, love. If you don't want me to hear, that's quite all right. I'm broad-minded enough, I think, for most things.

ANDREW. That's what she says.

STEVEN (*to* ANDREW). Look . . . I appreciated what you said. Last night.

As SHAW begins to intervene: 'Look . . .'

No, Dad . . . (*To* ANDREW.) But judgements, in certain situations, come very easily to hand.

ANDREW. You've got to make a decision sometime, Steve.

STEVEN. I've made my decision.

ANDREW. Decision! Steve!

STEVEN. I've *made* my decision. You, of course, can ignore it. If you like . . . But actually, I've made it.

ANDREW gazes at him for a while.

MRS SHAW stands watching them, puzzled, smiling.

ANDREW. I too, then, have a choice?

STEVEN. Yes . . .

ANDREW weighs his hand, as if he holds the handle of a sword.

ANDREW. Vengeance . . . is mine, then.

STEVEN. Yes . . .

ANDREW. Saith the Lord.

STEVEN. I don't want you doing any damage here.

ANDREW. Here?

STEVEN. I don't want you doing any harm.

ANDREW. Harm. (*Looks slowly round the room, his gaze finally coming to rest on MRS SHAW.*)

The others are rigid, silent: she still gazes at him, smiling, puzzled.

He smiles at her. Then:

Is it true . . . your father was a breeder . . .

MRS SHAW. A breeder?

ANDREW. Of livestock . . . And the like?

MRS SHAW. Well, he had a few . . .

SHAW. Look . . . Here . . .

ANDREW. I seem to remember . . . Kept in little pens.

MRS SHAW. That's right . . . (*Smiling.*)

ANDREW. Pigs . . . I remember you telling us, often. Not dirty animals at all, unless their environment was allowed to become polluted.

MRS SHAW. Yes . . . That's right.

ANDREW. Kept them very clean.

MRS SHAW. He did . . . He looked after them very well.

ANDREW. Habit.

MRS SHAW. What?

ANDREW. I say. A habit . . . cultivated by his daughter.

MRS SHAW. Well, I . . . (*Looks to the others, smiling.*)

COLIN. Look . . .

ANDREW. S'all right . . . S'all right. S'all right . . . No harm . . . no harm . . . (*To COLIN.*) Would you mind?

COLIN. What . . .

ANDREW. Warming up the engine . . .

COLIN. What . . .

STEVEN gestures at COLIN.

STEVEN. Go on then, Col . . . Go on.

MRS SHAW. Well . . . I don't know . . . I've always said we were a funny family.

COLIN, a wild look round, then goes.

ANDREW. Funny. I think we are. By any standard. A family of comedians. Clowns. Excruciating tricks. Everything, for your amusement, Ma . . .

MRS SHAW. Well, I'm not sure we're as good as that.

ANDREW. Oh, I think we are. Don't underrate us. Ask my Dad. The strongest here . . . Take all the weight. The lightest climb to the very top, and there . . . take all the praise. Acknowledgement . . . adulation . . .

MRS SHAW. Well, drink's done *him* no harm at all.

ANDREW. The harm that I was done, was done a very long time ago indeed.

MRS SHAW. He's nearly as bad as he was last night.

ANDREW. I am bad. I am . . .

STEVEN. Andy . . .

ANDREW. Do you remember when I used to cry outside that door . . . 'Let me in! Let me in!'

MRS SHAW. Oh, now . . .

ANDREW. Why wasn't it ever opened? *Why?*

STEVEN. Andy . . .

ANDREW. Why wasn't it ever opened, Steve?

STEVEN. *Andy* . . .

ANDREW (*shouts*). Why wasn't it ever opened, Steve?

ANDREW *gazes at* STEVEN. *Then he goes slowly to* MRS SHAW.

(*To* MRS SHAW.) Shall we dance?

MRS SHAW. Well, I . . . (*Laughs as he puts out his arms.*) Honestly, I don't know what we're coming to . . .

ANDREW. Salvation. I can feel it in my bones.

ANDREW *has started dancing with* MRS SHAW, *who is laughing, flushed.*

MRS BURNETT (*popping in her head*). Well, then. All up. I thought I'd have to come round and ring a bell.

MRS SHAW. You've come just at the right moment, love, I think! (*Disengaging herself.*)

MRS BURNETT. Has he been to bed? Or is he on his way?

ANDREW. We're on our way. About to take our leave. The others, as you can see, are somewhat overwhelmed. Events have caught up with them so to speak. While I . . .

well, I'm afraid that I too have been overrun.
Encapsulated. Caught well before my time . . .

MRS BURNETT. Well, I don't know . . .

MRS SHAW. Well, I don't either. It's some joke of theirs left
over from last night.

MRS BURNETT. If you want a bit of fun you know what
house to come to! (*Laughs*.)

REARDON (*appearing*). Hello. Hello. Hello. What's this?
What's this? What's this? Signs of departure. Sounds of
festivity and laughter . . . Colin warming up his aeroplane
outside . . .

SHAW. Aye. Come in, lad. Come in.

ANDREW. Just leaving. About to take our leave.

REARDON. So I see . . . So I see . . .

STEVEN. Look. I'll just pop up.

MRS SHAW. All right, love . . . I'm sorry you're going now,
so soon. (*To* MRS BURNETT.) They've all got work to
go to . . . except Andrew here, of course.

ANDREW. Always the sole exception . . . Compassion. I
can feel it in my bones.

REARDON. Men of the world. What a place they have to
go to.

MRS BURNETT. They have. They have. You're right.

REARDON. Brimful of opportunity . . . Round them on
every side . . . Wish I had my time over again, Harry.

SHAW. Aye.

REARDON. The journey to the stars! What a damn fine
future lies before them.

SHAW. Aye.

COLIN (*coming in, wiping hands on a cloth*). Well, then. All
set . . . A car like that. You'd think you'd have no
trouble . . .

SHAW. Aye.

COLIN (*sees* ANDREW). Yes. Well, then . . . If you're
ready.

ANDREW. Steven is on his way. Packing his few things
together.

COLIN. Right, then . . . Well. I'm sorry it's been so short,
Mother.

MRS SHAW. So am I, love. Maybe when you bring
your . . .

COLIN. Aye. Well. Tell them when I've gone, love.

MRS SHAW (*laughing*). Oh, all right, then . . . and maybe when *he* retires we'll be able to arrange something better.

ANDREW. Aye. Let's hope so. Keep my eye open, Dad, I shall.

MRS SHAW. Well, goodbye, love. (*Embraces* COLIN.) And I'm very pleased about you-know-what.

COLIN. Aye. Well. Goodbye, Mother . . . 'Bye, Dad. (*Shakes* SHAW's *hand*.)

SHAW. Aye. Goodbye, lad . . . And congratulations.

ANDREW. Look after them, Mr Reardon. They're very precious. Keep your eye on them, you know. (*To* MRS BURNETT.) He kept an eye on me once, you know, when I was a little lad. Never looked back since then.

REARDON. Nay, I wouldn't claim any credit for that. (*Laughs*.) I'll watch them.

ANDREW. Goodbye, then, Mother. Let's have a kiss.

They embrace.

MRS SHAW. Goodbye, love. And a bit less of that joking.

ANDREW. Aye. Aye. I promise that . . . Goodbye, Dad . . . Remember, now, when you're down that pit. Dig one out for me.

SHAW. Aye.

ANDREW *has taken his father's hand.*

ANDREW. Remember, now.

SHAW. Aye. I'll remember. (*Holds his hand a moment longer, gazing at him*.)

ANDREW. Right, then . . . Best be off.

STEVEN *has come on* . . . ANDREW *turns away and he and* COLIN *start saying goodbye to* REARDON *and* MRS BURNETT.

STEVEN. Goodbye, Mother.

MRS SHAW. Goodbye, love. And take care.

STEVEN. Aye. I will.

They embrace.

MRS SHAW. You'll remember, now?

STEVEN. Aye. I will . . . 'Bye, Dad.

SHAW. 'Bye, lad. (*Takes his hand.*)

STEVEN. Here . . . give you a kiss, an' all, shall I . . .

STEVEN *kisses his father's cheek, then embraces him.*
They're silent a moment.

ANDREW. Well, then. Off we get.

STEVEN. 'Bye, Mrs Burnett . . . Keep your eye on them.

MRS BURNETT. I will, love. Don't you fret. (*Shakes his hand.*)

STEVEN. Mr Reardon . . .

REARDON. Aye. Remember. Future of the nation in your hands . . . (*Shakes his hand.*)

STEVEN. Aye . . . I'll try.

MRS SHAW. And he's got four of his own to remind him.

They laugh.

COLIN. Right, then . . .

STEVEN. After you.

COLIN. No, no. Youngest first. Always shall be.

STEVEN. Goodbye, then . . .

SHAW. Goodbye, lad. Goodbye . . . We'll see you off.

REARDON. Aye . . .

STEVEN *goes.*

ANDREW (*to* COLIN). After you, old pal . . . First time I've seen him without a shave.

They laugh.

COLIN. Aye . . . Right.

COLIN *goes, followed by* ANDREW.

SHAW (*to* MRS SHAW). Are you coming out, love?

MRS SHAW. No, no . . . You go. I'll see them off from here.

REARDON. Come on, Mrs Burnett, we'll give them a shove. They'll need it.

SHAW. Aye . . . Come on. These city lads'll need a spot of muscle.

REARDON. Aye!

They go.

Laughter and shouts off: 'Make way! Make way! . . . Here he comes . . .'

MRS SHAW is left alone. She goes to the window, gazes out. Watches, moving back one of the curtains, slightly. She gets out a handkerchief, then wipes her eyes. Blows her nose.

Shouts from outside: she puts her handkerchief down and waves. After a while the shouting dies.

Silent. She gazes out a moment longer, then lets the curtain fall. She straightens it, turns back to the room. Abstracted, she straightens a cushion, etc.

After a moment SHAW comes back in, slow.

SHAW. Well, then . . . that's that, eh?

MRS SHAW. Yes . . .

SHAW. Did you enjoy it, love?

MRS SHAW. I did. Yes . . . And you?

SHAW. Aye . . . Aye.

MRS SHAW. They never change.

SHAW. Aye.

MRS SHAW. What was all that about, then?

SHAW. Nay, search me, love . . . Now then. Where do you want me? Here. Look. Let me give you a start. (*Goes to help her.*)

Light slowly fades.

THE MARCH ON RUSSIA

The March on Russia was first presented by the National Theatre Company in the Lyttelton auditorium of the National Theatre on 6 April 1989. The cast was as follows:

COLIN	Frank Grimes
PASMORE	Bill Owen
MRS PASMORE	Constance Chapman
WENDY	Rosemary Martin
EILEEN	Patsy Rowlands
POSTMAN	Michael Goldie

Directed by Lindsay Anderson
Designed by Jocelyn Herbert

The action of the play takes place in the Pasmores' bungalow.

Time – the present

ACT 1   Scene 1   Three a.m.
          Scene 2   Morning

ACT II   Scene 1   Evening
          Scene 2   Next morning

ACT ONE

Scene One
The Pasmores' bungalow. Three a.m.

We see the living-room and kitchen of the bungalow, linked by a passage. There are three doors leading off the passage — to Pasmore's room (bedroom 1), Mrs Pasmore's room (bedroom 2) and the bathroom. An exit leads to the front door and there are stairs leading to the dormer bedroom.

The rooms are furnished to suit the requirements of a retired working-class couple with affluent offspring, i.e. whilst retaining their own taste the contents of both interiors are in a much-used but good condition.

There is the usual furniture in the living-room together with an open fireplace and a window looking on to the street. The kitchen is furnished with units, a table (covered with a cloth), stools, an electric stove (with practical hob light and clock), fridge (switched on so it illuminates when opened), washing-machine and sink with practical tap. There is a door to the rear garden.

When the curtain rises it is dark. The coal fire has been allowed to die down, but the coals still illuminate the room. A glow from behind the drawn curtains of the window suggests a night-time illumination from a road outside.

COLIN, in pyjamas and dressing-gown, descends the stairs conscious of the silence of the house. He is middle-aged, early fifties, and stocky.

He goes into the kitchen, closing the door behind him, and switches on the hob light. He fills the kettle at the sink and plugs it in. He gets the teapot and a tea bag, putting the latter into the former and milk from the fridge.

A light goes on in bedroom 1, then goes out again. A moment later the door opens and PASMORE comes out. He is small, with a stocky figure, in his late eighties. He has preserved, however, a youthful appearance, if slow in movement. This is characterised by the formal way he does his hair, cut short and parted, with a fringe, and a figure

*which, as yet, hasn't gone to fat, despite his robust
proportions. He too is dressed in pyjamas and dressing-
gown.*

*He feels his way to the kitchen. He coughs as he moves,
clearing congestion, quietly so. He opens the kitchen door.*

PASMORE. You up?

COLIN. I hope I didn't wake you.

PASMORE. I'm often up in the night.

COLIN. Do you want a pot of tea?

PASMORE. I wouldn't mind. (*He sits on the stool by the
table.*) Keeps me going. (*He has an abstracted look, as if
he himself has been awake some time: incurious,
reflective.*) Once your mother's taken her pills it's as much
as she can do to wake in the morning. It was a great
surprise you coming. Done me and her a lot of good. (*He
coughs.*)

COLIN *sets another cup – his father's – on the table and
puts a tea bag into it.*

Are you warm enough up theer?

COLIN. All right.

PASMORE. These dormer bedrooms weren't really designed
for these bungalows. They had 'em put in later when the
houses didn't sell. (*He rises to move the curtain at the
kitchen window.*) Moors at the back, farm fields at the
front. Sea a mile off. (*He breathes in.*) Salt air. Kept me
alive. That and a good wife. It's paid its way, you buying
this house. How long has it to run on the mortgage?

COLIN. Five years. (*He makes the tea.*)

PASMORE. Better keep us voices down. (*He takes his cup.*)
What time is it? (*He goes to the kitchen door.*)

COLIN *stoops to look at the clock on the stove.*

COLIN. Three o'clock.

PASMORE. Can get world news.

COLIN. Hear it tomorrow.

PASMORE. Right. (*As he goes.*) Better put the milk back.

COLIN. Right.

PASMORE. Goes off if you leave it out.

COLIN, *having completed his own cup of tea, puts out the light over the stove, re-covers the milk and puts it back in the fridge.*

PASMORE, *entering the living-room, goes directly to the fire, stoops, coughs, picks up the poker, reignites the ashes. Colin follows, closing the door, and is about to put the light on.*

No: that 'un.

COLIN *puts on the reading-lamp.*

Good coal.

COLIN. It ought to be.

PASMORE. Aye. (*He straightens up.*)

COLIN. You've dug it long enough.

PASMORE. T'on'y collier round here, tha knows. All farmer's men. One or two schoolteachers. A dozen work at the radar station, up on Kielty Moor. Go past it in the car. Not a sign o' bloody life. Two hundred and fifty people work there, round the clock, twenty-four hours a day, three hundred and sixty-five days in the year. When it snows they sleep in bunkers. Watches Russia. (*He coughs.*) How long did it take you to drive up?

COLIN. Five hours. (*He sits.*)

PASMORE. A car like that. Do over a hundred, can't it?

COLIN. A bit.

PASMORE. I bet! (*He has taken a seat himself.*) How long are you up for?

COLIN. A couple of days.

PASMORE. We allus hope it'll be a bit longer.

COLIN. All I can manage.

PASMORE. How are your kiddies?

COLIN. Fine.

PASMORE. Kay?

COLIN. Terrific!

PASMORE *laughs.*

PASMORE. Married how long?

COLIN. Twenty-nine years.

PASMORE. Takes some beating.

COLIN. It does!

PASMORE. A good wife. Home. Children. I don't know
  what else it's all about.
COLIN. No.

Pause.

PASMORE. Put ought i' my cup she'd twig it i' the morning.
  'Have you been drinking?'! Drinking! (*He laughs.*)
COLIN. Get up once in the night or often?
PASMORE. Nay, up and down, in and out. Sometimes up
  once, then back. I rarely get to sleep afore three or four.
COLIN. You were tonight.
PASMORE. How could you tell?
COLIN. I heard you snoring.
PASMORE. Not me, old lad.
COLIN. Sounded to come from below.
PASMORE. Your mother.
COLIN. I remember that at home! (*He laughs.*)
PASMORE. Bennetts' one side, Cliftons' the other.
  Remember their dog? Gev us no sleep a night or two.
COLIN. The one next door isn't much improvement.
PASMORE. Sheepdog. Keep it penned up. *He* works at the
  radar station. Hasn't much time for a dog. (*He cocks his
  head to listen.*) Can sometimes hear one of their lads
  playing electronic music. The walls o' these houses aren't
  that thick.
COLIN. Does it keep you awake?
PASMORE. Can't grumble. Other people have bigger
  worries. What have you been doing?
COLIN. Working.
PASMORE. Ought to take a rest.
COLIN. I do from time to time.
PASMORE. I sometimes wonder if I haven't dreamt half the
  things I've done. Like living where we were afore: pit ten
  streets off, shop, pub, picture-house at the corner: I wek
  up at night and still think I can hear the dynamo, smell
  the smoke. Never late once, in forty-five years.
COLIN. Some record.
PASMORE. In the first twenty years, if I had a week off I
  had to work sixteen hours each day the week afore. It
  takes some beating.
COLIN. It does.

PASMORE. When I went back, afore we moved here. I f'und three men doing the job I'd done. Pit deputy, tha knows. (*Pause.*) I sometimes hear Bennett going down that path. He died twenty-five years ago. 'Standing around all day,' I'd tell him, 'i' front of a bloody furnace.' He wa're a steam locomotive driver, though when I first knew him he drove a hoss and cart. Worked for Bullcliff's, the farmer and coal merchant. Had bell-pits on his land. That's the time of your mother's father. He used to do his hosses. How's Kay?

COLIN. You've asked me.

PASMORE. And the children?

COLIN. Fine.

PASMORE. All earning their living.

COLIN. Just about.

PASMORE (*leaning forward, poking the fire*). Your sister Wendy's getting divorced.

COLIN. I know.

PASMORE. Your sister Eileen isn't much better. I've two daughters, both been married twenty-odd year, one wi' two kiddies, the other wi' none, and they've both gev up on their husbands.

COLIN. I thought Arnold gave up on Wendy.

PASMORE. Since she became a politician she's had no time for family life. They were going to adopt two kiddies. That went out of the window. In my day you struggled through these problems. You didn't give in after two or three year.

COLIN. They've been married over twenty.

PASMORE. We've been married fifty-nine. Sixty years tomorrow.

COLIN. Today.

PASMORE. Today!

COLIN. Here's to it! (*He toasts* PASMORE *with his cup of tea.*)

PASMORE. Watch that every night. (*He indicates the television.*) Destruction. People killing one another. Child molesting. Rape. Starvation.

COLIN. Wasn't it like that when you were young?

PASMORE. Nay, got sent to Russia. Gev a false age. Invaded the Crimea. Set off from Sebastopol. We'd

reached Rostov-on-Don when they decided we'd march
back again. I wa're in the Royal Naval Air Service.
Inducted at Gosport. Given six weeks training then taken
out, at night, in a launch, wi' another lad, into the English
Channel. Fu'st, out of nowhere, came a searchlight, then –
out of the darkness – came a voice. 'Pull alongside. Port
beam.' Ship plunging up and down. Ladder swinging from
side to side, then out and in. Waves higher than this
house. Half drowned. In the end they lowered a net.
Dumped on deck. Know the first words I heard when I
reported for duty in the Royal Navy? 'Take that man's
name fo' spitting on the deck.' Know what it wa'? A
merchant ship, with the superstructure taken off. The *Ark
Royal*. The first aircraft-carrier in the world.

COLIN. What was your job?

PASMORE. Patching planes. Made of wood and canvas. Put
your foot in the wrong place and you went clean through.
(*He laughs, coughs, then drinks his cooling tea.*) Crossed
the Bay of Biscay. Gibraltar: entered the Mediterranean.
Stopped at Taranto, at the foot of Italy, a big Italian naval
base. Cruised across the Ionian Sea to the Peloponnese.
Crossed the Aegean, past Macedonia, through the
Dardanelles, and entered the Black Sea. We anchored off
the mouth of the Danube, then we sailed to Odessa. Took
on a Russian General. Denisov. He had uniformed officers
and courtiers with him. Crying when he came aboard.
When he spoke to his wife he spoke in English. It was the
height of the Revolution. Orders came from Winston
Churchill. 'Save the Tsar!' We set off from Sebastopol.
Fighting Reds. Worst of all, starving groups of women.
Some had guns but most had pitchforks, shovels, knives
and axes. Used to come at night, in hordes. After the
food. Couldn't stop them. Kill anybody that tried. We had
marines, Gurkhas, and infantry. We fought all the way to
Rostov-on-Don. Six hundred miles. Then we fought all
the way back again. When we reached Sebastopol we
were told to ditch the aircraft – stores, spares, the lot –
and take on refugees. We filled up the holds with men,
women and children. Lots of them had jewels. One
woman with jewels round her neck, her fingers and her
toes, asked me if I'd marry her.

COLIN. Perhaps you should.

PASMORE. Nay, thy'd be a different cup of tea if I had! (*He laughs.*)

COLIN. What happened after that?

PASMORE. Took them to Constantinople. The Turkish authorities wouldn't let them ashore until they'd been deloused. Stripped 'em down: men and boys in one hold, women and girls in the other. Sprayed 'em down with hoses. Then a tender came out and took them off. After that we had to disinfect the ship, spray oursens, then, dive in off the stern, stark naked, and swim round to a ladder i' the bows. Sailed to Alexandria. We built an aerodrome at Abu Suar, out in the Egyptian desert. Played hockey. Boxed. Came home, sailing a torpedoed ship to Liverpool. I ended up in a Canadian air-force base in Lincolnshire, dismantling aeroplane engines. Then I came out. Within a year I wa' down the pit. Then I married. Had Eileen. You. Then Wendy. Forty-five years i' the coal-bin! A retirement home at the seaside. (*He coughs and reaches for the cup.*) Do you want another cup of tea?

COLIN. I'll get one.

COLIN *takes his cup and goes to the kitchen. He puts the light on over the stove and plugs in the kettle.*

A light goes on behind the second bedroom door. There is the noise of a chair being knocked inside. A few moments later MRS PASMORE *comes out. She wears a dressing-gown, and walks with a walking-stick. She is stout, but not plump, white-haired, aged 79.*

MRS PASMORE. Tom?

COLIN. It's me, Mother.

MRS PASMORE. What're you doing up at this time?

COLIN. Couldn't sleep. Dad's up as well.

In the living-room PASMORE *hastily rises, tidies the rug in front of the fire, the chair-cover and the cushion. Resumes his position.*

Do you want a cup of tea?

MRS PASMORE. If you're making one. Is it cold up there?

COLIN. It's fine. The fire's lit in the living-room. Why don't you go in and keep warm?

MRS PASMORE. Well, if you're all right. (*She goes into the living-room.*)

PASMORE. Congratulations, love. (*He rises.*)

MRS PASMORE. What's that?

PASMORE. Sixty years. (*He kisses her cheek.*)

MRS PASMORE. It's only three o'clock.

PASMORE. Just after.

MRS PASMORE. We didn't get married until midday.

PASMORE. Past midnight. Sixty years. (*Raising his voice to direct this to the kitchen.*) I don't regret a minute.

COLIN *raises his head and smiles, making tea.*

MRS PASMORE. It's a bit late if you did. (*She looks at the clock on the mantelpiece.*) This has stopped. You forgot to wind it.

PASMORE. So I did. So I did. (*To* COLIN *in the kitchen.*) A night like this. (*To* MRS PASMORE.) Must want the time to go back'ards, love. (*He pokes the fire.*)

MRS PASMORE. Put a bit of coal on, if you want it to blaze.

PASMORE. Your wish is my command. Always will be, always was.

COLIN *brings in the tea on a tray: a cup and saucer,* PASMORE's *cup, his own.*

MRS PASMORE (*to* COLIN). He's not like this when you're not here.

PASMORE. Nay, when you're not here, Colin, I'm on my knees. In adoration. Morning, noon and night. Eight hours of grovelling, eight hours of working, eight hours of sleep.

MRS PASMORE. He doesn't work at all, love. Thank you. (*She takes the cup and saucer after she sits.*)

PASMORE. I vacuum. I clean. I cut the lawn. I light the fire. I fetch the coal. I drive you to the shops.

MRS PASMORE. He makes it sound like a torment. He's in front of that television from five in the evening till twelve at night, children's programmes, the news, the lot. I don't know where to put myself at times. I get fed up of listening.

PASMORE. Watching. Watching. Women: they run this

house. When Wendy's here, or Eileen – or Wendy *and* Eileen – I go hide in a cupboard. No sooner show my head than it's fetch this, fetch that. I felt safer down the pit.

MRS PASMORE. You couldn't wait to get out.

PASMORE. Now I can't wait to get back in.

MRS PASMORE. Lies. All lies.

PASMORE. Don't worry. She can tell a tale or two.

MRS PASMORE. Should hear him over the fence to Mrs Halliday next door. She's twenty-five. You'd think *he* was twenty-seven.

PASMORE. The spirit is all that counts.

MRS PASMORE. Leaning on the fence to hold himself up: you'd think he was trying to court her.

PASMORE. She knows a good-looker when she sees one.

MRS PASMORE. You're old enough to be her father.

PASMORE. It's not age that counts, but spirit.

COLIN. You were commending the loyalty of marriage, Dad, a while ago.

PASMORE. She knows I wouldn't leave her.

MRS PASMORE (*to* COLIN). At his age, love, he wouldn't stand much chance.

PASMORE. One foot on that fence, she's off. (*He signals next door.*) She takes a joke. Her husband runs a boutique. In town. Gets his trade in summer, and scarcely ought for the rest of the year. He comes home and hangs about the house, a face as long as this. She prefers a bit of a joker.

MRS PASMORE. A joker!

PASMORE (*to* COLIN). I tell her one or two tales.

MRS PASMORE. As tall as this house. And always boasts.

PASMORE. Something to boast about, my love.

MRS PASMORE. She's heard it all. A thousand times.

COLIN. You're not quarrelling, are you?

PASMORE. This is light conversation, lad. (*He leans across and pats* MRS PASMORE'*s hand.*)

MRS PASMORE. I'm going back to bed. I only got up for a glass of water.

PASMORE. You've had a cup of tea.

MRS PASMORE. Colin made it. I wouldn't turn his offer down. Would I, love?

COLIN. You could have had water, if you'd preferred.

MRS PASMORE. I was glad to take it. (*She rises.*) I usually have a cup of water by the bed. I forgot tonight with your coming. Do you want any more blankets, love?

COLIN. I'm fine.

MRS PASMORE. You'll find them in that cupboard. In the little back room. It's the only time we use upstairs when you, or Wendy or Eileen come.

PASMORE. Didn't you take your pills?

MRS PASMORE. I did.

PASMORE (*to* COLIN). For arthritis. They make her sleep as well.

MRS PASMORE. It was the cup of water. (*To* COLIN.) I usually wake up, take a sip, and drop straight off. I won't stay longer.

COLIN. Good night, then, Mother.

MRS PASMORE. Good night, then, love.

COLIN. And congratulations.

MRS PASMORE. Oh, thank you, love. (*She nods to* PASMORE.)

MRS PASMORE *goes to her bedroom. The door closes behind her and the chair is knocked again with the walking-stick.*

PASMORE. Been through one or two hard times.

COLIN. You have.

PASMORE. Stuck together.

COLIN. That's right.

PASMORE. Thick and thin. Her thick, me thin. (*He laughs, picks up his tea and drinks.*) Be getting back myself. Stay down, if you want. There are one or two books to read. Adventure stories. Anything you want?

COLIN. No thanks.

PASMORE. Grand having you home.

COLIN. Good being back.

PASMORE. See you in the morning.

COLIN. Good night, Dad.

PASMORE. Good night, lad.

PASMORE *goes into the passage taking the cup with him. He coughs slightly and opens his bedroom door. He switches the light on.*

PASMORE *enters the bedroom and closes the door. There is a further cough from the other side.*

The light goes off in MRS PASMORE's *room. After a moment the light in* PASMORE's *room goes off too.*

COLIN *turns to the fire. He lies back in the chair, watching the fire. He draws his dressing-gown further round him. He drinks tea, then puts the cup down. He lies back, his eyes fixed on the fire.*

The lights fade to a blackout.

Scene Two
The same. Morning.

Light shines through the windows. The sound of the radio from the kitchen. The back door opens.

PASMORE *comes in with a bucket of coal. He wears trousers, a shirt, a pullover and slippers.*

He comes into the living-room and puts the bucket by the fire. He pokes the fire, and straightens up.

MRS PASMORE *comes out of her bedroom, wearing a dress and cardigan, and carrying her walking-stick.*

MRS PASMORE. Colin up?
PASMORE. Sleeps theer all day, tha knows.
MRS PASMORE. I don't think so. Not like some.
PASMORE. I only slept in after I gev up work. (*He indicates the fire.*) Stayed in. Bit o' coal on.
MRS PASMORE. We ought to order another ton. It's running out in the bunker.
PASMORE. I'll do it. Leave it to me.
MRS PASMORE. If I left anything to you it would never be done. Have you had any breakfast?
PASMORE. What I want.
MRS PASMORE. I only want a piece of toast. (*She goes into the kitchen.*)
PASMORE. The kettle's boiled. (*He picks up his cup of tea which is standing, hot, on the mantelpiece.*) The piece of toast is already cooked.

MRS PASMORE. How did you know I'd want one? (*She turns the radio off.*)

PASMORE. Toast is usually on the menu. This morning, I assume, no different from any other.

MRS PASMORE. It's hot.

PASMORE. I've just done it. I was going to bring it in, until I heard you moving about. Breakfast in bed.

MRS PASMORE. I never have breakfast in bed. (*She butters the toast.*)

PASMORE. Today, I thought, is special.

MRS PASMORE. Oh, today.

PASMORE (*calling through*). Many happy anniversaries, love.

MRS PASMORE. Thank you.

PASMORE (*to himself*). She doesn't give a damn. Yes, she does. No, she doesn't. Trying not to show it. (*He pokes the fire again and sits.*)

MRS PASMORE (*coming into the living-room*). Thank you, love. That was very much appreciated. And thank you for sixty years of a very happily married life.

PASMORE. Been one or two ups and downs.

MRS PASMORE. No more than most, and fewer than some. (*She kisses him, stooping to his chair.*) Thank you, love.

PASMORE *is clearly moved.*

Colin here as well.

PASMORE. That's right.

MRS PASMORE. Make a day of it.

PASMORE. We can. (*He weeps, without covering, however, or lowering his head.*)

MRS PASMORE. I'll just go get my breakfast. (*She returns to the kitchen, puts the piece of toast on a plate and pours a cup of tea from the pot.*)

PASMORE *sits by the fire, gazing at it.* MRS PASMORE *sits composedly in the kitchen, her air—and look—one of abstraction, as she eats her toast, about which she is fastidious; but not overly so.*

What were you talking about last night?

PASMORE. Sebastopol.

MRS PASMORE. You were never there. (*She eats.*)

PASMORE. Where do you think I got my wound?

MRS PASMORE. I thought it was Constantinople.

PASMORE. I was climbing over the wall when the eunuch got me with his sword. (*He bares a leg above his sock to examine the scar.*) Would you believe it, after all these years.

MRS PASMORE. You shouldn't have been there.

PASMORE. We took the wrong turning. This naval chap told us where to go. Said it was a club.

MRS PASMORE. I suppose it was.

PASMORE. His sword wa' like a razor. I've never jumped higher either afore or since.

MRS PASMORE. What's that got to do with Sebastopol?

PASMORE. I was in the Crimea before Constantinople.

MRS PASMORE. Of course you were.

PASMORE. You get dozier every minute.

MRS PASMORE. So do you.

PASMORE. I've some excuse.

MRS PASMORE. What excuse? And how can you hold a conversation when you're sitting in the other room?

PASMORE. I'm not holding a conversation. I'm sitting here and supping tea.

MRS PASMORE. You're talking to me.

PASMORE. I was answering a question. Do you want me to get up every time you talk?

MRS PASMORE. Why have you some excuse?

PASMORE. To do what?

MRS PASMORE. *To get dozier.*

PASMORE. I've lost half me lungs with pneumoconiosis. I've no circulation, and me heart's a quarter of the strength it should be.

MRS PASMORE. Who told you that?

PASMORE. The doctor.

MRS PASMORE. He never told me.

PASMORE. It wasn't you he was examining.

MRS PASMORE. He usually tells me when you go to see him.

PASMORE. This is the Pensions Board. When I asked for compensation.

MRS PASMORE. Oh, then.

PASMORE. If it wa're a quarter fifteen year ago it must be nearer a sixteenth by now.

MRS PASMORE. I've told you to watch it when you're carrying coal.

PASMORE. I do watch it. God damn it.

MRS PASMORE. You'll be waking Colin, shouting through.

PASMORE *slams the arm of his chair, but doesn't answer. He lifts his cup of tea to drink but doesn't bother; he puts it back down.*

What did you tell him about Sebastopol?

PASMORE. I told him we'd marched to Rostov-on-Don.

MRS PASMORE. I thought you went to save the Tsar.

PASMORE. The Tsar was shot. (*Pause.*) I told him how we'd marched all the way back again.

MRS PASMORE. To Sebastopol.

PASMORE. Fighting women.

MRS PASMORE. Women?

PASMORE. Every step.

MRS PASMORE. Why women?

PASMORE. Because they're all smiling and cooing and covering it up, but hell's own bloody demons underneath.

MRS PASMORE. There's no need to swear.

PASMORE. I wasn't swearing.

MRS PASMORE. I distinctly heard you swear. On Sunday morning.

PASMORE. It isn't Sunday morning.

MRS PASMORE. What is it?

PASMORE. God knows. (*He picks up the paper and tries to read without his glasses; he can't, so he puts it down.*) It's not Sunday.

MRS PASMORE. Every day is alike up here.

PASMORE. Except Sunday.

MRS PASMORE *finishes her breakfast and dusts her hands of toast.*

MRS PASMORE. What's so different then?

PASMORE. No milkman.

MRS PASMORE. I never hear him, in any case. (*She clears*

up, briefly, before bringing a fresh cup of tea through.
Calling.) Do you want another pot?

PASMORE. No, thank you.

MRS PASMORE. I can bring you one.

PASMORE. I said no thanks.

MRS PASMORE. If that's what you want.

PASMORE (*to himself*). If I didn't want one I should have
said I did.

MRS PASMORE (*entering*). What's that?

PASMORE. I said it's cold.

MRS PASMORE. It shouldn't be with that fire. (*She sits,
after setting the cup on the coffee-table.*) I thought Colin
might be.

PASMORE. I don't think he will.

MRS PASMORE. I think he might. (*She gets up, with great
difficulty, and moves her chair fractionally to a better
position. She adjusts the coffee-table, and sits again.*)
Well, then . . . (*She sips the tea; puts it down. Pause.*)
Have you heard the news?

PASMORE. You turned it off.

MRS PASMORE. I turned it off because no one was
listening.

PASMORE. I was listening.

MRS PASMORE. I didn't see you.

PASMORE. You don't have to see in order to listen.

MRS PASMORE. Don't you. (*Complacently, she sips tea.*)

PASMORE. Listened to it for long enough.

MRS PASMORE. We have.

PASMORE. How many years?

MRS PASMORE. Too many.

PASMORE. I thought you welcomed every year.

MRS PASMORE. I was married.

PASMORE. You are married.

MRS PASMORE. To you.

PASMORE. I know you're married to me.

MRS PASMORE. Oh, what's the use? Born stupid, stay
stupid.

PASMORE. You're referring to the chap next door.

MRS PASMORE. I'm referring to you. (*She picks up the
newspaper.*)

PASMORE. That's yesterday's paper.

MRS PASMORE. As a matter of fact (*She examines the top of the page.*) it's the day before's.

PASMORE. If you hadn't have turned off the radio we'd have heard today's.

MRS PASMORE. You'll hear it again this evening.

PASMORE. Might not be here this evening.

MRS PASMORE. Going somewhere, are you?

PASMORE. Might not be here. Full stop.

MRS PASMORE. You've been threatening to die for twenty-five years.

PASMORE. So have you.

MRS PASMORE. I had a hysterectomy.

PASMORE. I had pneumoconiosis. (*He coughs.*) Gets no better. Your condition gets no worse.

MRS PASMORE. I have other ailments.

PASMORE. Such as?

MRS PASMORE. Never you mind. (*She reads with no great attention, the newspaper raised above the level of her eyes.*)

PASMORE. Might be something contagious. If it is, I ought to know.

MRS PASMORE. If it's infectious.

PASMORE. Is it infectious? You never said.

MRS PASMORE. I said if it's infectious you ought to know. Since it isn't you can set your mind at rest.

PASMORE. What is it?

MRS PASMORE. You know well enough.

PASMORE. If I know well enough would I trouble to ask?

MRS PASMORE. Pity people who retire couldn't stay in work. (*She is absorbed in the newspaper.*)

PASMORE. I couldn't do a day's work to save my life.

MRS PASMORE. Don't I know.

PASMORE. You've nothing to complain of. No, she hasn't. Not a thing. I worked long enough to keep her going. Yes, I did.

MRS PASMORE. I'm appreciative of it. Don't you worry. You don't have to fret.

PASMORE. Might show it, in that case, from time to time.

MRS PASMORE. I do show it.

The back door opens. WENDY *comes in. She is slightly built, an attractive woman, in her mid-forties, well-preserved and well-dressed. She carries a bunch of flowers.*

MRS PASMORE *puts the paper down and half-turns, after listening.*

That's not Colin? (*She half-rises.*) He must have gone out. (*She gets up.*)

PASMORE. I'd have heard him if he had.

MRS PASMORE (*calling*). Colin?

WENDY *quietly closes the back door, aware of their voices.*

Did you leave the door unfastened?

PASMORE. I fetched a bucket of coal this morning. (*He rises and goes to the living-room door as* WENDY *takes off her coat.*) Colin?

They meet in the kitchen.

WENDY. Hello, Father.

PASMORE. Good God.

WENDY (*kissing him*). Happy anniversary, love! (*She hands him the flowers.*)

PASMORE. What are you doing here?

WENDY. I've come to see you!

PASMORE. Better give these to your mother.

MRS PASMORE (*crossing the room*). Wendy, love!

WENDY (*entering*). Happy anniversary, Mother.

MRS PASMORE. Thank you. Thank you, love. (*She takes the flowers.*)

WENDY *embraces her.*

WENDY. How are you?

MRS PASMORE. I'm well. What a surprise. Colin yesterday. Now this.

PASMORE *comes into the room.*

WENDY. What a welcome! (*She indicates* PASMORE.)
'What are you doing here?'
PASMORE. The shock. The shock.
WENDY. Give us a kiss!

She embraces PASMORE, *who kisses her cheek.*
Immediately, on being released, PASMORE *coughs.*

Choking to death, then, are you?
PASMORE. I'm off cigarettes. No more smoking for me.
WENDY. Better put these in water. (*She takes the flowers*
from MRS PASMORE.) Is there a vase in the kitchen?
(*She goes to the kitchen.*)
MRS PASMORE. In the cupboard, love.
PASMORE. Cupboard love. (*He indicates the newspaper.*)
MRS PASMORE. Eight letters. 'Stored affection.' (*She picks*
up the newspaper, which is folded back to the crossword.)
Cupboard. (*She puts down the paper and looks round for*
a pencil.)
PASMORE (*calling*). Are you staying?
WENDY. Of course I'm staying.
PASMORE. I wondered.
WENDY. Wonder no more. (*She gets a vase from the*
kitchen cupboard.)
PASMORE. Do you want a cup of tea?
WENDY. You both sit down. I'll do it. (*Having got the*
vase, she arranges the flowers in it, then makes herself a
cup of tea.)
MRS PASMORE. C.U.P.B. . . .
PASMORE. O.R.
MRS PASMORE (*writing, then*). It's not B.O.R.
PASMORE. B.O.R.E.
MRS PASMORE. It's B.O.A.R.D.
PASMORE (*calling through*). How do you spell cupboard?
WENDY. C.U.P. . . .
MRS PASMORE (*calling through*). B.O.A.R.D.
WENDY. Correct.
MRS PASMORE. Eight letters.
PASMORE. I'm ignorant. (*He sits back down.*) I'm only
good for shifting muck.
MRS PASMORE. You are. (*She prints letters in the paper.*)
Where it has P it should have W.

PASMORE. You've got it wrong.

MRS PASMORE. It's you who said cupboard.

PASMORE. I said cupboard love.

MRS PASMORE. The third letter should be W.

PASMORE. Cowboard.

MRS PASMORE. You see. I've got it wrong. Following your instructions.

PASMORE (*calling*). Have you driven over, Wendy?

WENDY. Two hours.

PASMORE. Shouldn't take as long as that.

WENDY. Rush-hour coming through the towns.

PASMORE. Do you want a hand?

WENDY. Sit yourself down.

PASMORE. Cowboard.

MRS PASMORE (*putting paper and pencil down*). When I met you, you were ridiculous. You're still ridiculous now.

WENDY *enters with the flowers.*

(*To* WENDY.) There! They look lovely, love.

PASMORE. Grand!

MRS PASMORE. Beautiful.

WENDY (*setting the vase down*). Sure you don't want another cup?

PASMORE. No, thank you.

MRS PASMORE. It was me she was asking.

PASMORE. Me an' all.

WENDY. Both of you shut up! (*She goes to the kitchen.*) I'll throw the teapot over you.

MRS PASMORE. You've upset her.

PASMORE. It's you's upset her.

MRS PASMORE. It was you.

PASMORE. I said nowt.

MRS PASMORE. It's you that keeps interfering.

PASMORE. I offered you a clue.

MRS PASMORE. Shut up!

Pause.

WENDY *comes in with her tea. She looks at both of them, chooses a chair and sits.*

Pause.

WENDY. That's Colin's car outside.

PASMORE. He came last night.

WENDY. Why didn't you tell me?

PASMORE. You never asked.

MRS PASMORE. I mentioned it, Wendy. In the rush you never heard.

PASMORE. You get your temper from her, tha knows.

WENDY. I get it from both of you, if the truth were known.

PASMORE. I'm as good as gold. I've nowt to complain at. It's she who's allus on a high horse.

MRS PASMORE. High horse!

PASMORE. Low horse, then.

MRS PASMORE (to WENDY). Isn't he ridiculous?

WENDY. I've driven seventy miles and all you do is bicker.

MRS PASMORE. I'm not bickering: it's him.

PASMORE. It's her.

MRS PASMORE. It's him . . .

Pause.

WENDY. There we are, then. (*She sips her tea.*)

PASMORE. Would you like a biscuit?

WENDY. No thank you, Dad. Do you want one, Mother?

MRS PASMORE. No thank you, love.

WENDY. Still in bed? (*She gestures.*) Colin.

MRS PASMORE. He was down here half the night.

PASMORE. Closer to a quarter.

MRS PASMORE. I'd say half . . .

WENDY. How's Kay and the children?

Pause.

MRS PASMORE. They're fine.

PASMORE. They're grand.

MRS PASMORE. How's Arnold?

WENDY. I haven't seen him for the past two months.

PASMORE. You're not divorced already?

WENDY. Not quite.

PASMORE. I don't know why you bother.

WENDY. Why not?

PASMORE. Nay, you've lived with him for twenty-odd year: if you didn't know what he wa' like till now you mustn't have had your head screwed on. (*To* MRS

PASMORE.) It's ever since she started with all these
bloody politics.

WENDY. What politics?

PASMORE. Labour Party. God Christ. A set o' Mary Ellens.

WENDY. I'm not with the Party any more.

PASMORE. What are you?

WENDY. I'm Independent.

PASMORE. You can bloody well say that again.

MRS PASMORE. Have you gone Independent, love?

WENDY. Don't make it sound like an infectious disease.

PASMORE. Contagious. We have that in this house.

A bang overhead.

Colin.

MRS PASMORE. I'm not surprised. The noise you make.

PASMORE. It's thy daughter does the shouting.

MRS PASMORE. It's your daughter as well.

PASMORE. Nay, the milkman wa' round a lot the year that
she wa' born. And the postman. Not to mention the
rentman. 'Rent and rates!' he'd call at the door, coming
in, tha knows, wi'out knocking.

MRS PASMORE. What a thing to say to your daughter!

PASMORE. You can say ought you like to her. Can't you,
love? She's a politician. You're not crying, are you?

WENDY. I'm blowing my nose.

MRS PASMORE. You were always harder on the girls than
you were on Colin.

WENDY. He was harder on Colin, I always thought.

PASMORE. Theer, then. I wa're hard on no one.

Pause.

WENDY *blows her nose and puts her handkerchief away.*

WENDY. Sixty years!

PASMORE. Sixty years o' penal servitude. (*He looks into
the cup and drinks.*)

MRS PASMORE. He's showing off to his daughter.

PASMORE. I'm not showing off.

MRS PASMORE. You are.

PASMORE. I'm not.

MRS PASMORE. I say you are.

Pause.

PASMORE. I said . . . (*Pause.*) If she's been married all these years – in sickness and in health – she might have hung on a little longer.

WENDY. I have hung on a little longer.

PASMORE. A little longer still.

WENDY. Until I die!

PASMORE. We're hanging on until we die.

MRS PASMORE. We're not hanging on at all.

PASMORE. We're not hanging on at all.

MRS PASMORE. That's right.

PASMORE. We accepted each other for what we are.

MRS PASMORE. We did.

PASMORE. I'm not sure what that is. But whatever it was – I accepted it.

MRS PASMORE. You're like two peas in a pod.

WENDY. Me and Arnold?

MRS PASMORE. You and your father.

PASMORE. I allus thought she wa' more like you. *Colin*, I thought, is more like me. Quiet and thoughtful.

WENDY *laughs.*

MRS PASMORE. I'm saying nothing.

PASMORE (*to* WENDY). Saint Hilda. (*He indicates* MRS PASMORE.)

WENDY *laughs again. She drinks her tea, looks round, puts the cup down.*

MRS PASMORE. Why should she make the rest of her life a misery if, by getting divorced, she can improve it?

PASMORE. She wept buckets when she first found out. 'Wendy,' she said. 'And *Arnold*.' You should have seen her.

MRS PASMORE. In principle I'm against it. In practice, though, I'm not.

PASMORE. She'll be asking me to divorce her next.

MRS PASMORE. It's not too late.

PASMORE. After sixty years.

MRS PASMORE. It's not too long.

PASMORE (*to* WENDY). In addition to which you were married in church.

WENDY. What's that got to do with it?

PASMORE. Your vows. Made before God. When you get
   up there you'll have a lot of bloody explaining to do.
WENDY. I got married in church because of you.
PASMORE. Me?
WENDY. And my mother.
MRS PASMORE. *Me?*
WENDY. And Arnold.
PASMORE. He'd never been inside a church.
WENDY. You said it didn't matter.
PASMORE. Nay, I've said enough. Here's Colin.

COLIN *comes down the stairs. He is dressed in trousers, a
pullover and an open-necked shirt.*

WENDY *rises.*

COLIN *goes to the kitchen with the cup he's brought
down. He rinses it out. He puts the kettle on. He sees
WENDY's coat flung over the stool, picks it up, puts it
down, and goes through to the living-room, opening the
door.*

COLIN. Wendy!
WENDY. Our kid! (*She embraces him.*)
COLIN. It's good to see you.
WENDY (*holding him at arm's length*). London not doing
   you much harm.
COLIN. It's had long enough to try.
WENDY. How's the family?
COLIN. Not bad. How's yours?
WENDY. Divorced. Or will be in a couple of months.
COLIN. Glad about it?
WENDY. Not half!
PASMORE. Don't mind us. We're not here. (*To* COLIN.)
   Do you want a pot of tea?
COLIN. I've put it on.
PASMORE. I'll mek it. Story of my life. Do this. Do that.
   Do t'other.
MRS PASMORE. It's a wonder he does anything at all, the
   advertising that goes on before he starts.
PASMORE (*to* COLIN). Sit down. It's done. (*He goes to the
   kitchen, leaving the door open.*)
COLIN. You should have said you were coming.

WENDY. I didn't know until I'd left.

COLIN. How're you going to make a living without your husband?

PASMORE (*calling*). She's got a job. She'll earn more inside six months in attendance money as a local councillor than you can earn in over a year.

WENDY. That's why I'm getting divorced. Give more time to the job.

PASMORE (*calling through*). She's gone Independent.

WENDY. I *am* independent. I haven't gone.

MRS PASMORE. That's always been her motto.

PASMORE (*calling*). Husband a company director; wife a working-class representative. It always did look bloody silly.

WENDY. 'It's either the Party or your husband,' they said. I decided to give up both.

PASMORE (*calling*). Your sister's sold out. Sold out on *us*. I wa' down the pit for forty-five years.

WENDY (*calling back*). You voted Conservative at the last election.

PASMORE (*calling*). I did not. (*He comes to the room door.*) Your mother voted Conservative.

MRS PASMORE. I wanted someone in charge who knew what they were doing. After fifty years of waffling I wanted to see someone in charge who believed in what they said, said it without equivocation, and went and did it. What's the word? (*She picks up the newspaper.*)

PASMORE. Nine across. Four letters.

MRS PASMORE (*finds it*). *Cant*! Sixty years as a collier's wife. It sums it up exactly.

WENDY. Stabbed in the back by my mother.

PASMORE. They're all Conservative round here. Boarding-house owners, shopkeepers. Farmers. Businesses. You couldn't raise a Labour vote round here if you looked from now till Christmas.

MRS PASMORE. Socialism's worn out. We voted for it, in power and out, for fifty-five years. Where's it got us? It isn't socialism that gives you better conditions. It's whether the country wants to work or not. Like Germany. Or France. Or Japan. They've leapt ahead and we, with labour disputes and demarcations – politicised trade

unions: I've heard it from him (*She indicates* PASMORE.)
– are one of the poorest industrialised countries in
Europe.

PASMORE. Ay up! Kettle! (*He goes.*)

WENDY. I never knew you were so militant, love.

MRS PASMORE. It makes you sick. Night after night.
Watching that. (*She indicates the television.*) *Asking* for
jobs. 'If I haven't got a job someone's got to give me one!'
There's never been such a gutless generation.

WENDY. An evangelist! My God.

MRS PASMORE. I won't have His name profaned. Not in
this house. You can profane God's name outside, but not
in here.

WENDY. You can see what affluence has done for them.

COLIN. Nay, don't blame me.

MRS PASMORE. Colin has done very well. He didn't sit on
his bottom and say, 'I want! I want!' He got up and
created . . . what did you create? My mind's confused at
the moment.

WENDY. *The Last Evangelist*, Mother.

MRS PASMORE. He wrote a book called *The Last
Evangelist*, the money from which he sensibly invested.

WENDY. Buying, amongst other things, a bungalow for
you.

MRS PASMORE. Taking the burden off the community.

WENDY. We could do with you on our Council, Mother.

MRS PASMORE. Don't worry. Your father and I have lived
through harder times than this. (*She indicates the
television.*) It makes me weep to see well-fed, well-clad
people, with subsidised housing and a National Health,
with state benefits and pensions, complaining they've
never had a chance. If their muscles were exercised as
much as their mouths they'd have created ten thousand
jobs apiece.

PASMORE (*coming in with* COLIN's *tea and a cup of his
own.*) Five across. Six letters.

MRS PASMORE. It's seven letters as a matter of fact. (*She
consults the newspaper again.*)

PASMORE. 'Needless complaining.'

MRS PASMORE. *Whining*.

PASMORE. She gets all the words from that.

MRS PASMORE. Not quite.

PASMORE. And all her ideas from the television. I'm ashamed to go out with her at times. A well-known socialist all my life and she'd make Mussolini look like the local vicar.

MRS PASMORE. How many union meetings have you come home from saying unions and politics shouldn't mix: the one holds back the other?

PASMORE. I said the other holds back the one. (*He laughs, sitting down.*)

MRS PASMORE. 'Workers, shirkers': that's what people are chanting now. It makes me ashamed to have been one.

PASMORE. You never were.

MRS PASMORE. I brought up three children! On wages that would be a pittance to the unemployed today. I hadn't a halfpenny in the house from Tuesday night till Friday lunch-time. No gas when we ran out of pennies. Pennies! Nowadays, if the gas is cut off they get a grant to put it back on.

WENDY. What did she have for supper, love?

PASMORE. Nay, all I do is bloody work. She has the ideas. A woman's world. It allus was.

MRS PASMORE. That's right.

PASMORE. Work down a coalmine, eight hours a day – day or night, as near as not – while she's up top, having ideas.

MRS PASMORE. If someone came complaining to me about what they can get for sitting on their bottom I'd give them a kick right up it. 'I haven't had this. I haven't had that.' I'd show them what they could have. There'd be no unemployment by the time I'd finished.

WENDY. No wonder she voted Tory.

MRS PASMORE. I voted for common sense.

WENDY. What're you doing for lunch?

PASMORE. Lunch?

WENDY. We'll take you out. (*She indicates* COLIN.) Have a spin along the front.

MRS PASMORE. I ought to choose some clothes. I'm not sure I've anything to go out in.

PASMORE. She's tons of clothes in theer.

MRS PASMORE. I've one wardrobe. One cupboard. One set of drawers.

PASMORE. I've two pair of trousers. Two jackets. One suit. Two pairs of shoes.

MRS PASMORE. By choice. (*She looks at him.*)

PASMORE. Her choice. (*He sees her look.*) Nay, I can only wear one pair of trousers and one jacket at a time. If one of them conks out I only need one other.

WENDY. We can go for a drive in the country, come back over the moors and have lunch at that hotel.

PASMORE. The Waldorf.

WENDY. The Waldorf! What do you think, our kid?

COLIN. Fine.

MRS PASMORE (*getting up; to* WENDY). I'm pleased you've come over, love. I want to find something special. (*She moves to her room.*)

PASMORE. I'd better look, an' all. I'll look at one shoe, then I'll look at the other. I'll look at the one coat, then I'll look at its mate. I'll look at one pair of trousers . . .

MRS PASMORE *disappears into her room, closing the door.*

PASMORE *looks from* COLIN *to* WENDY *and back again.*

I shan't be a minute. (*He winks from the door. He goes to his room and closes the door.*)

Pause.

WENDY (*sitting companionably beside* COLIN). What you been up to?

COLIN. A history of New York.

WENDY. New York!

COLIN. Purely as a hobby. I went there with the book. In a curious way it seemed like home.

WENDY. Home.

COLIN. The same provincial squalor. The same curious lack of guile. I've never met such an open-hearted people. Everything there is tenuous, despite its air of permanence and size . . . otherwise I'm back at college.

WENDY. Charles the Second.

COLIN. Right.

WENDY. 'The thought of England surges up before me. I

am recalling what is for me the most important historical period of all, the reign of the Puritans and Oliver Cromwell.'

COLIN. Freud, in a letter to his wife, on his coming to exile in England.

WENDY. I began to think it was you, you quoted it so often, Colin.

COLIN. Aye! (*He laughs.*) I haven't changed, our kid.

WENDY. Still out to impress.

COLIN. That's right.

WENDY. What drew you to The Evangelist?

COLIN. You're right. Not my period at all.

WENDY. 1808 to 1847.

COLIN. Remember the dates?

WENDY. I read the book!

COLIN. One summer vacation I was home from college, I was reading in the local library and came across *The Prophecies of Jonathan Wroe*. There I was, sitting at the edge of our parents' housing estate which stretched across a one-time moor where, one hundred and twenty years before, an impoverished youth, who worked in a local mill, had visions, or so he said, of heaven and hell. I looked up newspapers of that time and came across accounts of his last crusade: blowing up bridges, setting fire to mills, derailing trains – battles in the Pennine hills, with the local militia then with troops sent up from London. It came alive in a way that no other period ever could. It seemed remarkable that a product of the Industrial Revolution could see the consequences so far ahead, the despoilation, the conformity, the dilution of feeling – the de-spiritualisation, as our mother, if she ever found it in her crossword, might describe it – which have turned us into the people we are today.

WENDY. I never understood why he gave himself up.

COLIN. His father died when he was twelve. He became the sole provider for a family of seven. Was he, he asked himself, his mother's son, or was he his mother's husband? At the height of his campaign his mother was arrested. On the authorities' promise to release her he gave himself up. One day, in the City Museum, I came across a print: it showed a barrack-like square, the anonymous windows of a plain stone building, a line of red-clad soldiers, a scaffold, and two trussed figures: to add significance to their execution, they were hanged successively, the mother before the son, a few feet apart, and face to face. A short while later I stepped out into a cobbled yard not unlike the one in the print itself and decided that day to write the book.

Pause.

PASMORE *emerges from his bedroom carrying a dark suit on a hanger. He carries it down the passage to the back door.*

PASMORE (*as he passes* MRS PASMORE's *door*).
Mothballs.

MRS PASMORE's *door immediately opens.*

MRS PASMORE (*calling*). He's kept it in that cupboard so long it must be smelling musty.
PASMORE (*at the back door*). I've had no need to put it on. (*He exits, closing the back door behind him.*)
MRS PASMORE. We used to have mothballs. That was years ago. I shan't be a minute.
WENDY. You're not changing already?
MRS PASMORE. Not yet. (*She closes the door.*)
WENDY. Cant!
COLIN. *Cant!*

They laugh.

There is a tapping on the front door. WENDY *rises.*

WENDY (*calling*). I'll get it.
COLIN. You sit down. (*He goes out to the passage. He disappears towards the front door.*)

WENDY, *having risen, glances about the room. There is the sound of bolts being drawn, a key turned, a chain released.*

WENDY *picks up* MRS PASMORE's *folded newspaper.*

WENDY (*reading*). 'Needless complaining.'
COLIN (*off*). Eileen!
EILEEN (*off*). What on earth are you doing here?
COLIN (*off*). Come in!
EILEEN (*off*). I am in.

> EILEEN *appears in the passageway. She is well-built, middle fifties in appearance, though older. Robust; modestly dressed in a heavy coat and scarf.*

(*Off.*) How long have you been up?
COLIN (*off*). I came last night.
EILEEN (*at the room door*). I don't believe it!
WENDY. Great minds!
EILEEN. *Great minds.*

> WENDY *and* EILEEN *embrace.*

> PASMORE *enters the kitchen.*

When did you get here?
WENDY. An hour ago.
EILEEN. Must have passed me on the road. There's something the matter with the engine. (*She draws off her gloves.*)
WENDY. Engine?
EILEEN. The car's that slow.
WENDY. We could have come together.
EILEEN. Ridiculous. Both live in the same town. Last time I mentioned it you said you wouldn't be able.
WENDY. I found I could.

> COLIN *takes* EILEEN's *coat.*

EILEEN. And Colin. (*To* COLIN.) Thank you, love.
WENDY. Jack come with you?
EILEEN. Teaching.

> PASMORE, *having delayed himself at the sound of her voice, putting the kettle on in the kitchen, appears at the living-room door.*

PASMORE. It's you.
EILEEN. How are you, Father? (*She embraces* PASMORE.)
PASMORE. All right. (*He receives* EILEEN's *embrace.*)

EILEEN. Sulking, are you?

PASMORE. Suit's on the clothes-line. Full o' mothballs.

WENDY. It's not.

PASMORE. It's full o' summat.

WENDY. It's full of not being used.

EILEEN. Congratulations. (*She kisses his cheek.*)

PASMORE. What on?

EILEEN. We're not going to have to chase you with a stick? That's what he used to do with us. You are going to cheer up, Father.

PASMORE. I am cheered up.

WENDY. He was as bright as a penny until you arrived.

PASMORE. I should have had warning. My constitution's not used to all this noise.

MRS PASMORE *comes out of her room, having changed.*

MRS PASMORE. Is that our Eileen?

EILEEN. It is, Mother!

MRS PASMORE (*entering the living-room*). How are you, love?

EILEEN. Lovely to see you.

EILEEN *and* MRS PASMORE *embrace warmly.*

PASMORE. I thought we weren't going for another two hours. My suit's on the clothes-line. It'll be hours afore I'm ready.

MRS PASMORE. We can go whenever you like. (*To* EILEEN.) I thought I'd change. I'm so fed up of the same old clothes.

EILEEN. Congratulations, love. (*She embraces her mother again.*)

PASMORE. Keep your voice down.

MRS PASMORE. Whatever for?

PASMORE. Round here it's considered unnatural to be wed for more'n a year. Nob'dy'll bloody believe it.

A bang at the front door.

What did I tell you?

COLIN. I'll get it. (*He goes to the front door.*)

PASMORE. It can't be another. We only had three kiddies.

MRS PASMORE (*to* EILEEN). Do you want a cup of tea?

EILEEN. I'd love one.

PASMORE (*going*). I'll get it. The kettle's on. (*He goes to the kitchen.*)

EILEEN. Anybody'd think he wasn't glad to see you.

MRS PASMORE. That's the way he shows it, love. (*She raises her voice.*) That's the way he covers it up.

PASMORE (*calling*). In this house there's bloody well nowt to cover.

MRS PASMORE. And don't swear.

PASMORE (*calling*). I'm not swearing.

MRS PASMORE. I say you are.

PASMORE (*calling*). I'm expressing an opinion. (*He makes tea in the kitchen.*)

COLIN (*entering*). Post. (*He hands some envelopes to MRS PASMORE.*)

WENDY. Two telegrams.

MRS PASMORE (*calling*). Tommy!

PASMORE (*calling*). I can't mek it any faster. God damn and blast.

WENDY. Come and read your post.

WENDY *ushers* PASMORE *into the room as she goes out to the kitchen.*

PASMORE. What post?

WENDY. Come and read it.

PASMORE. Thy husband not with you?

EILEEN. Jack's in school, Dad. He sends you both his love.

PASMORE. Where is it? (*He looks round.*)

EILEEN. Give us a hug. (*She hugs him, bear-like, to her.*)

PASMORE. She's going to crush me to bloody death. How Jack's put up with it all these years I can't mek out. No wonder he's the size he is.

EILEEN. He's very well.

PASMORE. He's very thin.

EILEEN. He's very slender.

PASMORE. He doesn't weigh more than two or three pounds.

EILEEN. I'll give you a thick ear, if you don't watch out.

MRS PASMORE. Give over bickering and look at this.

(*Having opened the first envelope, she has removed a*

*card, read its message with great care, and now hands it
to* PASMORE.)

PASMORE. I can't see without my glasses. (*He screws up
his eyes to read.*)

MRS PASMORE. You can see well enough.

PASMORE. From Colin's children.

MRS PASMORE. All four of them have clubbed together.

PASMORE. It doesn't take much clubbing together to buy a
card. What's this squiggle?

MRS PASMORE. That's Susan.

PASMORE. Education: since these lot went to school, it's
gone to the dogs. (*He reads.*) 'Congratulations Grandma
and Grandpa.' Signed Susan, Cynthia, Kenneth and Paul.
That's very nice. Thank you, Colin.

MRS PASMORE. Thank you, love.

COLIN. It'll be Susan. She usually initiates these things.

MRS PASMORE. This is one of Eileen's. Thank you, love.

PASMORE. Aye, thank you, love.

MRS PASMORE. I always recognise Eric's writing. He
writes to us a lot.

EILEEN. What about your telegrams?

MRS PASMORE. I'll get to those, don't worry.

WENDY *brings in* EILEEN's *tea.*

WENDY. Sugar?

EILEEN. One, love.

WENDY *holds the bowl;* EILEEN *takes sugar.*

COLIN. I'll take it. (*He takes the sugar back to the kitchen.*)
Anyone else want tea?

WENDY. No thank you.

MRS PASMORE (*reading a card*). No thank you, love.

PASMORE (*shaking his head*). No thanks.

COLIN *puts the sugar bowl down in the kitchen. He sits
on a stool and gazes out of the back window.*

MRS PASMORE (*reading*). 'From Eric and Patrick.' Thank
you, Eileen. (*She kisses her cheek.*) They're both grand
children, love.

PASMORE. I know they're both grandchildren.

MRS PASMORE (*to* EILEEN). *Grand* grandchildren, love.

(*She tears open a telegram.*) Well, then. (*She reads it.*) That's very nice.

PASMORE. Won the pools, then, have we?

MRS PASMORE. It's from Arnold.

WENDY. Arnold!

MRS PASMORE. It's very thoughtful of him.

PASMORE. What's he want?

MRS PASMORE. To congratulate us, Tommy. 'On your diamond jubilee.'

PASMORE. Diamond. That's why I'm keeping quiet. I couldn't afford a bit o' glass.

COLIN *gets up and goes out into the garden through the back door.*

MRS PASMORE (*to* WENDY). That's very thoughtful of him, love.

PASMORE. Even though we aren't related.

WENDY. You will be for another month.

PASMORE. In that road, mek best on it we can.

WENDY. He's still very fond of you, I know.

PASMORE. Is he getting married again?

WENDY. We're not even divorced yet, Dad.

PASMORE (*to* EILEEN). Grab 'o'd of a woman one day, and grab 'o'd of another the next.

MRS PASMORE. I wish you'd moderate your language.

PASMORE. 'Four across. Three-letter word denoting modern marriage.'

MRS PASMORE. This is from you, love.

PASMORE. Bed.

MRS PASMORE (*to* EILEEN, *having opened the second telegram*). 'All our love and best wishes. Eileen and Jack.' Thank you, love.

EILEEN. Not at all, Mum. (*They embrace.*)

MRS PASMORE. I've always hated 'Mum'.

EILEEN. That's what I call Jack's mother. (*To* PASMORE.) She can't stand 'Mother'.

PASMORE. My mother I called 'Mam'.

MRS PASMORE. It always sounded common.

PASMORE. She was a wonderful woman.

MRS PASMORE. She couldn't control her children.

PASMORE. It was my father who didn't have much control.

MRS PASMORE. She had control over your discipline, but not your education.

PASMORE. I left school at eleven.

MRS PASMORE. You were twelve.

PASMORE. I was expelled at twelve. I left at eleven.

WENDY. What were you expelled for, Dad?

PASMORE. For never bloody well being there.

EILEEN. Where were you?

PASMORE. Wukking! What some people nowadays have never heard of. Twelve-hour day, six days a week. Seven miles walk at four in the morning; seven mile back at night. I went to sleep with my clothes on.

EILEEN. I don't believe it.

PASMORE. In a cupboard.

EILEEN. Rubbish.

PASMORE. On a shelf. Out of a family of twelve sons and three daughters, I'm the on'y one still living.

MRS PASMORE (*handing him the second telegram*). That's Eileen's and Jack's.

PASMORE. Didn't need to come as well. Could have saved a couple of bob.

EILEEN. Do you want me to go back home again?

MRS PASMORE. He doesn't, love.

WENDY. Where's Colin?

EILEEN. He took that sugar out.

WENDY. Colin? (*She goes out to the kitchen, sees the back door open and goes out.*)

PASMORE. I'd better go and get changed, if we're off for a drive.

EILEEN. Are we going out?

MRS PASMORE. We've planned to, love.

PASMORE. We can go in Colin's car.

EILEEN. Mine almost came to a stop.

PASMORE. Summat i' the carburettor. I'll have a look afore you leave.

MRS PASMORE. He mended our car last week. We had to ask a mechanic to come and get the blessed thing restarted.

PASMORE. I'd forgotten a nut. You'd think I'd forgotten a bloody wheel.

MRS PASMORE. It wouldn't go.

PASMORE. You could sit in it, couldn't you?

MRS PASMORE. In the garage?

PASMORE. I don't know what she wants.

MRS PASMORE. I don't know whether it's old age or he simply puts it on.

PASMORE. She lived in a henhouse once.

MRS PASMORE. I did not.

PASMORE. Her father was out of work.

MRS PASMORE. He never lived in a henhouse.

PASMORE. Talk about meking jobs. All her father made were bloody complaints.

MRS PASMORE. He was wounded in the war! (*To* EILEEN.) The Boer War, love. It affected the use of his lungs. He worked as hard as any man. He kept being dismissed. They didn't think he worked hard enough. (*She gets a handkerchief from her sleeve and wipes her eyes.*) He never explained he was wounded.

PASMORE. You did.

MRS PASMORE. I went to his employer. I said, 'Do you know you have put a man out of work who gave his health for his country?'

EILEEN. What did he do?

MRS PASMORE. He laughed in my face.

PASMORE. Ask her what she did.

EILEEN. What did you do, Mother?

MRS PASMORE (*pause*). I picked up a teapot standing on his desk and emptied it into his lap.

PASMORE. He shot out of his bloody chair! Wouldn't strike a woman. Not in those days. Wi' equality, nowadays, o' course, he'd have knocked her around all day.

MRS PASMORE. We never lived in a hen-coop.

PASMORE. It had been a hen-coop.

MRS PASMORE. A shed. We were only there seven days.

PASMORE. After that, the doss-house.

MRS PASMORE. The People's Home.

PASMORE. Used to be called the workhouse.

MRS PASMORE (*weeping*). A man who had given his health for his country and he was condemned to take his wife and children to the People's Home.

PASMORE. The dregs of the earth is that place.

MRS PASMORE. You see how far I've come. All this, from where we started.

PASMORE. All my generation, tha knows, are dead. Most of them within eighteen months of retiring. Pneumoconiosis, heart disease, silicosis. I'm the only one left from a generation of colliers that went down the pit just after the First World War. A whole generation: gone.

MRS PASMORE. But for you.

PASMORE. And my wife.

Pause. WENDY comes in the back door, followed by COLIN, who is carrying PASMORE's suit.

WENDY (*in a lowered voice*). Are you all right?

COLIN. Fine.

WENDY. You sure?

COLIN. I'd better take this in. (*He indicates she should go before him.*)

MRS PASMORE. Are you going to get ready?

PASMORE. I'm off. Shan't take more than two minutes.

COLIN (*entering the living-room*). Spot of rain. (*He sniffs the suit.*) Seems all right.

PASMORE. How do you mean, seems? Good bit o' cloth is that. On'y been in it twice. Both times to local funerals.

MRS PASMORE. He has not.

PASMORE. His next door but one's. Hers across the road.

MRS PASMORE (*after a pause.*) That's right.

PASMORE. In principle I'm allus wrong. Three across: 'Put-upon man. Seven letters.'

EILEEN. Husband!

PASMORE. Right. (*He goes, taking the suit, and closes his bedroom door.*)

MRS PASMORE (*to EILEEN*). I'll go and finish love. Thank you for your cards. Would you put them out? I shan't be long. (*She goes to her room and closes the door.*)

EILEEN *begins to lay the cards and telegrams. WENDY adjusts them on the mantelshelf.*

COLIN. Remember when he got a septic thigh? A cut that became infected. In the hospital they said they'd have to cut his leg off. One last chance they said was to put on boiling fomentations. I'd just left him, after a visit. I heard him scream. I went back to the door. Two nurses were holding him down. When two of the other nurses came past, one of them said, 'I don't think a human being can stand it. Boiling water, every two hours.' At school, I'd gaze out at the hospital across the road. 'If he can suffer like that,' I thought, 'I have to work much harder.'

EILEEN. I remember him going to work with ulcers on his legs.

WENDY. He treated them with onions.

EILEEN. The smell!

WENDY. And covered them with a piece of oilcloth that smelt even more than they did.

EILEEN. In the bus he used to stand at the back holding on to the seats. When the conductor asked him to sit, he said he couldn't.

WENDY. It was true.

EILEEN. When he came home from work, his legs were covered in pus. He used to sit, groaning, while my mother fed him in the bath.

WENDY. The stench.

EILEEN. How the hell did he stay alive?

WENDY. Beats me.

COLIN. There's no known medical reason why he is alive. Verdict of the local doctor.

EILEEN. Put a great burden, of course, on you.

COLIN (*moving away*). I don't think so.

EILEEN. The only son. (*She watches him.*) How's America?

COLIN. Fine.

EILEEN. I got your card.

COLIN. Good.

WENDY. Never sent me one.

COLIN. I did.

WENDY. I never received it.

Pause.

COLIN. Perhaps I didn't. (*He sits, abstracted.*) I intended writing a letter. (*He exchanges a look with* WENDY. *Then:*) Bloody freezing up there last night. There's no heating in that bedroom.

WENDY. Did you tell them you were coming up?

COLIN. I didn't.

EILEEN. None of us did.

WENDY. We've never got on well. Two by two, but not the three of us together.

COLIN. We've hardly had the chance.

WENDY. Once or twice.

EILEEN. I suppose it's true. Wendy and you: me and you.

COLIN. Wendy's mercurial. You're phlegmatic. Me: saturnine.

They laugh.

EILEEN. Remember the occasion when Father said we'd have been much better if we'd reversed the sexes?

WENDY. I don't think Colin was cut out to be a woman.

EILEEN. You were cut out to be a man.

WENDY. Me?

EILEEN. Me too.

WENDY. I never wished it.

EILEEN. Neither have I.

WENDY. I'm looking forward to living on my own. Or maybe, our Eileen, with another chap.

EILEEN. Young or old?

WENDY. Young.

EILEEN. How young?

WENDY. Very. See what you've been missing, love.

EILEEN. Poor old Jack isn't all that bad.

WENDY. Got his headship?

EILEEN. He will never get a headship. A head of department is all he'll rise to.

WENDY. How about Colin?

COLIN. My career took a leap backwards with *The Last Evangelist*. A readership might come up in two or three years. 'Too close to popular mythology and not enough to scholarship.' My Professor. *Swainton*. 'It surprises me to see, nowadays, Pasmore, what they can do with popular biography.'

EILEEN laughs.

Some mornings I set off for college, get there, return home, and I can't recall a word I've said. I assume I've passed the day in a normal way: when I go back the

following day, there's no sign that I haven't. The other
morning I woke so terrified that all I could do was cry for
help: in the middle of a bedroom, in a quiet house, in the
middle of a sedate neighbourhood near the heart of
London. Kay called her doctor. I sat clinging to a chair.
When you're in the grip of this thing every second
becomes an hour. And then, in the wake of this feeling,
comes despair.

PASMORE *comes out of his room in suit, shirt and socks,
carrying his shoes. He goes to the kitchen and gets
cleaning materials from a cupboard. He looks round for
somewhere to clean the shoes. He goes out of the back
door.*

I'd gone to New York hoping to distract it. The
opportunity came up when they publicised the book. I
kept gazing out of the window, on the plane, wanting it to
crash. I could see the ocean – like flecks of dust on a pane
of glass – each fleck the crest of an Atlantic roller. At one
point, I saw an irregular shape of the intensest white
enclosing a second irregular shape of opalescent green –
gleaming, iridescent – and suspended, or so it seemed,
midway between the aircraft and the sea. The fear went
from me. Moments after that I felt ecstatic. An iceberg, a
pool of water melting at its centre. In New York I'd walk
up and down outside my hotel not knowing who or where
I was. I'd go into a bar, order a meal, sit over it, and,
without having touched it, get up and leave. One Sunday,
I sat on a flight of steps near Central Park: joggers ran
past, a man sold second-hand books from a stall. I
couldn't move. I sat transfixed – gripped by a dementia
which even now I couldn't describe.

The bedroom door opens and MRS PASMORE *comes out
dressed for an outing, but with her stick and a coat and
handbag over her other arm. She is aware of the back
door being open and, seeing* PASMORE's *door open too,
she calls:*

MRS PASMORE. Tommy?
PASMORE (*off*). Out here.
MRS PASMORE. Have you got a handkerchief? (*She has*

one in her hands. She goes to the kitchen and checks the switches of the kettle and stove.)

COLIN. Why I let that out I've no idea. You get careless, at times, about how you feel.

EILEEN. What did the doctor say?

COLIN. There's not a great deal he can do. After a while, I sobered up. I go to work. I give out notes. There was a time when I couldn't work at all. I'd walk the streets. Or weep. Not through despair, you know, but terror.

MRS PASMORE (*glancing out of the back door*). Never mind talking to Mrs Halliday. (*Calling.*) He was supposed to be cleaning his shoes. (*Pause.*) Tell him, love. He takes no notice of me. (*She looks at the tiny watch on her wrist.*) Come in, then. (*Calling.*) Thank you, love.

PASMORE *comes in past her.*

You've been standing out there in your socks.

PASMORE (*aware he has his shoes in his hands*). I had no time to put them on.

MRS PASMORE. You've had time to talk to Mrs Halliday.

PASMORE. She asked me.

MRS PASMORE. She's usually at her shop by now.

PASMORE. She's on her way.

MRS PASMORE. Are you leaving all those cleaning things out there?

PASMORE. Oh, yes. (*He goes to retrieve them.*)

MRS PASMORE. Too busy talking.

PASMORE (*off*). It's t' on'y chance I get. (*He brings in the shoe-cleaning material in a box and puts it away in the cupboard.*)

MRS PASMORE. And wash your hands.

PASMORE. Aye.

MRS PASMORE. And put your shoes on.

PASMORE. Shoes.

MRS PASMORE. Before you wash your hands.

PASMORE. By God. How would I live without you?

MRS PASMORE (*indicating the handkerchief*). I'll put this in your pocket.

PASMORE *continues putting on his shoes. MRS PASMORE goes to the living-room.*

EILEEN. Lovely, Mother.

MRS PASMORE. Thank you, love.

PASMORE (*calling*). Are you ready for off?

WENDY. We are, old man!

PASMORE (*calling*). I shan't be a minute. (*He goes to the sink to wash his hands, murmuring to himself.*) 'Wash hands, wash feet, wash nose.'

MRS PASMORE. Is that the time? (*She checks the clock on the mantelpiece with her watch.*)

PASMORE *barely rinses his hands and dries them. He uses a towel, after glancing up to see if he's observed, to give his shoes a final polish. He ducks to the window to see his reflection: he can't. He smooths down his hair with one hand. He hangs up the towel and dusts it down to obviate stains.*

He's like a child. (*To* COLIN.) His second childhood, love.

EILEEN. You look lovely, love. (*She gives* MRS PASMORE *a kiss.*)

MRS PASMORE. I can't tell you how much it means to us. To see you all together. (*Calling.*) Tommy!

PASMORE. I'm coming. I'm coming. God damn and blast! Do this, do that, do t'other. Yes you shall. Oh no you shan't . . . Where's this, where's that, where's t'other?

MRS PASMORE. Tommy!

PASMORE. I am coming. (*He takes a last look at the kitchen, and finally puts the towel in the cupboard, closes the kitchen door, and comes through. To himself.*) God Christ. (*Then, entering.*) How am I looking?

WENDY. You're looking grand!

EILEEN. Lovely.

WENDY. Champion! (*She kisses him.*)

COLIN. I'll get my coat. (*He goes to the stairs, and exits.*)

PASMORE (*to* MRS PASMORE). Let me help you on with yours.

MRS PASMORE. Thank you, love.

EILEEN. Get the glad rags on!

WENDY (*who has watched* COLIN *depart*). Right.

EILEEN. Remember the church dances we used to go to?

WENDY. *You* used to go to. I used to follow.

EILEEN. You were always popular, love. (*To* MRS
  PASMORE.) Used to ask me who my sister was.

WENDY. One of her chums would come across: fists like
  melons, feet to match. 'Can I have this 'un, lovely?'

EILEEN. Everyone was awed by Wendy. Brilliant at sport,
  brilliant at maths.

WENDY. Changed when I got married.

EILEEN. Arnold!

WENDY. Oh, Arnold!

  WENDY *and* EILEEN *laugh.*

MRS PASMORE. I don't see why.

  PASMORE *departs to the hall for his coat.*

WENDY. Under-manager at the age of thirty-one. Managing
  director at forty-five.

EILEEN. The boy-wonder of Maccleswade Grammar.

WENDY. Chairman of the Board at forty-seven.

MRS PASMORE. *Is* he Chairman of the Board?

WENDY. It's then he began casting round, our Mother, for
  a younger wife.

MRS PASMORE. It can't be that.

WENDY. And me for a younger husband.

MRS PASMORE. Really, love. Your father doesn't know
  you're pulling his leg.

  PASMORE *returns with his coat.*

PASMORE. It's been a house of women. I just earned the
  money. Come home exhausted: yak, yak. Ten to the
  dozen. If women could work as much as they talk, this
  house would be stacked to the roof with money.

WENDY. It is stacked to the roof.

PASMORE. What with?

EILEEN. Affection. (*She embraces him and kisses his cheek.*)

PASMORE. Words! I never know where I am. (*He is pleased
  by their attention, flustered.*)

EILEEN. Live here like a king.

PASMORE. I don't know about a king: she queens it over
  me enough. Do this. Do that. Yes, your majesty. My
  beloved.

MRS PASMORE. Put your coat on.

PASMORE. Right!

WENDY. I'll hold it for you.

PASMORE. Thank you, love. Right!

The sounds of COLIN *coming downstairs.*

Are we ready?

WENDY. Ready!

EILEEN. Ready! (*She gives* PASMORE *a kiss.*) Mother?

MRS PASMORE. Yes, love.

PASMORE. Looks a picture. Just like when I first saw her.

COLIN *enters with his coat, dropping it in a chair.*

Your car, Colin?

COLIN. Right.

MRS PASMORE. Through the country.

PASMORE. Just fancy a drink.

MRS PASMORE. I hope you're not going to embarrass us.

PASMORE. I've never embarrassed anyone.

MRS PASMORE. The last time we celebrated anything,
    Colin had to carry you upstairs.

PASMORE. I was tired.

MRS PASMORE. Tired! (*To* EILEEN.) Our fiftieth wedding
    anniversary, love.

PASMORE. We're off. Ladies before gentlemen.

EILEEN. Off we go, Mother.

COLIN. I'll lock the back door. (*He goes to the kitchen.*)

MRS PASMORE. Bring out the front-door key, love. Put the
    fire-guard round.

PASMORE. It's on. It's on. (*He does so.*)

MRS PASMORE (*to* EILEEN). A mother's instinct, love.

PASMORE. We're off!

MRS PASMORE *leads the way to the front door. It is
heard to open.*

PASMORE *follows.*

WENDY *indicates for* EILEEN *to go before her.*

EILEEN. After you, our kid.

WENDY (*calling*). Colin!

EILEEN *and* WENDY *go.*

COLIN (*calling*). Right! (*He locks the back door, bolts it and chains it. He comes back to the living-room, picks up the coat he's dropped there and looks round at the room.*)

WENDY (*off*). Colin!

EILEEN (*off*). Colin!

COLIN *pulls himself together, starts to put on the coat, and goes.*

The sound of the front door closing and the key being turned is heard.

PASMORE (*further off*). Come and get this car unlocked.

COLIN (*calling, off*). Right!

EILEEN (*off, fainter*). Colin!

WENDY (*off, fainter still*). Colin!

The lights fade to blackout.

ACT TWO

Scene One
The same. Evening.

Evening light at the window and the low glow of the fire.

The front door is unlocked.

MRS PASMORE (*off*). You had a peggy-stick. It had three legs, like a stool, with a broom-handle, and you thrashed it up and down. My arms! They used to ache!

She comes into sight in the passage, from the front door.

Sometimes the clothes would get wound up, more with the handle than anything else – (*She goes into the living-room.*)

EILEEN *follows her, switching on the light.*

– then you'd have to reach into the tub. The water we'd heat in a copper and ladle it out with a metal jug. That took some time: *emptying* the tub with buckets. I used to be that exhausted I'd sit on the stairs and cry. (*She gasps and holds her chest.*) My breath! I could never catch it! (*She lays down her handbag, suddenly conscious of the room.*) When you were young the buckets were heavier than you could handle: so much would spill on the floor.

She allows EILEEN *to help her off with her coat.*

Then the mopping-up.

WENDY *comes in the front door and along the passage. She carries a box of chocolates.*

We'd be wet through at times. (*She catches sight of* WENDY *entering.*) When Wendy was old enough, she'd pitch in. Those *were* wash-days! When it rained – a house of clothes for the better part of two days drying round the fire.

WENDY (*to* EILEEN). Your car keys, love. (*To* MRS PASMORE.) There's your chocolates. (*She hands them to* EILEEN *to give to* MRS PASMORE.)

EILEEN. Mother: your box of chocolates.

MRS PASMORE. Thank you, love. (*She kisses her.*) What a lovely picture. Almond blossom.

EILEEN. Cherry.

WENDY. Plum.

MRS PASMORE. I couldn't eat another thing. That meal went on for hours. I'll just put on the kettle.

WENDY. I'll do it, Mother.

MRS PASMORE. Mend up the fire. I shan't be a minute. (*She goes to the kitchen.*) There you are. (*She switches on the kitchen light.*)

PASMORE *comes in, rather slow on his feet.*

EILEEN. You poke. I'll shove on the fuel.

WENDY *removes the fire-guard and pokes the fire.*
EILEEN *lifts the scuttle and tips on the coal.*

PASMORE (*at the living-room door, pausing*). Women working. Don't often see it nowadays.

WENDY. Nowadays, Father, you see nothing else.

PASMORE. This house, lass, I'm talking about. (*He covers his mouth, glancing back to the kitchen.*)

MRS PASMORE *is in the kitchen filling the kettle. She plugs it in, then re-straightens the curtains. She washes her hands during the following action.*

WENDY. You were bad enough in the restaurant, Dad.

PASMORE. Can't stomach well-dressed people.

EILEEN. You're well-dressed.

PASMORE. I'm only well-dressed when I'm going out with you. (*He puts his arm round* WENDY *and kisses her cheek.*) Thy's putting on some weight.

WENDY. I am not.

PASMORE. Eileen was as plump as a chicken. Thy'd disappear inside your clothes and we'd never know you wa' theer. How are you, Eileen?

EILEEN. Champion, Dad. (*She gives him a kiss.*)

PASMORE. Grand meal.

EILEEN. It was.

PASMORE. Even if Colin paid for it.

WENDY. We all paid for it, Father. Except you.

PASMORE. The exception that proves the rule!
EILEEN. That's right.

Having washed her hands, MRS PASMORE *has gone to
dry them, but the towel is not there. She looks round and
finally locates it in the cupboard.*

MRS PASMORE (*to herself*). Where's that towel?
WENDY. Where's Colin?
PASMORE. Locking up his car.
EILEEN. Bought it with the money from his book.
PASMORE. Nothing beats hard work. Motto of my life.
  That fire could do with poking.
WENDY. I've poked it.
PASMORE. You've dabbed at it. God Christ! (*He pokes the
  fire himself.*) This fire and me are close together. I often
  talk to this on a morning. 'How are you?' 'I'm fine.'
  'Want a bit o' feeding?' 'Right!' A house wi'out a fire is
  like a home wi'out a woman.
MRS PASMORE. Have you seen this?

PASMORE *turns as* MRS PASMORE *comes in, holding
up the towel which she has extracted from the cupboard.*

PASMORE. What is it?
MRS PASMORE. It's a towel.
PASMORE. A towel.
MRS PASMORE. From the kitchen.
PASMORE. The kitchen.
MRS PASMORE. Just look at it!
EILEEN. It's only a towel, Mother.
MRS PASMORE. It's my towel, love. That's polish.
PASMORE. I had an accident.
MRS PASMORE. An accident!
PASMORE. If I've muckied it, I thought, I'll give 'em a little
  rub.
MRS PASMORE. You've used it on your shoes!
PASMORE (*holding one foot out, then the other*). Can see
  yourself in that.
MRS PASMORE. After all these years! It'll never come off.
  (*She weeps.*) He has his own towel in the bathroom. I
  don't know what he does with his hands.

PASMORE. I make the fire. I empty it every two or three days.

MRS PASMORE. It's too much. (*She sits.*) I keep the house clean. All he does is dirty it up.

COLIN *comes in, closing the front door and emerging in the passage. He now stands in the living-room doorway.*

WENDY (*with her arm round* MRS PASMORE'S *shoulder*). You're surely not going to get upset?

MRS PASMORE. I'll never use it again.

WENDY *takes it from her.*

EILEEN. You'll wash it.

MRS PASMORE. It'll never come out. It's too much.

PASMORE. Are we having us some tea or aren't we?

WENDY. I'll put it on.

MRS PASMORE (*calling*). Don't put that towel with the washing.

WENDY (*going*). Why not?

MRS PASMORE. It needs special rinsing.

COLIN. What's the problem?

WENDY. Towel. (*She holds it up as she passes him in the door.*)

EILEEN. Dad has used Mother's towel to polish his shoes.

PASMORE. A final flick. It fell on the floor. I must have put on too much polish.

MRS PASMORE. It never fell.

PASMORE. How do you know what it did?

MRS PASMORE. You picked up the closest thing to hand. The story of my life.

PASMORE. Like I picked up you, you mean?

MRS PASMORE. *You never picked me up*! You never did!

PASMORE. I don't know where I am. Go out and celebrate and we end up here in tears.

MRS PASMORE. It's your thoughtlessness. Your never counting what comes next. It was me who made this family. Saving every week. Penny after penny.

PASMORE. I'm off to bed.

MRS PASMORE. You'll do no such thing.

PASMORE. I'll run off wi' Mrs Halliday to her boutique.

MRS PASMORE. You'd like that, I know.

PASMORE. Life at the seaside, Colin!

MRS PASMORE. We're not at the seaside. We're in the country. I couldn't live in a seaside town. (*To* COLIN.) It's far too crowded in the summer.

PASMORE. Autumn now.

MRS PASMORE. I don't care when it is.

Pause.

WENDY *makes tea and arranges a tray in the kitchen. She has put the towel in the empty washing-machine.*

PASMORE. A towel isn't that important.

MRS PASMORE. It is to me.

PASMORE. I'll buy you another. As it is, I've bought you this. (*He gives her a box from his pocket.*)

MRS PASMORE. What is it?

PASMORE. Open it and see.

MRS PASMORE. Well, I don't know . . .

EILEEN. Open it, Mother.

MRS PASMORE. Well . . . (*She gazes at it.*)

COLIN. Open it.

EILEEN (*calling*). Wendy!

WENDY, *in the kitchen, pauses.*

COLIN. Wendy!

EILEEN (*calling*). Come and look at this!

WENDY *comes back through.* PASMORE *shifts his position to another chair.*

Father's given Mother a present.

WENDY. That's quick. He was in the doghouse a minute ago.

EILEEN. Well, then, Mother . . .

MRS PASMORE. Are you ready?

PASMORE. We're ready.

MRS PASMORE *opens the box.*

MRS PASMORE. You might have chosen a better moment.

PASMORE. When?

MRS PASMORE. Sooner rather than later.

PASMORE. The restaurant, I thought, wa' far too crowded.

MRS PASMORE. It's lovely, love. What is it?

PASMORE. A ring.

MRS PASMORE. A ring. (*She puts it on.*) It's made to fit a giant.

PASMORE. They'll alter it.

MRS PASMORE. Where did you get it?

PASMORE. What does it matter?

WENDY. Let's have a look.

MRS PASMORE. It looks like a brooch.

EILEEN. Let's have a look, Mother.

WENDY. It is a brooch.

EILEEN. No, it isn't.

MRS PASMORE. Can you see it, Colin?

COLIN. It looks grand.

PASMORE. I've been saving up for that.

MRS PASMORE. Where did you get the money?

PASMORE. I've saved it.

MRS PASMORE. You haven't spent our contingency fund?

PASMORE. What contingency fund?

MRS PASMORE. For our funeral!

EILEEN. You've not been saving up for that?

MRS PASMORE. Everybody did in our day, love.
  Sometimes not more than a halfpenny a week.

PASMORE. I haven't touched it. You'll be buried when you
  dee. I'll be buried. We'll all be buried.

MRS PASMORE. Where did you get it?

PASMORE. It's a present. What is this place? A prison?

WENDY. Why don't you say thank you, love?

MRS PASMORE. Thank you.

PASMORE. Theer, then.

MRS PASMORE. Let me give you a kiss.

PASMORE. If you think that I deserve it.

MRS PASMORE. Of course you deserve it. (*She holds both
  arms out.*)

PASMORE *crosses to her, leans down and is kissed.*

There. You see. It's already dropped off.

WENDY. I'll get it, Mother.

MRS PASMORE. Where he's got it from . . .

PASMORE. Where do you think I got it?

MRS PASMORE. I'm sure I couldn't guess.

COLIN (*having picked it up*). Gold. (*He examines it.*)

PASMORE. He's the same, you see.

MRS PASMORE. It's such an unusual ring.

PASMORE. An antique.

MRS PASMORE. Did you buy it second-hand?

PASMORE. It has a motto.

COLIN. 'From E.T. to U.N.'

WENDY. It's a 'B'.

MRS PASMORE. It is second-hand.

COLIN. 'Amo . . .'

PASMORE. It means 'I love'.

WENDY. Who's 'B.T.'?

EILEEN. Who's 'U.N.'?

PASMORE. In Latin.

WENDY. 'Te Amo.'

PASMORE. 'I love you.'

MRS PASMORE (*taking it back in her outstretched hand*). It is second-hand. (*She examines it.*)

PASMORE. It doesn't make any difference.

MRS PASMORE. It's like someone else's clothes.

PASMORE. I wanted to buy you a present.

MRS PASMORE. You could have bought me flowers.

PASMORE. Flowers don't last.

MRS PASMORE. I'd never let one of these wear someone else's clothes. I'd stay up all night mending rather than take in someone else's rejects. (*She puts the ring back in its box.*)

PASMORE. That's not a reject.

COLIN. For God's sake, Mother: he's bought you a present.

MRS PASMORE. Like all his presents, Colin.

PASMORE. That's not true.

WENDY. Not true at all.

MRS PASMORE. Not all his presents. Just like some. (*She takes out her handkerchief.*)

PASMORE. What did I have to buy you ought?

MRS PASMORE. You had your pension.

PASMORE. You look after that.

MRS PASMORE. You could have asked.

PASMORE. I did. (*He sits and weeps bitterly to himself.*)

EILEEN. There's the kettle.

COLIN. I'll get it. (*He goes to the kitchen.*)

WENDY. The two of you behave. Both of you say sorry.

MRS PASMORE. If I give him too much he goes and spends it. He has to be watched. I can't let your father out of my sight. On those fruit machines. As well as something else.

EILEEN. Now what is it? What's been happening?

MRS PASMORE. It's nothing that I want to talk about. I'll take the ring. I appreciate the thought. I mean that.

WENDY. I'll get the tea. (*She goes to the kitchen and signals to COLIN to return to the living-room. She finishes the tea-making and setting the tray.*)

COLIN (*returning*). Sorted it all out?

MRS PASMORE. There's nothing to sort out, love.

PASMORE. All fine and dandy. (*He blows his nose.*) All a picture.

MRS PASMORE. Getting old: it has its problems. It's true for everyone, I suppose.

PASMORE (*blowing his nose*). I thought of buying flowers. Then I saw that. Amo means I love. *Te Amo* means I love you. (*He weeps into his hand.*)

Pause.

COLIN. There's no need to get upset about it, Dad.

PASMORE. It's just today. You all being here.

MRS PASMORE. We hadn't a farthing when we married.

PASMORE. We wouldn't have now if it wasn't for these.

MRS PASMORE. Neither of Tommy's parents came to our wedding. Mine thought I should have stayed at home. All my sisters and brothers were working or married. The youngest in those days had to help around the house.

PASMORE. A domestic servant.

MRS PASMORE. Your brothers came.

PASMORE. Four. Four of 'em came. And seven not.

MRS PASMORE. None of your sisters.

PASMORE. None of my sisters.

MRS PASMORE. The church was a bowling-alley last time I saw it.

PASMORE. When we got on the train for the honeymoon I had to stand. She sat i' the carriage, next to a chap who chatted to her all the way.

MRS PASMORE. He was very handsome.

PASMORE. A square moustache, eyes as big as saucers, flushed cheeks. I went in a time or two and said, 'Are you all right?'

MRS PASMORE. I was all right.

PASMORE. Would you believe it? The fourth or fifth time I went in this chap said, 'Is this man troubling you, my dear?'

WENDY (*coming in with the tray and hearing this*). What did you tell him?

MRS PASMORE. I said he was!

They laugh.

EILEEN. Why didn't you tell him he was your husband?

MRS PASMORE. I was too embarrassed.

PASMORE. Embarrassed!

MRS PASMORE. I hardly knew anything about the world. I was nineteen. I'd worked in a mill before my mother asked me to help at home. Tommy was the first man I ever went out with. (*She pulls her skirt over her knees.*) If a young woman couldn't be spoken to by a young man on a crowded train, I don't see where else she could be spoken to. He was very polite. 'Is this man pestering you?' he said.

PASMORE. He asked, at the other end, if he could carry her case.

MRS PASMORE. I don't know why you didn't let him. Thank you, love. (*She takes a cup of tea from* WENDY.)

PASMORE. If it's not been one man, it's been another. (*He takes a cup of tea from* WENDY.) Thank you.

MRS PASMORE. I can't help it if I'm attractive.

PASMORE. With a walking-stick?

MRS PASMORE. You should have seen him oggle me in my costume.

PASMORE. God Christ, it was longer than a nightdress. 'Do you think I should show any ankles?' You couldn't even see her bloody toes! (*He laughs; and then chokes, holding his tea. He drinks.*)

MRS PASMORE. This is a conversation to have in front of our children.

PASMORE. If they are our children. From what you're telling us, they might only be yours.

MRS PASMORE. He doesn't know when to stop. He carries a joke too far.

COLIN. When you were married, where did you live?

MRS PASMORE. We lived in a room at my mother's.

PASMORE. About the size o' that kitchen. A street, tha knows, at the back of a mill.

EILEEN. Thank you. (*She takes a cup of tea from* WENDY.)

MRS PASMORE. We had a bed against one wall.

PASMORE. One cupboard.

MRS PASMORE. One chair.

PASMORE. A window the size of a matchbox.

MRS PASMORE. It was.

PASMORE. In the middle of summer you had to burn candles to see where you were.

MRS PASMORE. Water from a tap in the yard outside.

PASMORE. We had to wash in the basement.

MRS PASMORE. We had Eileen at that time.

PASMORE. Aye.

MRS PASMORE. The Council came one morning – Tommy was working nights and asleep in bed. I was washing Eileen in a little bath. They took one look at this tiny room and said, 'We'll get you a home, Mrs Pasmore.'

PASMORE. Got us a council house after that.

MRS PASMORE. A godsend.

PASMORE. A palace.

EILEEN. You don't have to tell us, Mother.

MRS PASMORE. No. No. Of course. That's right.

PASMORE. Today's been one to remember.

MRS PASMORE. It has. (*Looking at the clock, then her watch.*) Must have been eight hours.

PASMORE. Six.

MRS PASMORE. That ride over the moor. I don't think I've been that route before.

WENDY. Good job you told them at the restaurant it was you arriving, Dad.

PASMORE. They know me there by now.

MRS PASMORE. We've never been there in our lives.

PASMORE. Nay, about town.

MRS PASMORE. You've hardly been into town without me.

PASMORE. I've been a time or two on my own.

MRS PASMORE. He talks to anybody. You, me: out it comes. All about his children. Colin's book. Wendy's council. Eileen's children.

WENDY. Something to be proud of.

PASMORE. That's what I tell her. She never listens.

MRS PASMORE. He spoke to one man one morning and the man said, 'Are you trying to solicit me?'

PASMORE. He was mad.

MRS PASMORE. He said he'd call the police.

PASMORE. All I said to him was, 'How are you going?' He said, 'Are you trying to . . .' What was the word?

MRS PASMORE. Solicit.

PASMORE. Harmless. (*He drinks tea.*)

MRS PASMORE. I've never seen you move off as quick as that.

PASMORE. I'll be buggered if I'm had up for being a homosexual.

MRS PASMORE. He's been had up for a lot of things.

COLIN. What things?

MRS PASMORE. Matches. (*She watches* PASMORE.)

PASMORE. Matches.

MRS PASMORE. He had matches down the pit.

PASMORE. Three.

MRS PASMORE. We had to come back from our honeymoon for him to appear in court.

PASMORE. Ten shillings for every match.

MRS PASMORE. It was more than he earned each week.

WENDY. How did you pay them back?

PASMORE. A bob a week.

MRS PASMORE. Thirty shillings altogether.

PASMORE. An accident! I'd forgotten all about them.

MRS PASMORE. Endangering lives.

PASMORE. Endangering nothing.

MRS PASMORE. Why did they have you up in court?

PASMORE. If I had a pound for every man I've seen with a matchbox down the pit, I'd be the richest man alive. I'd have summat on my back you could call a coat.

MRS PASMORE. That is a good coat. I bought you that last Christmas.

PASMORE. It's a very good coat.

MRS PASMORE. In that case, why disparage it?

PASMORE. If you have bought it, my love, it's good enough for me.

MRS PASMORE. He doesn't know when he's well looked after.

PASMORE. I do. I do. After all these years.

MRS PASMORE. Fancy giving me a present with someone else's inscription.

EILEEN. It's not worth going into, Mother.

MRS PASMORE. It's typical, love. He could have bought me something.

WENDY. Have you bought him something?

MRS PASMORE. Why should I?

WENDY. You don't have to sit there and let it all come to you.

MRS PASMORE. Let what come to me?

WENDY. Openness. Generosity. Strength.

Pause.

MRS PASMORE. You were never very fond of me.

WENDY. I am very fond of you. I love you. I always have.

MRS PASMORE. There are feelings and feelings.

WENDY. Are there?

MRS PASMORE. I shan't say any more. (*She draws her skirt over her knees.*) Certainly not on a day like this.

WENDY. What have we to hide?

MRS PASMORE. What have we, indeed?

WENDY. You haven't anything, Colin?

COLIN. I don't believe I have.

WENDY. Eileen?

EILEEN. None of your usual habits.

WENDY. What habits?

MRS PASMORE. As a child she was always stirring up things that were better left alone. (*To* EILEEN.) That's why she became a politician.

WENDY. That's right. I did. What's the point of leaving anything alone? Particularly the way things are at present.

MRS PASMORE. Or are some people so born to mischief that they won't leave things alone in order to damage others?

PASMORE. I'll go get out of these clothes. (*He rises.*) I'm not used to being in a suit. (*He staggers.*)

EILEEN. You've had too much to drink.

PASMORE. A little goes a long way in my book. Any road, (*He starts to leave.*) each day is a celebration. You being here, tha knows, is good enough for me. (*He coughs. He goes out of the room.*)

EILEEN (*to* WENDY). You've driven him off.

PASMORE (*popping back in the doorway*). As for drinking: it wasn't me that drank a bottle of wine. Don't look at our Colin. He was driving. Your mother and I had a glass of champagne.

WENDY. A bit before, old man.

PASMORE. A drop. A drop. (*He closes the living-room door and goes to his bedroom. He opens the door and goes in, but doesn't completely close it.*)

MRS PASMORE. I think I'll go and lie down.

EILEEN. Do you want any help, Mother?

MRS PASMORE. No thank you, love.

COLIN *holds the door for her.* MRS PASMORE *goes. She opens her bedroom door, goes inside and closes it.*

EILEEN. You've had too much to drink.

WENDY. I had sufficient.

EILEEN. Why spoil a lovely day?

WENDY. Why, indeed? (*She sits.*) Aren't you going to say anything, Colin?

COLIN. Not much.

MRS PASMORE *comes out of her room and goes to the living-room.*

WENDY. No wonder he writes a book about an evangelical who blew up half the industrialised world and retires into an academic shell the next.

MRS PASMORE. I worked hard all my life. I brought up all of you on next to nothing, with a husband who had an eye for women like he had for nothing else, and who drank when I first knew him.

WENDY. He was a very good father.

MRS PASMORE. You don't know the half of it. You don't know your father, love, at all.

WENDY. I know he coughed his guts out at the coalface for the better part of fifty years. What did you do, Mother?

MRS PASMORE. She always had a vicious streak. (*To* EILEEN.) You can see what I had to put up with. If she gets it from anyone it's not from me.

WENDY. Your life was no harder, Mother, than that of many women, and a good deal easier than most. I have women in my office every day of every week begging for guidance, begging for peace. Broken in mind, broken in spirit. *Broke*. With homes that reek like sewers, with minds racked by anxiety and depression – and by a hatred which, if you brought it into this room, would set this place alight. I do my job as best I can. I get no satisfaction – except that of knowing that, if *I* didn't do it, someone else might do it worse.

MRS PASMORE. It seems to me, my dear, you are full of despair.

WENDY. So are you. But mine, my dear, is on the move.

EILEEN. What's got into you, our kid?

COLIN. It's better, far better she lets it out.

EILEEN. Is it? Is it? Aren't some things, Colin, better left unsaid?

MRS PASMORE (*sitting weeping*). Don't you think I haven't despaired? Don't you think I haven't been full of it myself? Day after day. Most women from our neighbourhood never raised their sights higher than the local pub. I did. I'd have given anything to have been able to get out of the house. When you were children, your father's wage was four pounds ten. No matter how hard I struggled, I couldn't get our housekeeping lower than five. New shoes would throw my budget out for months. A new suit would throw it out for years. I baked, I cooked, I cleaned, I sewed. To wash your father's clothes took half a day. My father was a farrier. His trade was in decline. He was wounded in the war. He could scarcely stoop to shoe a horse. I saw him try. He had a bullet through his lungs. I loved him. Oh, I loved him! (*She weeps.*) He never complained. Not once. Never! (*She weeps bitterly into her hands.*) He was a saint. A *saint*! (*Pause.*) You were married to a managing director. You have a lovely house, on the edge of a wood. I'm not saying it's cost you nothing – but nothing to the price that some of us have had to pay. (*She covers her face in her hands.*)

WENDY *moves to the door of the living-room, which has been left open from* MRS PASMORE's *entrance.*

WENDY (*calling*). You can come out of there, old man.

Pause.

PASMORE's *bedroom door is finally drawn back.* PASMORE *comes out, white-faced, perhaps the effect of too much drink – though not otherwise apparent – and of what he has heard through the open door. He has changed into trousers, an open-necked shirt and a pullover, his hair ruffled. He, too, behind the door has wept.*

Are you all right?
PASMORE. Grand! (*He rubs his hands together.*)
EILEEN. Do you want more tea?
PASMORE. No thanks. (*He comes in with a fearful look to* WENDY.)
WENDY. It's unusual, with our domestic arrangements, that we get the chance to come together. In most families that I know of, the brothers and sisters are out of touch.
EILEEN. Aren't you casting round with a flail?
WENDY. A flail?
EILEEN. Because you've lost your husband.
WENDY. Husbands may, my dear, be everything to you. They are nothing at all to me.
EILEEN. And children?
WENDY. Children?
EILEEN. You haven't any, Wendy.
WENDY. I've tried.
EILEEN. And didn't succeed.
WENDY. Alkaline douches, I'm afraid, didn't do the trick. Neither did sexual positioning, temperature graphs, or artificial insemination – techniques which, in my case, came too late. Ten years younger, our kid, I might have had a child. How about you? What do you do that's so important?
EILEEN. I go out to work.

WENDY. Do you?

EILEEN. Part time.

COLIN. Eristic argument: it used to dominate our house. It's what often drove me out of it.

MRS PASMORE. What's 'eristic'?

WENDY. Two down: seven-letter word.

COLIN. Arguing not to establish a truth but for effect. I have no time for it. I never had.

EILEEN (*speaking generally*). More tea?

PASMORE. No thanks.

PASMORE *shakes his head, the only one to respond.*

WENDY. Eileen always thought you went out as our protagonist, Colin. Our crusader. The heathen being anyone our parents took an exception to.

MRS PASMORE. We sent him out to better himself.

WENDY. Did you better it, Colin? This self you never knew you had. Or did you half destroy it?

MRS PASMORE. We gave you all an education. The best there was to have.

WENDY. I see Colin labouring night after night: Latin, Greek, Maths, History. Ah, *History*! I had to forgo a dress, Eileen a skirt, our mother a coat. Science. Art. When I followed him all I saw was Colin's back, *heaving*. 'Every shovelful of coal I dig, I dig it out for you.' Isn't that what you used to tell him, Dad? I never felt it, of course, myself. Digging out a spadeful for a daughter didn't carry the same weight as it did for a son. Nevertheless, I made it count. I made it count.

PASMORE. He had a better life than me.

WENDY. Has he? Did he? (*She looks at* COLIN.) It wasn't enlightenment they were shaping you towards, but work conducted from a sitting position, equated with a profession, not a job, with a salary, not a wage.

COLIN. It wasn't that.

WENDY. What was it, Colin?

COLIN (to MRS PASMORE). Do you remember how you used to say you never embraced me as a child?

MRS PASMORE. As a *baby*.

COLIN. I wonder why.

MRS PASMORE. I always thought if you had too much

cuddling you'd grow up soft. I cuddled Eileen, of course, a lot. And Wendy. She used to cuddle me. She was always cuddling. You were always very cuddly, love.

WENDY. Yet never Colin.

MRS PASMORE. He didn't seem to want it, love!

WENDY. As a baby?

MRS PASMORE. As a boy. I used to let him lie.

WENDY. What for?

MRS PASMORE. I wasn't very sure of men. I was always blushing when the rentman came.

PASMORE. What did I tell you! What did I say!

MRS PASMORE. It was modesty, that's all. With Tommy working shifts, I was often alone in the house at night.

WENDY. Our father helped when he was there.

MRS PASMORE. He was very fond of all of you. With Colin he always fought. On his knees. In front of the fire. With you two, of course, it was always games. Hiding and chasing. You used to love it. There it is. The joys and tribulations.

EILEEN. It's not a great deal, to go by default.

WENDY. Default?

EILEEN. When you measure it against their virtues.

WENDY. Virtues?

EILEEN. *Strengths*!

MRS PASMORE. After all, you were all three loved!

WENDY. Loved!

MRS PASMORE. Believe me: I never meant you, nor Colin, nor Eileen, any harm.

WENDY. Dad?

PASMORE *shakes his head.*

EILEEN (*to* COLIN). Are you all right?

COLIN. I'm fine. (*He glances at* EILEEN, *then turns away.*) I'm grand!

Pause.

MRS PASMORE. And what of your father?

EILEEN. What about him?

MRS PASMORE. If you have your traumas, what of his?

COLIN. What are your traumas, Dad?

PASMORE. Never you mind.

WENDY. Out with it, Dad.

PASMORE. On with the dance!

MRS PASMORE. If everything's coming out, it might as well.

PASMORE. It's nowt.

MRS PASMORE. Nothing!

PASMORE. To make a fuss.

MRS PASMORE. He's been stealing from a shop.

PASMORE. I pick things up. I can't remember.

MRS PASMORE. He puts things in his pocket. A life of honesty thrown away. We've never taken a penny – not a halfpenny – not from anyone. We've always paid our way. Now this.

WENDY. Why didn't anyone tell us?

MRS PASMORE. He asked me not to. You've got your troubles. We've got ours.

PASMORE. It's nowt.

MRS PASMORE. The shopkeeper said he'd take him to court. The local shop. The only one we've got.

PASMORE. I shan't ever show my face again. (*To* MRS PASMORE.) I told you it was coming.

MRS PASMORE. How did you tell me?

PASMORE. I said I didn't feel well. I had a headache whenever I went in.

MRS PASMORE. I have a headache whenever I go in. But not because I steal.

COLIN. You've been left too much on your own up here.

MRS PASMORE. Wendy's too busy. Eileen has her lads. You're in London.

COLIN. I'll come up here more often.

WENDY. I'll come over. (*To* EILEEN.) We'll both come over. (*To* PASMORE.) It's nothing to go on about.

PASMORE. It is to me.

MRS PASMORE. He doesn't sleep at night for worry.

PASMORE. I'll go to prison.

WENDY. You will not.

PASMORE. I've read cases in the paper.

EILEEN. You're not giving in after all these years?

PASMORE. In?

WENDY. Fighting, Father!

PASMORE. It's not fighting, lass. It's nought I understand.

WENDY. Have you seen the doctor?

MRS PASMORE. Doctor?

WENDY. You don't think he's a thief? He needs someone he can talk to.

PASMORE. I got up thinking this was a special day. I bought that ring.

MRS PASMORE. Where did you get it?

PASMORE. I got it in the market.

MRS PASMORE. The market!

PASMORE. He sells antiques.

MRS PASMORE. We've never bought anything from a stall in the market.

PASMORE. Lots of things. Lots.

MRS PASMORE. Not as a present.

PASMORE *shakes his head in disbelief: he cannot make sense of what he feels.*

PASMORE. I *saved* for it! I paid good money.

MRS PASMORE. What out of?

PASMORE. I *saved*! (*He goes to the door.*)

MRS PASMORE. And don't rush off.

PASMORE. I'm not rushing off.

MRS PASMORE. I've had to sit here and take abuse.

WENDY. It's not abuse.

MRS PASMORE. I've had to sit here and take criticism, haven't I?

PASMORE. I don't know what's happening to me. I don't know where I am any more.

MRS PASMORE. You're at home, with your wife, your son and your daughters.

PASMORE (*to* COLIN). At your age, one neet – on night shift – I lost my head. One chap wa' going on at me. I wa' supposed to be in charge: he wa' telling me what to do – foul-mouthed, half drunk. I said, 'If you don't do what I tell you, I'll ram you through wi' this.' A rock-drill: a bit as sharp as a needle and twice as long as this. (*He indicates his arm.*) 'Go so-and-so yourself,' he said. I would have killed him. I wa're on'y half his size. I couldn't get to him. For the best part of an hour I chased him round that face. After that it wa', 'Go so-and-so yourself,' to everybody. To me it was, 'Yes, Tommy,' and

'No, Tommy,' and 'I'll do that, Tommy.' He knew I'd meant it. *I* knew I'd meant it. That man came as close to deein' that night as he ever came to deein' wukking on that face. (*Indicating* MRS PASMORE.) I used to come home and fall asleep wi' the pit muck on me. I'd fall asleep at the table. Everything wa' black. It lasted two or three year. She used to say, 'Whatever's happened?' I couldn't explain it. There's scarcely a day goes by when I don't feel I've ever quite got over it. I worked for every penny. I wa're at the coalface at sixty-five . . .

WENDY. I'll go see this shopkeeper and sort it out.

PASMORE. All I wanted to do was buy you a present. You tell me I went and stole it.

MRS PASMORE. I asked.

PASMORE. Does it make any difference? I gave him money – my money. (*He holds his head.*) I wish you'd never told them. I wish to God they'd never come back.

MRS PASMORE. I'm glad they did.

PASMORE. To run me down.

MRS PASMORE. To run you nothing!

WENDY. All a lot about nothing.

EILEEN. Right!

WENDY. On with the dance!

PASMORE. Every tale has a happy ending.

WENDY. Every?

PASMORE. Almost . . .

EILEEN. What about this one, Father?

PASMORE. I don't know. (*He shakes his head.*) I don't know.

Pause.

WENDY. We'll get this shop business sorted out. We'll come up here more often.

PASMORE. There isn't much longer for either your mother or me to go.

WENDY. Quite a bit.

PASMORE. Not much. Not much.

WENDY. It's all the more important, in that case, to relish what we have. (*She puts her arm round* PASMORE.)

PASMORE. Aye . . . I suppose that's true.

WENDY. You don't honestly think I'm wicked, love? (*She*

sits on the arm of the chair beside MRS PASMORE,
putting her arm around her shoulder.)

MRS PASMORE. If you'd had a child you'd understand.
PASMORE. I'm going to have a rest.
MRS PASMORE. I'll lie down too.
PASMORE. What time are you leaving?
WENDY. Eileen?
EILEEN. I've got to get back this evening.
WENDY. Me too.
PASMORE. In that case, I'd better stay up.
EILEEN. Lie down for an hour. We'll still be here.
PASMORE. Hilda?
MRS PASMORE. I'll lie down too.
COLIN. Do you want a hand?
MRS PASMORE. Thank you, love.

COLIN *holds her arm to the door.*

PASMORE. How about me?
EILEEN. Here. I'll carry you! (*She takes his arm.*)
PASMORE. It'll take more than you to lift me, love. I could
  lift all three of you in one arm afore. How long ago is
  that?
EILEEN. A long, long time.
PASMORE. If I don't wek up just let me know.
WENDY. We'll wake you, Dad.

COLIN *and* MRS PASMORE *get to her bedroom door.*

COLIN. Are you all right, Mother?
MRS PASMORE. Thank you, love. (*To* EILEEN.) Wake us,
  won't you, before you leave?
EILEEN. We will.

PASMORE *and* MRS PASMORE *go into their rooms.*
The bedroom doors are closed. Pause.

COLIN *and* EILEEN *go back into the living-room.*
COLIN *closes the door.*

WENDY. I hate driving in the dark.
EILEEN. I'll give Jack a ring before I leave.
WENDY. You're very quiet.
COLIN. I'm not leaving until tomorrow.

WENDY. I'll stay.

COLIN. You don't have to.

WENDY. I'll ring the office. (*She indicates the bedrooms.*) If they're distressed then so am I.

EILEEN. Do you remember your 'throne'? That chair you used to stand on?

WENDY. Our father used to cheer.

EILEEN. He'd say, 'Tell us why the nationalisation of the coal industry will do us all a bit of good.'

COLIN. That went down like a bomb.

WENDY. I enlightened every one of you. Him (*She indicates COLIN.*) and you especially.

COLIN. Better close the door. (*He makes sure the living-room door is closed.*)

EILEEN. Like when father was on shifts.

COLIN. 'Speak in whispers.'

EILEEN. 'Don't run about.'

WENDY. His bloody snores would wake the dead.

EILEEN. 'Why can't we make a noise when Dad is snoring?'

COLIN. Precocious.

WENDY. Are you staying on as well?

EILEEN. That's right.

WENDY. I'll take these through. (*She collects the tea-things and goes to the kitchen.*)

EILEEN. There was a time when Wendy was a hausfrau.

COLIN. Before Arnold got loose-handed at the office.

EILEEN. Was it really as bad as that?

COLIN. Aren't really words to describe it. Still.

Pause.

EILEEN. Could put more coal on that.

COLIN. Right.

WENDY (*entering*). Found this. (*She holds up a bottle of wine.*) I'll get three glasses. Keep them here. (*She stoops to the sideboard and gets glasses out.*)

EILEEN. Don't fancy a drink.

COLIN. Nor do I.

WENDY. I'll have one. (*She hands a glass to COLIN as he rises from the fire.*) Pour one out.

COLIN. I think I'll have one.

WENDY. Eileen?

EILEEN (*glancing at* COLIN; *pause*). Right.
WENDY (*to* COLIN). Three.
COLIN. Wake them, shall we?
WENDY. No.
EILEEN. No.

> WENDY *takes her glassful, holds it up to examine it, and sips.*

WENDY. Not bad.

> COLIN *pours less than half into each of the other two glasses and hands one to* EILEEN.

Here's to it.
COLIN. Mother and Dad. (*He toasts.*)
WENDY. Mother and Father.
EILEEN. Mother and Father.
ALL. Mother and Father.

> *They drink.*

> *The light fades.*

Scene Two
The same. The next day.

Daylight shows through behind closed curtains; the fire has died down.

WENDY, her head on a cushion, and covered by a blanket, is curled up on the settee, asleep.

The light is stronger in the kitchen, where the curtains are open.

COLIN comes downstairs, dressed. He goes to the kitchen, after drawing the living-room door to as he passes. He picks up the pot of tea steaming there, as is the kettle, and drinks.

WENDY raises her head in the living-room, and looks over to the door. She rises. She stretches, goes over to the curtains, and draws them back. She flinches at the daylight.

COLIN, *hearing sounds, pours tea into a cup from the teapot, puts in milk and sugar, and stirs it. He brings it to the door and taps on it.*

WENDY (*stretching*). Oh, it's you.

COLIN. You up?

WENDY. That's very kind of you. (*She takes the cup.*)

COLIN. Milk and sugar.

WENDY. Anyone up?

COLIN. I've taken them a pot of tea. Remember how Eileen used to sleep with her head hooded in a blanket? Still does. Fire in. (*He picks up the bucket.*)

WENDY. What time are you leaving?

COLIN. Soon.

WENDY. Have a wash.

COLIN. My mother put out a towel. Pink. I've told them you're still here. (*He takes the bucket and goes and unlocks the back door. He goes out.*)

WENDY *goes to the bathroom and closes the door.*

PASMORE's *door opens. He comes out in his trousers, shirt, pullover and slippers. He goes to the bathroom door and tries it.*

PASMORE. Sorry. (*He comes into the living-room and sits, gazing at the fireplace. He raises his head at the sound of the bucket at the back door.*)

COLIN *comes in, closing the back door.*

COLIN *goes to the living-room.* PASMORE *rises.*

COLIN. There you are, Dad.

PASMORE. Aye . . .

COLIN. Still in. (*He indicates the fire.*)

PASMORE. I'll do it.

COLIN. No, no. Sit down.

PASMORE. My job.

He sits and watches COLIN *rake the fire then set in pieces of coal.*

Concessionary coal. Pay for the haulage. Comes half-price. (*Aimlessly.*) Call this 'the coal-house', tha knows, round here.

COLIN. Sleep all right?

PASMORE. Not bad. Where did you lot sleep?

COLIN. Eileen up. Wendy down here. I offered her my bed. She wouldn't have it.

PASMORE. I thought they had to be off last night.

COLIN. Decided to stay over.

PASMORE. It'll not burn up. (*He watches the fire.*) You need to pull that shutter. Push it to the left.

COLIN *pushes a lever above the fire itself, let into the metalwork within the tiled façade.*

You can see it drawing.

COLIN. Were you upset last night when I came in?

PASMORE. When did you come in?

COLIN. Before I went to bed.

PASMORE. I don't remember.

COLIN. I didn't hear you snoring.

PASMORE. I don't snore. (*He looks up in the direction of* MRS PASMORE's *room.*) That's put about by your mother.

COLIN. I've taken her a cup of tea. We have to get off, I think, quite soon.

PASMORE (*rubbing his face*). I remember scarce ought about last night. (*Pause.*) I don't remember too much about this morning. (*He looks up.*) I can never mek any sense on it. You look for a bit o' peace. (*He shakes his head, then bows it.*) All you get is nowt and nothing.

Pause.

WENDY *comes out of the bathroom.*

Pause. She listens to the silence in the living-room then comes in.

WENDY. Sleep all right? (*She stoops to* PASMORE *and kisses his forehead.*)

PASMORE. Not bad.

WENDY. Lifted the roof. It's a wonder you've a tile left on.

PASMORE. That's your brother.

WENDY. Not your wife?

PASMORE. Could be her, an' all. (*He watches her.*) Sleep in here, then, did you?

WENDY *folds the blanket.*

WENDY. That's right.

PASMORE. Off in one or two minutes?

WENDY. Correct.

PASMORE. I used to get a kick out of that. Leaving the house. The three of you asleep. Your mother in bed. Sun rising. There's never once, going down, I didn't feel sick. Home-time, you'd see the colliers crawl in at the bottom: two minutes later, up top, they used to run. That glad to get out of it for ten or twelve hours. There we are, then. (*He claps his hands.*) On with the dance!

COLIN *picks up the wine bottle from last night.*

WENDY (*indicating the bottle*). We had one or two drinks last night.

PASMORE. Didn't know we had any.

WENDY. Found it in the bottom of a cupboard. Forgotten you had it.

PASMORE. That's right.

COLIN. I'll wash my hands. (*He goes out to the kitchen and puts the bottle in the waste-bin there.*)

WENDY. None of this misanthropy, Father.

PASMORE. What's that?

WENDY. Thinking that life has come to an end.

PASMORE. It has.

WENDY. That's misanthropy.

PASMORE. Is it?

WENDY. Or despair.

PASMORE. I dreamt I met my brothers last night. Like we used to meet each Sunday.

WENDY. Church?

PASMORE. Evensong; door wide open, windows lit. Organ playing. (*Pause.*) My mother wa' very religious. (*Pause.*) If there isn't a God, we've certainly made a fine excuse for one.

Pause.

WENDY. Have you had any breakfast?

PASMORE. Save up till lunch-time.

WENDY. More tea?

PASMORE. No thanks.

WENDY. I'll talk to the shopkeeper.

PASMORE. Will you?

WENDY. When you go to the shop, let my mother go in, or, if you do go in, just watch yourself.

PASMORE. I do nowt else. Don't worry. (*He looks up.*) I'll go get washed.

He goes to the bathroom, passing COLIN coming into the room from the kitchen.

PASMORE goes into the bathroom and closes the door.

COLIN. How is he?

WENDY. Fine. You're not despairing, are you?

COLIN. No.

MRS PASMORE's bedroom door opens. She comes out, dressed, with her walking-stick. There is daylight in the room behind.

She takes a cup and saucer to the kitchen, rinses them under the tap, and looks round to tidy the room. She finds it tidy already.

WENDY. Relax.

COLIN. I am relaxed.

WENDY. Odd meeting here like this.

COLIN. Yes.

WENDY. Same flesh and blood.

COLIN. Yet different.

WENDY. Right. (*She watches him.*)

Pause.

MRS PASMORE pauses in the kitchen and contemplates going through to the living-room. She hesitates.

What's she doing?

COLIN. Tidying.

WENDY. You think so?

COLIN. Yes.

MRS PASMORE hesitates with her hand on the kitchen door. She releases it as:

EILEEN comes downstairs, briskly, noisily. She is dressed. She goes to the bathroom and finds it locked.

EILEEN. Sorry! (*She comes into the living-room.*) Sleep all
  right?
WENDY. Splendid.
EILEEN. Breakfast?
COLIN. Had some.
EILEEN. Wendy?
WENDY. No thanks.
EILEEN. Parents?
COLIN. Up.

  MRS PASMORE *has 'girded' herself. She opens the door
  and emerges.*

EILEEN. There you are, then, Mother.
MRS PASMORE. This is a surprise, finding you all here.
WENDY. It is!
EILEEN. Slept well, I should think, after all that drink. (*She
  kisses her cheek.*)
MRS PASMORE. Not that much, love. Though I did sleep
  well.
EILEEN. Anything I can get you?
MRS PASMORE. Colin brought me tea. That's all I have on
  a morning.
EILEEN. Can't face the world without something inside.
  (*She goes.*)
MRS PASMORE (*calling*). You'll find the food in the
  cupboard. And, if not in the cupboard, the fridge.

  PASMORE *emerges from the bathroom.*

EILEEN. 'Morning, Father!
PASMORE. 'Morning, love.
EILEEN. All right?
PASMORE. Champion.
EILEEN. Anything in the kitchen?
PASMORE. No thanks. Empty, if you want. (*He indicates
  the bathroom.*)
EILEEN. Right. (*She goes into the bathroom and closes the
  door.*)
PASMORE (*to MRS PASMORE*). They're leaving soon.
COLIN. Better get off early.
MRS PASMORE. Yes, love.

WENDY. Best get off.
PASMORE. Aye . . . Right.

Pause. PASMORE sits.

WENDY. If I leave now, I may get back in time for my
  committee. (*To* PASMORE.) I'll drop by at the shop.
PASMORE. Right.
WENDY. We'll sort it out.
PASMORE. Aye.
WENDY. Don't worry.

Pause. WENDY *looks at* COLIN.

EILEEN *comes out of the bathroom and goes through to
the kitchen.*

I'll ring you both this evening.
PASMORE. Right.
WENDY. Goodbye, then, Dad. (*She kisses his cheek,
  stooping to him.*)
PASMORE. Goodbye, then, love. (*He allows his arms to be
  held.*)
WENDY (*as* MRS PASMORE *rises*). Goodbye, then,
  Mother. No need to get up.
MRS PASMORE. I'll get up, love.

They embrace, MRS PASMORE *almost formally,*
WENDY *warmly.*

WENDY. Bye, Colin.
COLIN. Bye, love.

They embrace and kiss each other's cheek.

WENDY. I'll say goodbye to Eileen in the kitchen.
MRS PASMORE. Right, then, love.
WENDY. See each other more often.
MRS PASMORE. Yes.
WENDY (*after a pause*). Goodbye. (*She goes, without a
  backward glance, to the kitchen, taking her coat.*)

PASMORE *rises.*

Goodbye, our Eileen.

EILEEN. Are you off?

WENDY. Just. (*She nods back to the living-room.*)

EILEEN. I'll see you out.

They depart through the back door, WENDY drawing on her coat, EILEEN following.

In the living-room, MRS PASMORE has gone to the window. COLIN stands behind her, gazing out. MRS PASMORE, after gazing out, turns away. She goes back to her chair. PASMORE goes to the window and gazes out.

PASMORE. Neat car.

MRS PASMORE. Has she?

PASMORE. Didn't you see it?

MRS PASMORE. I did.

PASMORE (*waving*). She'll be asking Eileen to give her a shove. (*Pause.*) There's Mrs who-is-it looking out next door.

MRS PASMORE. Which next door?

PASMORE. Across the street.

MRS PASMORE. It's not a street.

PASMORE. The road.

MRS PASMORE. She can't be next door if she's across the road.

PASMORE. She's off. (*He waves, watches for a moment, then turns.*)

MRS PASMORE. It's herself she's hurt more than anything else.

COLIN. She's gone to catch the shopkeeper, Mother.

MRS PASMORE. Has she?

COLIN. Before he opens up.

PASMORE. She's given me my instructions.

EILEEN comes in the back door. She feels the teapot, finds it hot, under the cosy, and pours a cup.

MRS PASMORE. What are they, pray?

PASMORE. I come to the door to carry your shopping.

MRS PASMORE. That's all you do at present.

PASMORE. I shall go on doing it, in that case.

MRS PASMORE. I'll look forward to it, love.

COLIN. I dreamt last night that all this was a dream.

MRS PASMORE. It is.

PASMORE. It doesn't feel like one. (*He sits.*) 'Our dream of life is o'er.' Five letters. (*He indicates the newspaper.*)

Pause.

MRS PASMORE. I don't know, love. (*She is abstracted.*)

Pause.

EILEEN, *having sipped her tea, comes through to the hall. She gets her coat and comes into the living-room.*

EILEEN. I'm off! Goodbye, Mother.

MRS PASMORE (*rising*). Goodbye, love.

EILEEN *embraces her and kisses her cheek.*

EILEEN. I'll be over again quite shortly.

MRS PASMORE. Right, love.

EILEEN. Goodbye, Father.

PASMORE. Goodbye, love.

He rises to be embraced. EILEEN *kisses his cheek.*

EILEEN. Cheerio, Colin.

COLIN. Cheerio.

She kisses and embraces him.

EILEEN (*to* MRS PASMORE). I'll give you a call as soon as I'm back.

MRS PASMORE. Right, then, love.

EILEEN. I'll go the back way. Cheerio. (*She goes, crossing the kitchen. She takes an apple from the bowl and puts it in her pocket. She closes the back door behind her.*)

MRS PASMORE *goes to the window.* PASMORE *sits.* COLIN *watches from behind* MRS PASMORE.

MRS PASMORE. She always drove too fast.

PASMORE. Always?

MRS PASMORE. Don't you remember how many goes she had to get her licence? (*She waves.*) She almost took the gatepost off. (*Pause. She watches, then turns back to the room.*) You left, Colin.

COLIN. Yes.

MRS PASMORE *sits.*

MRS PASMORE. Don't have to rush.

COLIN. No.

MRS PASMORE. You've a longer drive than either.

COLIN. I'd better make a start.

MRS PASMORE. Did you sleep any better last night? (*She gazes at him keenly.*)

COLIN. I did. (*Pause.*) I'll get my things. (*He goes. He pauses outside the door, then continues upstairs.*)

MRS PASMORE. You can turn off the drawer.

PASMORE. Right. (*He gets up and moves the lever over the fire.*)

MRS PASMORE. Burnt up.

PASMORE. It has.

MRS PASMORE. Got the coal?

PASMORE. Colin got it.

MRS PASMORE. You shouldn't have let him.

PASMORE. Why not?

MRS PASMORE. That's your job.

PASMORE. All my life.

MRS PASMORE. Don't feel so badly done to.

PASMORE. I don't.

MRS PASMORE. I had such a funny dream last night. I dreamt I died. I called, 'I'm dying'. You were fast asleep.

PASMORE. I dee'd as well.

MRS PASMORE. Is that what dying's like?

PASMORE. Like what?

MRS PASMORE. Like waking from a sleep.

Pause.

COLIN *comes down. He appears in his overcoat carrying a holdall.*

COLIN. I've stripped the beds.

MRS PASMORE. Thank you, love. (*She stands and puts out her arms to be embraced.*)

COLIN. Goodbye, Mother.
MRS PASMORE. Goodbye, love.

They hold the embrace for a moment. Then COLIN *kisses her on the cheek.*

PASMORE *stands, looking on.*

COLIN. Goodbye, Dad.
PASMORE. Goodbye, lad.

COLIN *embraces* PASMORE.

COLIN. Look after yourselves.
PASMORE. We shall.
COLIN. I'll go out the back door: the front one's locked.
Bye, then.
MRS PASMORE. Bye.

COLIN *goes out to the passage. He crosses the kitchen to the back door. He looks round at it briefly, glances towards the living-room, then goes, closing the back door behind him.*

You ought to have seen him off.
PASMORE. I can see him off from here. (*He stoops to the window and waves.*) Mrs who-is-it's out again.
MRS PASMORE. I wish you wouldn't call people something that they aren't.
PASMORE. How do I know who she is? (*Pause. He waves.*)
He drives slower than our Wendy.

Pause. He watches a moment longer, then turns and comes back to the room.

MRS PASMORE. Well, then. (*Pause.*) Oh, now.

PASMORE *shields his face.*

Oh, now. (*Not moving.*)

PASMORE *weeps.*

Oh, now, Tommy.

PASMORE, *his face still shielded, is silent.*

Tell me – that time – when you marched in Russia.

PASMORE. Russia.

MRS PASMORE. General Denisov.

PASMORE. Denisov.

MRS PASMORE. He came aboard at Odessa.

PASMORE. Odessa.

MRS PASMORE. In tears.

PASMORE. In tears.

MRS PASMORE. With his wife.

PASMORE. His wife.

MRS PASMORE. As the ship steamed out . . .

PASMORE. As the ship steamed out . . .

MRS PASMORE. He took her hand.

PASMORE. He took her hand. (*Pause.*) He said. (*Pause.*)
'Oh, where are we going to, my love?'

*Her gaze, full of tears, is turned on her husband; his grief-
stricken face is turned on hers. The anguish of their past
and present life is evident between them.*

The light slowly fades.